POLITICS OF PRESIDENTIAL RULE IN INDIA

POLITICS OF PRESIDENTIAL RULE IN INDIA

K. Indramani Singh

AKANSHA PUBLISHING HOUSE
NEW DELHI -110 002 (INDIA)

AKANSHA PUBLISHING HOUSE
4649/21-B, Ansari Road
Daryaganj, New Delhi - 110 002
E-mail: ektabooks@yahoo.com
Phones: 011-23263193, 09435116718
Visit us: www.akanshapublishinghouse.com

Politics of Presidential Rule in India

First Published, 2009

ISBN 978-81-8370-169-3

PRINTED IN INDIA

Published by Akansha Publishing House, New Delhi - 2 and Printed at Capital Offset Press, Delhi.

Dedicated to

My Grandmother

Smt. Gulapchaobi Devi

Contents

	Preface	ix
1.	Introductory	1
2.	President's Rule in the States and Union Territories: A comparative study	24
3.	The Position and Role of the Governor During the President's Rule in the State	99
4.	Role of Central Government Under President's Rule in the State and Centre-State Relations	137
5.	President's Rule: Feedback and Reality	163
6.	Conclusions and Observations	188
	Appendices	194
	I. Chronology of President's Rule in Manipur with Relevant Details	194
	II. President's Rule in States and Union Territories	202
	Bibliography	228
	Index	232

Preface

At the very outset, I acknowledge my deep sense of gratitude to G P Singh, Professor of History in the University of Manipur, Imphal, for all his valuable suggestions and advice in the course of preparation of this volume. It would be have been well-nigh impossible for me to accomplish my task without his help.

I am extremely grateful to Prof. Ksh. Bimola Devi, Dept. of Political Science, presently Dean, School of Social Sciences, Manipur University, and Dr. S. Rajen, Associate Professor, Dept. of Political Science, Manipur University, for encouraging me to undertake this research work.

I extend my grateful thanks to the librarians and staff of Manipur University Library, Central State Library, Imphal and Manipur Assembly Secretariat Library for all the help and cooperation they extended to me in having access to the books and other documents useful for my purpose. My special thanks go to R. K. Rajen, Deputy Secretary, Manipur Assembly Secretariat, for providing me some very important documents. My thanks are also due to all my friends and well-wishers for their good wishes for success in my endeavours.

I am thankful to Mrs. Kiran Singh for all her good wishes and encouragement to me. Lastly, I shall never forget of my beloved partner Th. Memcha Devi who always assist in my life. I thank to Shri L. Suraj Singh, Lecturer of Political Science, D.M. College of Arts, Imphal, for his incessant help in various academic pursuance.

K. Indramani Singh

1

INTRODUCTORY

The primary purpose of this work is to provide, as far as possible, a detailed account of President's rule in different States and Union Territories of India covering the period mainly from 1951 to 1976 and in the state of Manipur from 1972 (the year in which it attained full-fledged statehood) till 2001-02 in a systematic manner within a chronological framework stating the reasons thereof and throwing light on the role of the Governor during the President's rule in the state, the role of Central Government in the decision-making process with regard to the imposition, promulgation, extension and revocation of the President's rule in the state and its bearing or centre-state relations, the advantages and disadvantages of President's rule and so on. The present work also aims at offering some solutions to the problems relating to the invoking of Article 356 and its approval by the parliament for bringing the concerned state under the President's rule if the need so be. A work containing all the relevant details of the subject is still a desideratum. We, therefore, find a fair scope to undertake this research work. There is an ample scope to throw fresh light on the subject on the basis of the available sources. Our study of the subject is based on the data available in the primary and secondary sources. The data collected from all the relevant sources have been properly analysed, harmonized and arranged. Some of the hypotheses relating to especially the theoretical aspect of the subject have also been examined.

The present work, we hope, will be of some use for the political scientists, parliamentarians and legislators, constitutional experts, state Governors and for those who want to make further study of the subject.

General Background

India is a Union of States, but the Constitution is more specific about the Union than about the states. The latter have been made dependent upon the Union Government in many spheres even in normal times and much more so during the periods of emergency.

Article 249 of the Indian Constitution authorises the Parliament to enact legislation on any subject on the state list provided the Rajya Sabha by two thirds majority empowers it to do so. Under Article 312, Parliament is empowered to create new all India services common to the Centre and the states provided again the Rajya Sabha passes a resolution to this effect by a two-third majority. In accordance with the provisions of the Article, in 1963 the Central Government decided to set up three new All India Services of viz., the Indian Forest Services, the Indian Medical and Health Services and the Indian Services of Engineers, although only the Indian Forest Services has been created.

Article 256 places a State Government under an obligation to so exercise its executive power as to ensure compliance with the law made by Parliament and to this end the Centre is empowered to issue necessary directions to it. Article 257 places the states under the control of the Central Government in certain cases. It says, "the Executive Power of every State shall be so exercised as not to impede or prejudice the exercise of the executive power of the Union and the executive power of the Union shall extend to the giving of such directions to a State as may appear to the Government of India to be necessary for that purpose. The executive power of the Union shall also extend to the giving of directions to a state as to the construction and maintenance of means of communication declared in the direction to be of national or military importance, the executive power of the Union shall also extend to the giving of directions to a state as to the measures to be taken for the protection of the railways within the states". Further, Articles 200 and 201 empowered the Governor who is the President's appointee to reserve a Bill passed by the State Legislative Assembly for the consideration of the President who has right to veto it. Finally, an unusual feature of the Indian federalism is that even the very identity of States has not been protected. Article 3 of the constitution provided that the Parliament may By - law (a) form a new state (b) increase the area of any state (c) diminish the area of any state (d) alter the name of any state. And as Article 4 confirms, such a law is not to be construed as an amendment of the Constitution. It is notable that the Central Government has made ample use of the provision contained in Article 3.

The Constitution even provided for the dismissal of a popularly elected ministry in a State by the President. The suspension of the constitutional provisions relating to a responsible government in the state is by all accounts an extraordinary feature which is not to be found in any other Federal Constitution except that of Pakistan. This unusual constitutional feature and its invocation constitute the theme of the present work. And further, it attempts to find out the relationship between Centre and State political administration, and its impact towards the socio-politico and economic development of the particular States and whole country in general.[1]

In the true sense, if the President is satisfied on receipt of a report from the Governor of a State or otherwise that a situation has arisen in which the government of the State cannot be carried on in accordance with the provisions of the Constitution, he is empowered under Article 356(1) of the Constitution to issue a proclamation to that effect. Under such a proclamation, the President may (ii) assume to himself or any of the functions of the Government of the State and all or any of the powers vested in a or exercisable by or under the authority of Parliament, and (iii) make any other incidental or consequential provision necessary to give effect to the objects of the proclamation. The President however cannot assume to himself any of the powers vested in a High Court. A proclamations issued under clause (1) of Article 356 may be revoked or varried by a subsequent proclamations under clause (2) of the Article 356 and has to be laid before each House of Parliament except where it is a proclamations revoking a previous proclamation. The proclamation ceases to operate at the expiration of two months unless before the expiration of that period it has been approved by resolutions of both Houses of Parliament under Article 356(3). Under clause (4) of article 356, as amended by the Constitution (forty-fourth Amendment) Act 1978 and approved by the Parliament it remains in operation for six months from the date it was issued unless, of course, it had in the meanwhile been revoked. Extension of the operation of proclamation beyond the first six months is contingent on necessary approval by the Parliament. Under the first provisions to Article 356(4), if and so after a resolution approving the continuance in force of such a proclamation is passed by both Houses of Parliament, the proclamation would remain unless revoked within six months, but no such proclamation shall in any case remain in force more than three years.[2]

Since the coming into force of he Constitution on January 26,1950, President's rule has been promulgated 75 times upto 1989 in 23 States. Punjab was the first State in the Union where President's rule was necessitated within two years of the commencement of the Constitution.

The causes which have led to the proclamation of President's rule in States are varied in nature, such as defections by the Members of Legislatures,, breaking of coalitions due to withdrawal of support by alliance partners, passing of no confidence motions against the Council of Ministers, resignation of Chief Ministers for various reasons, absence of Legislatures in newly formed States, public agitations in States leading to instability in the administration, complete breakdown of constitutional machinery in the States, failure of the State governments to tackle law and order problem, etc. Though defections leading to imposition of President's rule became a matter of rather frequent occurrence only after the 1967 General Election, it was as early as in

Andhra Pradesh. Other States where similar situations, have arisen over the years are Bihar, Gujarat, Haryana, Karnataka, Kerala, Manipur, Mizoram, Orissa, Punjab, Sikkim and Tamil Nadu. Instances of President's rule being necessitated by break up of ruling coalitions are Kerala (1979,1981 & 1982), Orissa (1961 and 1971), Punjab (1968) Tripura (1979) and Uttar Pradesh (1970).

The passing of no confidence motions against the Council of Ministers in the State Legislatures of Andhra Pradesh and Kerala led to President's rule there in 1954 and 1964 respectively as no other party was then in a position to form a Ministry,

In Gujarat, President's rule was introduced in 1976 after the Chief Minister had resigned following an adverse note in the State Assembly on a Demand for Grants. There have been other cases as in Kerala (1970 and 1979), Punjab (1951), Sikkim (1979), Uttar Pradesh (1968 and 1975), and West Bengal (1970) when the Chief Ministers resigned on their own due to various reasons which resulted in the Governor's recommendations for taking over the administration of these States by the President. Public agitations among other causes led to President's rule in Andhra Pradesh in 1973 , in Assam in 1979, in Gujarat in 1974, in Kerala in 1959 and in Punjab in 1983 and 1987.

The formation of new States like Kerala in 1956, Punjab in 1966, and Manipur and Tripura in 1972 created situations in which the administration had to be taken over by the Centre till the new Legislative Assemblies could be duly elected and the popular Ministries ushered in. In Kerala in 1965, in Orissa in 1971 and in Rajasthan 1967, in spite of the formation of new Legislative Assemblies after fresh elections no single party emerged with an absolute majority or was in a position to form a Ministry in collaboration with other parties, and consequently President's rule under Article 356 was promulgated in those States.[3]

Proclamation issued in respect of nine States on April 30, 1977 constituted a distinct class and may be said to have set a new precedent. The March, 1977 elections to the Lok Sabha had thrown up an unprecedented political situations in that in as many as nine States, Bihar, Haryana, Himachal Pradesh, Madhya Pradesh, Orissa, Punjab, Rajasthan, Uttar Pradesh and West Bengal, there was a total or near total rejection of the candidates belonging to the party which was then ruling in these States as well as at the Centre. The Union Government took the view that this implied a complete lack of confidence on the part of the electorate in the Governments of the nine states. In these circumstances, the then Union Home Minister suggested to the Chief Ministers of the nine States that they should advise the Governors to dissolve the State Assemblies and seek a fress mandate. The suggestion was not accepted by the concerned State Government who chose to contact the constitutional validity of the Centre's suggestion and of the impending action under Article 356 before the Supreme Court. The Supreme Court by its Order of April 29, 1977, dismissed the suits and injunction applications filed by the States and declined to interfere in its judgement, delivered a week later i.e., May 6, 1977.[4]

The Supreme Court cannot interdict the use of Article 356 taking undue advantage of a conflict between the Executive or Judiciary in a particular State. The most that one could say in that a dissolution against the wishes of the majority in a State Assembly is a grave and serious matter. Perhaps it could be observed that it should be resorted to under Article 356 (1) of the Constitution only when a critical situation has arisen. But the question is whether the State Assembly and the State Government for the time being have been so totally and imphatically rejected by the people that critical situation has arisen or is bound to arise unless the political soverign is given an opportunity of giving a fresh verdict. A decision on such a question undoubtedly lies in the executive realm.

Meanwhile, on April 30,1977, proclamation under Article 356 were issued in respect of the afore-said none States by the acting President The Legislative Assemblies of the States were simultaneously dissolved and the Chief Election Commissioner approched to hold fresh election for them.

Following the Mid-term Lok Sabha Elections held in January, 1980 proclamation under Article 356 were issued in respect of nine States (viz., Bihar, Gujarat, Madhya Pradesh, Maharashtra, Orissa, Punjab, Rajasthan, Tamil Nadu and Uttar Pradesh) on 17th Feb. 1980, and the Legislative Assembly of the States were the break down of constitutional machinery. Any such proclamation would however, cease to operate on the expiry of the period of six months from the date on which it was first issued except where it is a proclamation revoking a previous proclamation. The provision for extending President's rule to Jammu and Kashmir was promulgated in 1954 by Constitution Order 1954.

A proclamation issued under article 3 56 (1) may contain an express provision that the Legislative Assembly of the State concerned be dissolved simultaneously with the proclamation. This has been done so far on 49 occasions. In most other cases where it was thought that there was some chance for the formation of stable Ministry even dissolved simultaneously as the Union Government felt that having suffered an overwhelming defeat in Lok Sabha elections the Ruling Party in these states no longer represented the people.

President's rule in the States of Jammu and Kashmir was promulgated on 7/9/1986 and ceased to operate from 6/11/ 1986 after expiration of two months period. A popular government of National Conference was installed in the State with the support of Congress (I) Party. The State had earlier remained under Governor's Rule for 3 months and 14 days from 27/3/ 1977 to 9/7/79 and again for 6 months from 7/3/ 1986 to 6/9/ 1986. The Section 92 of the Constitution of Jammu and Kashmir provides for Governor's Rule in the State with the concurrence of the President of India in case of after the issue of the proclamation the State Assembly instead of being dissolved was kept in a State of suspended animation. However, in Gujarat 1974, Nagaland 1975, Karnataka 1971, Orissa 1971, Punjab 1985, Uttar Pradesh 1968, West Bengal 1970 though the State Assembly was only suspended in the first instance it was subsequently dissolved. In a few other cases, Karala (1970,1979 and 1982),

Punjab (1971), Sikkim (1979) and West Bengal (1971), the Legislative Assembly had already been dissolved by the Governors concerned before the Presidential proclamations were issued.

While laying a proclamation on the table no obligation is cast on the Government to lay also a copy of the Report of the Governor of the State concerned in cases where the President has acted on such a Report. During the discussion in Lok Sabha on November 19,1954 on the proclamation issued in respect of the State of Andhra Pradesh, it was stated by the Government that the Report of the Governor was a secret document and as such could not be made available to Members. In the case of the proclamation in respect of the State of Kerala in 1959, however a summary of the Governor's Report was laid on August 17,1959. The subsequent practice has been that a summary of the Governor's Report or the Report itself in extension is laid on the table of both Houses of Parliament.

Under Section 51 of the Government of Union Territories Act, 1963, the President on receipt of a report from the administrator of a Union Territory, may by order suspend the operation of all or any of the provisions of the Act for such a period as he thinks fit and make such incidental and consequential provision.

Since the coming into force of the Government of Union Territories Act 1963. President's rule had been promulgated ten times in four Union Territories Pondichery came under President's rules 5 times and former Union Territory of Mizoram and Goa two times each followed by Arunachal Pradesh where it had been proclaimed only once up to 1985.[5]

Early History

The Government of India Act 1935, contained section 93 which empowered the Governor to dismiss the popularly elected government and take over the administration of the province. Before the enactment of the Government of India Act 1935 India was unitarily governed and as such a need to provide for the take-over of provincial government did not arise. Section 93 of the Government of India Act 1935, provided, power of Governor to issue proclamations (1), If at any time the Governor of a province in satisfied that a situation has arisen in which the government of the province cannot be carried on in accordance with the provisions of this act, he may by proclamation (a) declare that his functions shall to such extent as may be specified in the proclamations be exercised by him in his discretion, (b) assume to himself all or any of the powers vested in or exercisable by any provincial body or authority and any such proclamation may contain such incidental any consequential provisions as may appear to him to be necessary or desirable for giving effect to the objects of the proclamation including provisions for suspending in whole or in part the operation of any provisions of this act relating to any provincial body or authority.

It did not take the Central Government long to invoke section 93 of the Government of India Act 1935, shortly after the commencement of the second world war, the congress Governments in seven out of could be formed in them. These were Bombay, Madras, the United Provinces, Bihar, and the central provinces. In these was proclaimed section 93 and such provinces came to be known as 'Section 93 provinces'. Lord Wavell, the viceroy of India, was even in favour of introducing this section in Bengal stricken as it was by famine, but was virtually overruled by the Home Government, Bengal came under it in March 1945 and Punjab in March 1947.

History has the uncanny knack of often thrusting on people and institutions role of which they were at one time outspoken critics, section 93 of the Constitution of India Act 1935, had constituted during the period of the British Raj, the proverbial mote in nationalist Indian eyes, conferring as it did drastic powers on the Governor of the province. When, however, the nationalist leaders, into whose hands the power of governance of India passed in 1947, began framing the constitution of free India, they took at leaf out of the Government of India Act 1935, and became votaries of the once condemned provision.

The Draft-constitution, prepared by the drafting committees of the Constituent Assembly of India, contained Article 188 which empowered the Governor to proclaim to taking over of the state Government such a proclamation was to have the maximum validity of two weeks. The Article ran as follows.

"If at any time the Governor of the state is satisfied what a grave emergency has arisen which threatens the peace and tranquillity of the state and that it is not possible to carry on the Government of the state in accordance with the provisions of this constitution he may by proclamation, declare that his functions shall, to such extent as may be specified in the proclamation, be exercised by him in his discretion and any such proclamation may contain such incidental and consequential provisions as may appear to him necessary or desirable for giving effects to the objects of the proclamation including provisions for suspending in whole or in part the operation of any provisions of this constitution relating to any body or authority in the state. Provided that nothing in this clause shall authorise the Governor to suspend, either in whole or in part the operation of any provisions of this constitution relating to any body or authority in the state. Provided that nothing in this clause shall authorise the Governor to suspend, either in whole or in part, the operation of any provision of this constitution relating to High Courts."[6]

The proclamation shall be forthwith communicated by the Governor to the President who may, thereupon, either revoke the proclamation or take such action as he considers appropriate in exercise of the emergency powers vested in him under Article 278 of this constitution.

A proclamation under this article shall case to operate at the expiration of two weeks unless revoked earlier by the Governor or by the President by public notification.

The function of the Governor under this article shall be exercised by him in his discretion. Moreover Article 278 in the Draft constitution sought to bring the President's rule into the picture. The Governor was under a constitutional obligation to transmit his proclamation to the President who, if satisfied that the Government of the state could not be conducted in accordance with the provision of the constitution, could take over in his hands the functions of the state Government and declare that the powers of the legislature of the state shall be exercisable only by parliament.

Such was the original provision made in the Draft constitution. It, however, underwent three important changes in the course of the debates in the Constituent Assembly. Article 188 was completely deleted, thereby empowering the President alone to assume the functions of the state government in the event of a break down of the constitutional machinery there.

The Constituent Assembly discovered the two-phase intervention in the State sphere, first by the Governor on his own and later by the President to be plainly anomalous. First, if the President was ultimately to saving himself into the state field it would be more logical that he come into it at the very beginning. Second, the President may issue the proclamation of takeover on the basis of a report by the Governor or on his own initiative. This marks a departure from the earlier stipulation under which the President could not act except on a report by the Governor duly preceded by the Governor's proclamation under Article 188. The original provision of the Governor's report being obligatory for the invocation of the President's rule was made flexible, or rather optional. If the centre is responsible for protecting the constitutional machinery in the states, as is the acknowledged position under the constitution, why make the Presidential action absolutely dependent on the Governor's report.

Finally, the functions of the state legislature were, according to the provisions of the Draft constitution to be assumed by the parliament which was not explicitly authorised to confer such powers on the President. No such bar on the party of parliament operates now.

Though an extraordinary feature in a federal constitution,

the provision seeking dismissal of state government by Presidential action gained acceptance in the Constituent Assembly with surprising case. In a way, this was a reflection of the times. The nation was at this time passing through a critical period in her history in the wake of partition, communal riots and other different disturbances. The Constituent Assembly itself, which originally contemplated a rather weak federal government, ultimately became the champion of a powerful centre. Article 278 (which later became article 356) was but one manifestation of the prevalent national sentiments. In addition to the observations of constitutional experts they observed. If the central Government and parliament are given the power that Article 277, 278 and 278 A read together propose to confer on them, there is a serious danger that whenever there is dissatisfaction in provinces with its Government, appeals will be made to the central Government to come its rescue. The provincial elections will be able to throw their responsibility on the shoulders of the central Government. Responsible government is the most difficult form of government. It requires patience and it requires the courage to take risks. If we have neither the patience nor the courage that is needed, our constitution will virtually be stillborn.

Under the constitution, the central government has assumed the ultimate responsibility of assuring constitutional government in the state. If the President is satisfied on the report of a governor or otherwise that there has occured a constitutional breakdown in a state, he may assume any or all the functions of the state government and declare the state legislature exercisable by or under the authority of the parliament. However, he cannot assume any of the functions of the High Court or modify any provision of the constitution relating to the High Courts. Finally, the duration of President's rule in a state has the outer limit of three continuous years.[7]

Another significant Article is 357 which describes the manner of exercise of the legislative powers. During the President's rule in a state the powers of the legislature become exercisable by or under the authority of Parliament. The latter may confer on the

President the power of the State Legislature to make laws and even authorise him to delegate this power to any other authority. The President, may also authorise, when the Lok Sabha is not in session expenditure from the consolidated fund of the state pending its parliamentary sanction.

Laws enacted by Parliament or President or other authority which fall within the field of the legislative powers of the State cease to have effect on the expiration of a period of one year after the proclamation has ceased to operate unless they have been repeated earlier or reenacted by the state legislature.

In short, the article which finally emerged out of the Constituent Assembly read as follows:

"If the President, on receipt of a report from the Governor or Rajpramukh of a state or otherwise is satisfied that a situation has arisen in which the Government of the state cannot be carried on in accordance with the provisions of this constitution, the President may by proclamation, assume to himself all or any of the functions of the Government of the state and all or any of the powers vested in or exercisable by the governor or Rajpramukh as the case may be, or any body or authority in the state other than the legislature of the state.

"Declare that the powers of the legislature of the state shall be exercisable by or under the authority of Parliament. Make such incidental and consequential provisions as appear to the President to be necessary or desirable for giving effect to the object of the proclamation, including provisions for suspending in whole or in part the operation of any provisions of this constitution relating to any body or authority in the state.

One must take not of two points, including one which is purely terminological relating to this article. Article 356 did not apply to Jammu & Kashmir till 20 Dec. 1964, although it is one of the states of the Indian Union. Secondly, the words House of the People and Council of States have since been substituted by Lok Sabha and Rajya Sabha, respectively and the words Governor or Rajpramukh as the case may be have since been deleted, having become meaningless in the course of time.

The Attitude of Central Government

It is to be noted that the constitution does not provide for President's rule at the centre. The President is always a constitutional head and even when a ministry falls he has to go on inviting political parties to form the government or to order mid term poll. The reason for not incorporating provision for Presidential takeover of the Central Government cannot be that instability in a state should cause the country wide concern than instability at the centre. This is truly a recognition of the constitution's faith in the political parties of the land and ultimately in the electorate.

The Pattern of Assembly Dissolution

The dissolution of a State Assembly in India may be effected in two ways. The Governor himself may dissolve the Assembly a power which he enjoys in the Constitution. This right which he invokes on the advice of the Chief Minister has been exercised under two circumstances. The Governor as a provided that nothing in this clause shall authorise the President to assume to himself any of the powers vested in or exercisable by a High Court, or to suspend in whole or in part the operation of any provision of this constitution relating to High Courts. Any such proclamation may be revoked or varied by a subsequent proclamation.

Every proclamation under this article shall be laid before each House of parliament and shall, except where it is a proclamation, revoking a previous proclamation, cease to operate at the expiration of that period it has been approved by resolutions of both Houses of Parliament.[8]

Provided that if any such proclamation is issued at a time when the House of the people is dissolved or the dissolution of the House of the People takes place during the period of two months referred to in this clause, and if a resolution approving the proclamation has been passed by the House of the people before the expiration of that period, the proclamation shall cease to operate at the expiration of thirty days its reconstitution unless before the expiration of the said period of thirty days by the House of the people.

A proclamation so approved shall, unless revoked cease to operate on the expiration of a period of six months from the date of the passing of the second of the resolutions approving the proclamation under clause (3). Provided that if and so often as a resolution approving the continuance in force of such a proclamation is passed by both houses of parliament, the proclamation shall, unless revoked, continue in force for a further period of six months from the date on which under this clause it would otherwise have ceased to operate, but no such proclamation shall in any case remain in force for more than three years. Provided further that if the dissolution of the House of the People takes place during any such period of six months and a resolution approving the continuance in force of such proclamation has been passed by the Council of States but no resolution with respect to the continuances in force of such proclamation has been passed by the Houses of the People during the said period, the proclamation shall cease to operate at the expiration of thirty days from the date on which the House of the People, first sits after its resolution unless before the expiration of the said period of thirty days a resolution approving the continuance in force of the proclamation has been also passed by the House of the People rule, dissolves the Assembly when in the normal process fresh elections to it are to be held, and in all such cases the popular ministry remains in powers though on a somewhat caretaker basis. Also, he has terminated the life of the Assembly on a few occasions of legislative turmoil continuing in office.

The second set of circumstances has been, in practice, been the prelude to the President's rule in the state, what is more, in such situations President's rule may even turn out to be a constitutional inevitability. If the Assembly did not pass the budget before its dissolution, state administration may come to a complete standstill unless the budget is passed by the parliament which derives this necessary authority only when Article 356 has been imposed on the state. Under either circumstances the governor's dissolution of the Assembly does not dispensed away with the Council of Ministers, the latter institution is dispensed away with only when Article 356 in unfolded. The truly distinguishing feature of President's rule is the absence of a Council of Ministers. It needs to be noted that while the Legislative Assembly may be dissolved or suspended under President's rule, the upper house, wherever it exists remain intact.[9]

Modality of President's Rule

President's rule has been generally imposed without prior warning to the States to set right their affairs. Article 356 is invoked very much like the proverbial bolt from the blue without giving them an opportunity or notice to settle the problems concerned. This is contrary to the intention of the framers of the Constitution, B.R. Ambedkar, the Chairman of the Drafting Committee, told the Constituent Assembly that "before Article 356 is brought into operation it will be prudent to take proper precautions before actually suspending the administration of the provinces. I hope the first thing to do would be to issue a mere warning to a province that has earned that things were not happening in the way which they were intended to happen in the Constitution. If that warning fails, the second thing to do will be to order an election allowing the people of the province to settle matters by themselves. It is only when these two remedies fail we may resort to this article. I do not think we could then say that these Articles were invoked in vain."

A word about the actual declaration of President's rule is also called for. Out of the thirty six cases, President's rule has lasted for two months or less on five occasions, for six months or less on fifteen occasions, for any duration between six and twelve months ten times, and the duration has exceeded one year in eight instances. By keeping the validity of parliamentary approval of President's rule to a period of six months the Constituent Assembly considered that return of popular

Government should be possible within this period. As can be seen in a majority of cases this did nct happen.[10]

The process of heralding President's rule is formally set into motion with the Governor transmitting his report to the President in which he makes a definite recommendation for the application of Article 356 of the Constitution to the State concerned.

In this matter, the Governor does not act on the aid and advice of his Council of Ministers nor is he answerable to any court of law on whether his report is based on any extraneous facts. But the President to whom the report is addressed takes action on it on the advice of his Council of Ministers. In fact, the President's rule can be imposed only on the advice of his Council of Ministers and in this way, the President's satisfaction becomes the Council of Ministers satisfactory. Also the source of information on which the President bases his satisfaction has been kept very wide indeed. This use of the word otherwise in Article 356 is full of import for it does not in any way seek to restrict or limit the channel of information on which he reaches his satisfaction. The information of the failure of the constitutional machinery might have for instance emanated from any one of Centre's own sources. Also the very amplitude and undefined character of the information on which the President is to be satisfied indicates that satisfaction and the source there of are not justifiable.

Although constitutionally the Governor's report is not obligatory for the promulgation of President's rule in a State convention has made it so. The Governor's report is as a rule now placed on the table of each House of Parliament along with the President's proclamation. Being above party politics the Governor is to look upon to give to the President an objective assessment of the political situation in his state and under a convention his recommendation is to prevail upon the centre in the matter of President's rule.

The following chart shows the dates of proclamation and their revocation in the States:

State		*Date of Proclamation*	*Date of Revocation*
Kerala	(i)	23 March, 1956	1 November, 1956
	(ii)	1 November, 1956	5 April, 1957
	(iii)	31 July, 1957	22 February, 1960.
	(iv)	10 September, 1964	24 March, 1965
	(v)	4 August, 1970	3 October, 1970
Punjab	(i)	20 June, 1951	17 April, 1952
	(ii)	5 July, 1966	1 November, 1966
	(iii)	23 August 1963	17 February, 1969
	(iv)	15 June, 1971	17 March, 1972
Uttar Pradesh	(i)	25 February, 1968	25 February, 1969
	(ii)	1 October, 1970	18 October, 1970
	(iii)	13 June, 1973	18 November, 1973
	(iv)	30 November, 1975	21 January, 1976
Bihar	(i)	29 June, 1968	26 February, 1969
	(ii)	4 July, 1969	16 February, 1970
	(iii)	9 January, 1972	19 March, 1972
Gujarat	(i)	13 May, 1971	17 March, 1972
	(ii)	9 February, 1974	18 June, 1975
	(iii)	12 March, 1976	24 December, 1976
Orissa	(i)	25 February, 1961	23 June, 1961
	(ii)	11 January, 1971	3 April, 1971
	(iii)	3 March, 1973	6 March, 1974
West Bengal	(i)	20 February, 1968	26 February, 1969
	(ii)	19 March, 1970	12 April, 1971
	(iii)	29 June, 1971	20 March, 1972
Andhra Pradesh	(i)	15 November, 1954	23 March, 1955
	(ii)	18 January, 1973	10 December, 1973
Haryana	(i)	21 November, 1967	21 May, 1968
Mysore	(i)	27 March, 1971	17 March, 1972
Nagaland	(i)	22 March, 1975	—
Pepsu (Patiala and east Punjab State Union which merged with Punjab in 1956)	(i)	4 March, 1953	7 March, 1954
Rajasthan	(i)	31 March, 1967	May, 1968

Tamil Nadu	(i) 31 January, b 1976	—
Tripura	(i) 21 January, 1972	20 March, 1972[11]

The total period of President's rule in the States exceeds twenty years. The significance of this period becomes amply obvious if one but recalls that the Constitution itself is not more than twenty six years old. The following table describe the chronology of President's rule in the State:

Name of State	*Date of Pro-clamation*	*Date of Revocation*	*Period of President's Rule (in days)*
Punjab	20 June, 1951	17 April, 1952	302
PEPSU	4 March, 1953	17 March, 1954	378
Andhra Pradesh	15 November, 1954	23 March, 1955	128
Travancore Cochin (named Kerala in Nov. 1956)	23 March, 1956	5 April, 1957	378
Kerala	31 July, 1959	22 February, 1960	206
Orissa	25 February, 1961	23 June, 1961	118
Kerala	10 September, 1964	24 March, 1965	145
Kerala	24 March	6 March, 1967	721
Punjab	5 July, 1966	1 November, 1966	118
Rajasthan	13 March, 1967	26 April, 1967	44
Haryana	21 November, 1967	21 May, 1968	181
West Bengal	20 February, 1968	25 February, 1969	371
Uttar Pradesh	25 February, 1968	26 February, 1969	367
Bihar	29 June, 1968	26 February, 1969	248
Punjab	23 August, 1968	17 February, 1969	178
Bihar	4 July, 1969	16 February, 1970	227
West Bengal	19 March, 1970	2 April, 1971	377
Kerala	4 August,1970	3 October,1970	64
Uttar Pradesh	1 October, 1970	18 October,, 1970	18
Orissa	11 January, 1971	3 April, 1971	82
Mysore	27 March, 1971	20 March, 1972	359
Gujarat	13 May, 1971	17 March, 1972	313
Punjab	15 June, 1971	17 March, 1972	280

West Bengal	29 June, 1971	20 March, 1972	365
Bihar	9 January, 1972	19 March, 1972	70
Manipur	21 January, 1972	20 March, 1972	59
Tripura	21 January, 1972	20 March, 1972	59
Andhra Pradesh	18 January, 1973	10 December, 1973	326
Orissa	3 March, 1973	6 March, 1974	341
Manipur	28 March, 1973	4 March, 1974	341
Uttar Pradesh	13 June, 1973	18 November, 1973	158
Gujarat	9 February, 1974	18 June, 1975	494
Nagaland	22 March, 1975	—	—
Uttar Pradesh	30 November, 1975	21 January, 1976	52
Tamil Nadu	31 January, 1976	—	8
Gujarat	12, March, 1976	24 December, 1976	287[12]

A Glimpse at the History of President's Rule

The history of President's rule in India can be traced in a chronological order. The history of this rule can be divided into three broad periods or phases. The first phase begins with the inauguration of the Constitution in 1950 and may be said to have come to an end with the Fourth General Election held in 1967. The occasions of President's rule during this period were few in comparison to the frequency with which article 356 was invoked after this election until then the political map of the India was unvarying. The above data available only up to 1976. Since the materials are depending to government publications, specially Parliamentary Debates and Parliamentary Secretariat, I would not have an ample chance to collect further publication for details for my research purpose. However, I must try to analyse very much further regarding the proclamation of President's rule in the States and Union Territories of the country. The Congress Party, the ruling Party at the Centre as well as in the States and the problems and issues were normally tackled in the party network. As a result the constitutional provision entailing central takeover of State administration did not acquire any significant measure of urgency. Rather, it was a period of over stability.

The first phase came to an unexpected end in 1967 when the General Election threw out of power the erstwhile Ruling Party, the Congress in many States but at the same time did not bless any single party with majority in the Legislative sufficient enough to constitute the Ministry single handed. The defeat of the Congress was a reflection of peoples disenchantment with it and their increasing economic hardships, which the various five year plans did little to alleviate. The Indian scene at this time was characterised by political fluidity of an extreme nature, the non-Congress parties, suddenly aware of their new strength and opportunities responded to such a situation by forgoing alliances with each other and constituting coalition governments in the States. This was the era of Samyukta Vidhyak Dal (United Legislators Parties) and United Leftist Fronts in the country, this was the golden age of defections in Indian politics and marks the advent of politics of manipulation and manoeuvre in the country. Understandably, the majority thus contrived generally proved to be technical not emotional consequently the non-Congress parties swung into political power with rapidity and surprise, but thanks to coalitional politics they began disintegrating and bowing out of office as swifting. They were saddler but one is not sure it they became wiser after a short-lived but intensive experiment in coalitional government making in the country.[13]

The second phase may be said to have come to a formal end in 1971 when in March of that year the election to the Lok Sabha was held, earlier in February, 1969 Midterm Assembly Election were held in as many as four States—Punjab, Uttar Pradesh, Bihar and West Bengal, but its verdict broadly followed the earlier pattern set by the 1967 poll. The United Front gained absolute majority in West Bengal and formed the Government. The Akali Dal emerged as the single largest party in Punjab and formed the coalition government its other partner being the Jana Sangh, In Uttar Pradesh the Congress gained an almost absolute majority and formed the ministry. This party was the single largest one in Bihar and formed a coalition government.

In December 1969, within a few months of the mini-General

Election occurred the historic spirit in the Congress Party as a consequence of which the ruling Congress lost its majority in the Lok Sabha but continued in power with the support of the Communist Party of India (CPI) and Darvida Munnetra Kazhagam (DMK).

At the end of 1970 the Lok Sabha was abruptly dissolved and Parliamentary election was held in March 1971. This election signified the passing away of the second phase of the President's rule in India.[14]

The electoral verdict was the clearest ever in the annals of Indian polling. The Congress obtained an embarrassingly huge majority 352 of the 518 seats in the Lok Sabha. Most other parties limped back to Parliament with greatly depleted numbers, their position being as follows:

Congress (I) 16 seats (from 65 in the previous Lok Sabha), Jana Sangh 22 (from 35), Swatantra Party 8 (from 44) and Samyukta Socialist Party (SSP) 3 (from 23). The CPI retained its 23 seats while the Communist Party of India Marxist (CPI-M) increases its strength from 19 to 25 seats. In 1971 the Lok Sabha Election was for the first time delinked from the State Assembly Elections but West Bengal, Orissa and Tamil Nadu went to the poll at the same time. The Congress success at the State Level was much less flattering nevertheless, the landslide victory of the Congress in the Lok Sabha Election totally obscured the significance of assembly results and instead indicated the turn of the tide in favour of the Congress and particularly Indira Gandhi, the Prime Minister and the leader of the party. The Congress success at the polls was due to the unprecedented popularity which Indira Gandhi personally commanded all over the country, the period of political flux came to an end.

The Third Phase begins in 1971 and characterised, more than anything else, by an emergence of a substantially different framework within which the concept of President's rule discovered for itself. The defeat of Pakistan and Liberation of Bangladesh by the end of 1971 tremendously raised Gandhi's political stature nationally as well as internationally when, therefore in March, 1972 the 16 States of the Indian Union went to the polls to elect their Assemblies, she was easily the greatest mobiliser of votes for the Congress, and the electoral tide continued running in its favour of the total number of 2,757 seats in the Assemblies, the Congress captured 1,936.

Before one moves further one would like to add that nine instances of President's rule occurred in the first Phase lasting sixteen years eleven days during 1967-71 and sixteen in the final phase.[15]

REFERENCES

1. President's rule in the States and Union Territories, Lok Sabha Secretariat, New Delhi 1989, p. 10.
2. President's rule in the State and Union Territories, *op.cit.*, p. 11.
3. *Ibid.*, p. 14.
4. Annual Report of the Ministry of Home Affairs, Government of India, 1977-78, pp. 10.
5. S.R Maheshwari, *President's rule in India*, p. 33.
6. *Ibid.*, p. 34.
7. Durga Das Basu, *A Shorter Constitution of India*, p. 216.
8. *Ibid.*, p. 218.
9. *Lok Sabha Debates*, Second Series, Vol. IV, No 52, 22 March, 1951.
10. *Constituent Assembly Debates*, Vol. IX, Col. 177.
11. S.R. Maheshwari, *op. cit.*, p. 18.
12. *Ibid.*, p. 14.
13. *Ibid.*, p. 19.
14. *Lok Sabha Debates*, Secondaries, Vol-XXXIII, No. 11, 17 August, 1959.
15. *Ibid.*, Col. 2872.

2

Presidents's Rules in the States and Union Territories: A Comparative Study

1. STATES:

SECTION-A

[1950-1966]

Punjab

First, it is remarkable that the State in which Article 356 of the Constitution was invoked for the first time was the State of Punjab and the this happened within one and a half year of the inauguration of the present Constitution much before the First General Election under the Constitution. Being the first case of the President's rule in a State, it deserves a somewhat detailed analysis.

The Congress Party in Punjab, which was then the Ruling Party in the State, was deeply faction-ridden. Although Gopi Chand Bhargava was the Chief Minister and Leader of the Congress Legislative Party, there was within party a faction led jointly by Bhimsen Sachhar and Paratap Singh Kairon. The Congress Parliamentary Board in an attempt to resolve the political tangle directed Bhagava in the Summer of 1951 to make his Cabinet composite and broad-based, Bhargava resisted such a move, which was interpreted by the central leadership of the party as a defiance of the Congress Parliamentary Board's directive. Quite understandably, the board could ill afford to let Nehru go and quickly responded to Nehru's protest by formally asking Bhargava on 11 June, 1951 to resign forthwith from the Chief Ministership. Meanwhile, the central leadership of the Congress Party made up its mind to seek President's rule in Punjab in view of the factions within its State Level Organisation and to form a government only after the General Election. Secure behind the influencing support of majority of the Congress Legislators of Punjab, Bhargava even toyed with the idea of defying the central directive of Legislators to form a non-Congress government in the State. However, ultimately Bhargava veered round the directive to the Board and on 16 June, 1951 handed in his resignation to the Governor Chandu Lal Trivedi the five lines letter of this resignation began with under instructions from the Central Parliamentary board. In reply to the Governor's question he expressed his inability as Leader of the Congress Assembly Party, again under instruction from the Central Parliamentary Board to form a new Ministry.[1]

Evenwhile bowing out of office, Bhargava observed, as it is the Parliamentary Board's decision to give the administration of Punjab into the hands of the Governor is on, rounds of principles of democracy far from desirable rule by the Governor of Punjab is a retrograde step which the elected representative of the people can never agree to and can never be a substitute to a rule by the duly elected representatives.

The Governor sent his report to the President on 18 June, 1951 recommending the imposition of President's rule in Punjab. It was however not until 20 June, 1951 that the State could be formally brought under President's rule one cannot miss the significance of such an event Gopichand Bhargava, the Chief Minister was not only Leader of Congress Legislative Party but commanded the allegiance of the majority in the party. The constitutional machinery in Punjab did not face any cheats immediately or potential and President's rule was sought simply to rescue the State Level Party from its internal factional politics.

The President's proclamation on failure of the constitutional machinery in Punjab came up for Lok Sabha approval on 9 August, 1951. C. Raja Gopalachari, the Home Minister, referred to the constitutional breakdown in the State as a result of Gopichand Bhargava's resignation. He continued this is not the same as the old picture under Section 1935 by which provincial autonomy was substituted by arbitrary authority under certain circumstances.[2]

Patiala and East Punjab State Union (PEPSU)

The Second State to have witnessed President's rule was PEPSU or the Patiala and East Punjab States Union formed by integration of the Princely State in Punjab and Punjab neighbours. PEPSU was merged with Punjab under the state Reorganisation Act, 1956.

The First General Election in PEPSU along with the rest of country in 1952 did not throw up any single party which commanded absolute majority in the State Assembly out of 60 members, the total strength of the Assembly, the Congress secured 26 seats, Akali Dal 22, Jana Sangh 1, Communists Party 3, KMPP 1 and Independent 7. Immediately after the General Election, the Congress though minority part formed the Ministry which however, went within a few weeks of its assumption of power because of defections of its Legislators and the United Front Party (UFP) formed the government on 22 April, 1952. The political activity in the State became confined to manoeuvring for position by each party by luring Legislators from the opposite camp. The facility with which Congressmen joined the ministerial party and the Ministerial joined the Congress in Opposition was truly adjusted. Most of the time of the Legislative and of the Ministry was, as a result, taken up with trying to maintain the balance after the Budget Session, the State Assembly never met for more than seven day altogether due to the shifting allegiance of Legislative the Ministry was afraid effacing the Assembly, consequently, not much legislative business could be transacted throughout the even though important legislation had been pending in the Assembly and demanded action meanwhile, another awkward development took place. In February, 1952 the Election of nine members including three Ministers of whom Geani Singh Rarewala, the Chief Minister was one, Morally

Shken, Rarewala resigned from the Chief Ministership of 1 March, 1952 eight days after the setting a side of his election. The delay owed itself to the UFP'S repeated claims that it still had a majority in the Assembly and was confident of continuing a stable government in the State. The invalidation of nine Election Results reduced strength of the Assembly to 51, the Party position being as follows:

United Front 25, Congress 21, Communists 3, Independents 2. As a result a number by-elections became due. It was the fear of the Central Government that fair and free elections were not possible under the prevalent political setup, and therefore, the Centre's takeover of State administration was thought to be necessary.[3]

In view of these considerations the President's rule in PEPSU. The only State where the Sikhs were in the majority was introduced on 5 March, 1953. Thus ended the experiment of the first ever non-Congress Ministry in the country and the only one at the time while placing the Presidential Proclamation before the Lok Sabha on the same day, the Home Minister, Kailash Nath Katju charged that parallel administrative authority had been established in many areas of the State and that the entire administration had become weak. He indicated that the law and order situation had deteriorated and Agrarian reforms and developments plans held up. He emphasized that the State was in a need of efficient administration.

On the same day i.e. 5 March, 1953 the Central Government laid before Parliament a copy of the President's proclamation of the takeover of PEPSU Government but the Resolution asking for Parliamentary approval was moved at a latter date and passed V.B. Pillai I.C.S. was immediately appointed as Adviser to the Rajparamukh, but on 7 March 1953 P.S. Rau was appointed as adviser and V.B. Pillai continued as an additional adviser. This was the first time in the history of President's rule under the present Constitution that Advisors were appointed. It is also notable that the announcement of Adviser's appointment was made in the Parliament itself, a privilege which has remained denied to Advisors appointed subsequently.

Soon after taking over charge of his duties P.S. Rao addressed a Press Conference in which he explained the range and nature of his task. The Rule of the President, which is of a temporary character is designed to put down violence and lawlessness at all costs to reinstate the Rule of Law, to discourage communalism to eradicated corruption in the public service and generally to restore the decencies of public life in the State. He further observed that the Government was to be carried on in the name of the Rajpramukh during President's rule in the State. But the Rajpramukh would act in all matters on the advice of the adviser, he emphasized. He went on to say that the law and order situation in the State was bound up with Agrarian Reforms, the Legislative measures introduced in the PEPSU Assembly which had lapsed with the President's proclamation were to be duly enacted by the President when the Parliament passed the enabling act vesting in him the law making power provided under the Constitution. In May, 1953 the Parliament passed the PEPSU Legislature Act as well as the Budget for the State. In September, 1953 the Parliament extended President's rule in the State for another term of six months as the delimitation of constituencies and the preparation of electoral rolls had not been completed.[4]

Andhra Pradesh

Next came Andhra's turn when in November, 1964 the Ministry led by the veteran T. Prakasam fell by a majority of but one vote. This Ministry formed in October, 1953 was coalition one to begin with. In November, 1953 the party position in the Assembly stood as follows:

Congress 45, Communists 42, Praja Socialist Party (PSP) 16, Krishikar Lok Party 14, Independents 13 (of whom 6 were with the Congress and 4 with the Communists), Krishak Mazdoor Praja Party (KMPP) 6, Scheduled Caste Federation 2, Socialists 1. The Government's Prohibition Policy which proved to be its nemesis was a subject of intense controversy in the State.

In March, 1954 an expert committee under the chairmanship of Ramamurty which had been appointed by the Government to examine this problem recommended the virtual abolition of prohibition on the ground that it had failed. This Report of the Committee was approved by the State Assembly in June, 1954 but the Government took no action on its recommendations. On 4 November, 1953 a vote of no confidence in the Ministry was moved in the Assembly.

The resolution said that this Assembly expresses its want of confidence in the Ministry for they had failed to respect and implement the recommendations of the RAMAMURTHY Committee as decided by the Assembly on 27 May, 1954.[5]

On 6 November the motion was carried by 69 votes. The position was, Communists 40, Congress 2, Praja Socialist 7, Krishikar Lok Party & Praja 2 and Independents 10 to 68 (Congress 48, Praja Socialist 1, Krishikar Lok Party 1, Praja Party 5, KMPP 1 and Independents 12) with one Independent abstaining and one Praja Socialist Legislator absent thus dealing amoral below to the Prakasam Ministry. The Government suffered the defeat on account of two Congress Members and two members of the Praja Party (the pro-government group) defecting and voting with the opposition.

Soon after the defeat, T. Prakasam along with his Council of Ministers submitted his resignation to Governor, and also advise him in favour of dissolution of the assembly. The Leader of the Communist Party (which was the second largest Party in the assembly). Nagi Reddy thereupon met the Governor to press his claim to form the Government. He later hold the press. "I urged on the Governor that the Communist Party as the first party in the elections had the right to form an alternative Government here and now, according to democratic principles, I have also told the Governor that my Government when formed would be stronger and more stable than the previous Ministry. The Governor, Chandu Lal Trivedi (who was earlier Governor of Punjab) ignored the plea, and on 15 November 1954 President's rule was imposed in Andhra and the state Assembly too was dissolved. Trivedi did not consider the appointment of any adviser necessary, as he did in Punjab in 1952.[6]

The decision to impose President's rule in Andhra was a controversial one indeed the most controversial one since Article 356 was first invoked in 1952. The various political parties of Andhra were highly critical of President's rule imposition as they believed that it was done without fully exploring the possibilities of forming an alternative Ministry by the Opposition Parties. When in November the President's proclamation was placed in the Lok Sabha for its assent, it was approved but not without sharp criticism. The Home Minister defended the imposition ofPresident's rule in Andhra on the ground that in Parliamentary Democracy, the Ministry, when defeated in the Legislature, enjoyed the prerogative of recommending to the head of state to dissolve this Assembly and seek fresh Election. A.K. Gopalan, the Communist Member, he asserted is very good and I submit it is a precedent which ought to be followed, on the other hands, alleged that all principles, conventions and traditions pertaining to Parliamentary Democracy had been cash to the winds when the opposition was not asked to form government. In my opinion, he said a constitutional crisis happens only when there is no confidence, against a Ministry, then there are other parties and the leaders of other parties have to be called, and they are to be given a chance to form a government. If they are not able to form a government and if either the Governor or the crown in authority finds that there is no possibilities of running of administration and there is nobody to take charge of the administration then and then only there is a constitutional crisis.[7]

Kerala (Then Travancore-Cochin)

Kerala was the fourth state to have come under President's rule. After the General Election in the state held in February, 1964 the party position in the 118 members Legislative Assembly was as follows:

Congress 45, Communists 23, Praja Socialist (PSP) 12, Travancore Tamilnadu Congress (TTNC) 12, Revolutionary

Socialists 9, Kerala Socialists Party 3, Independents 6 and Anglo Indian representative 1. On 16th March, 1954 the PSP's Patton Thenu formed the Ministry with the support of the Congress. The Pillai Ministry fell when the Congress withdrew its support thereupon the Congress itself formed the Government early in 1955. This strength at this time Congress 45, PSP 19, Communist 27, TTNC 12 and Independence 2. The state Assembly was scheduled to commence voting on the Budget Demands on 15 March, 1956 but on 10 March six legislators belonging to the Congress resigned from the party to mark their protest against the proposed transfer of five Tamil speaking districts to Madras thereby reducing the Ruling Party into minority. Thereupon, the Chief Minister, Govinda Menon, submitted to the Rajpramukh the resignation ofhis Ministry. Effort at forming an alternative stable government having failed the Rajpramukh recommended to the President to proclaim President's rule in the state. The President's issued the necessary proclamation on 23 March, 1956. The State Legislature was dissolved and it was made clear that fresh election would be held in the state in February, 1957 when its country was to go to the polls. P.S. Rau, who had been the adviser in PEPSU, was appointed as Adviser to the Rajpramukh according to the official notification during the President's rule. The administration of the state will be carried on by the Rajpramukh acting upon the advice of Mr.P.S. Rau, ICS, who had been appointed adviser.[8] A week later, the Lok Sabha approved the President's proclamation enforcing Article 356 in Kerala. Defending this measures, the Home Minister, Govind Ballabh Pant told the Lok Sabha that the leader of the Praja Socialist Party which had a strength of fifteen in a House of 118 (excluding the speaker who also belonged to the PSP) reported to the Rajpramukh at one time that he had the support of fiftynine members but two of them withdrew their support to the PSP later. The Rajpramukh found that the PSP was not able to muster more than fifty seven out of 118 members. This number arithmetically less than hatf of State Assembly) and the PSP was not in a position to form a Ministry he asserted A.K. Gopalan denounced the imposition of President's rule in Kerala as being undemocratic, unjust, irregular and against all norms of democratic functioning in this country.[9] He said that although the Congress did not command a majority, it was invited by the Rajpramukh to form the Government which it did with the help of TTNC. It (the Congress Ministry) was not a stable Government, but it was allowed to be formed. The practice in Travaneore-Cochin, PEPSU and Andhra has shown that where it was helping others there has been a Ministry, but if the other parties could come together and form a majority there could be no Ministry at all with President's rule. Thus, the life expansion the Ministry and State Legislative Assembly was subdued by the inspiration of Central Government and its agent i.e. Governor of the state. The people and political leaders were not in favour of imposing President's rule in the state at any cost it was in vain, when the situation prevail uponits politics.

Kerala

The credit of having the Communist Party of India as the ruling Party for the first time under the Indian Constitution goes to Kerala.This happen after the Second General Election held in 1952. The Communist came into power in the State through democratic processes but the opposition parties in Kerala, especially, the Congress showed little sign ofbeing reconciled to the political spectacle of the Communists being at the helm of affairs in the state even since the Communists Ministry took office, the Opposition parties have done all in their power to bring it down. Especially the Congress have cared little about the means. This seem to have forgotten that the Communists were returned to power through the ballot box and should be removed by that means alone. In some places at least, the Congressmen applied the provocation that led to the unfortunate incidents.[10]

In June, 1959, the Congress, the Praja Socialist Party and Muslim League combined their forces and formed a Joint Action Committee to launch a non-violent movement to bring to an end the Communist Rule or misrule according to them in Kerala. The Joint Action Committee issued a 37 points charge sheet containing their allegation against the Communist Government in Kerala, the main ones being as follows:

It had negligently failed to carry out development programmes in accordance with the Fifth Plan, and fundamental rights were denied, there was no security for life and property, and the rule of law had ceased, corruption was rampant and increase like a flood etc.

The charge sheet concluded the administration of the state is being carried on by the Communist Ministry on the principle that the Government and the party were the same. It has planted as many of the party members as possible in the Government. The Opposition is concerned about it because it would pave the way for a Communist Party dictatorship. The popular movement against the communist ministry was intensified and it quickly snowballed. Processions, strikes, mass arrests became the order of the day and the Government did not lose its legislative majority. The Governor, Rama Krishna Rao, sent his report to the President, recommending imposition of Article 356 of Kerala. The Governor, Ramakrisna Rao himself recommending President's rule in Kerala by reporting many defects of the Communist government in the State.

Since then on 31 July 1959 the Central Government announced the President's rule in Kerala. It was an altogether extraordinary contest for the invocation of Articles 356. The Nambodripad Ministry continued to enjoy majority support within the Legislature and thus, did not present a situation of constitutional breakdown in the State.[11]

When the Presidential Proclamation came for the Lok Sabha's approval on 17 August, 1959, Govind Ballabh Pant the Home Minister explained why the Central Government's intervention in Kerala became necessary. The foremost among the reason cited by him in support of the central action was the virtual abrogation of rule of law by the Communist Government, which had discriminated in favour of its party members, directed the police not to take preventive measures, released those who had committed heinous crimes and withdrawn cases on Communist supporters. On the other hand, S. A. Dange accused the Centre of hatching a conspiracy against the Communist government in Kerala which always was like the provincial note in the Centre's eye.

The Communist government in Kerala, he said, began implementing the accepted policies and objectives of the country, which frightened the Centre. He observed the problem is not one of programmes or objectives, Socialism is the objective. Actually, the centre did not want to strength the opposite political ruling in the state, mainly Congress Centre Government have strong willing to install the same political structure with the Centre. This was the overtaking position of Centre-State relation the contrary in spite of federalism in India. Indian Constitution has double standard in implementation of the constitution. Therefore Communist Party is their opposite in the context of politics.

Orissa

Orissa has been a state lacking political stability. As the state included a number of former princely states feudal politics have always had a fairly commanding influence on the people. Besides, the sizable tribal population in the state has been anxious and keen to maintain its distinct social completion, thus providing the political base for the Jharkhand Party. After the General Election of 1957, the strength of the various parties in the 140 members Assembly stood as follows:

Congress 56, Ganatantra Parishad 51, Praja Socialist Party 11, Communists Party 1 and Independents 7. In April 1957 (that is after the announcement of the election result) the single largest party in the state, the Congress, although not commanding an absolute majority, was invited by the Governor to form the Government. The Government went on and functioned well on the whole. But the position remained somewhat unstable because of the substantial strength of the Ganatantra Parishad in the Legislature that some members of one party joined the other party, and some members of the other party joined the first party. The floor crossing was a frequent affair in Orissa and the result was that the Congress also had to carry on the administration in a somewhat difficult situation.[12]

The situation became so difficult that in 1958 the Chief Minister Hare Krishna Mahatab tendered his resignation but was persuaded by the Governor to withdraw it and continue as head of Government. Haunted by political uncertainties, Mahatab suggested at this stage the formation of a coalition Government in the state. In May, 1959 the Congress, Ganatantra Parishad coalition Government, the country's first coalition between a National Political Organisation i.e. Congress and a Regional Party i.e. Ganatantra Parishad, was formed with Hare Krishna Mahatab as the Chief Minister. This coalition government, on the whole, functioned well, and there was cooperation also between the two parties insofar as the administration of Government was concerned. However, there were various of opinions and concepts between the two parties. Hardly did the Government function for about a year and nine months when difference between the partners of the coalition arose, ultimately wrecking the coalition. The immediate bone of contention was how long the coalition arrangement was to last. The congress had in its mind the idea of keeping the coalition intact only till the end of the Budget Session. On the other hand, the Ganatantra Parishad leader and the Finance Minister R.N. Singh, insisted that he be assured of the continuance of the Coalition Government until *six* months prior to the General Election before he would agree to present the Budget in the Assembly. There was deadlock between the partners. On 22 February, 1961 Hare Krishna Mahatab submitted the resignation of his Congress Ganatantra Parishad coalition Government to the Governor. Explaining the reason for such a move Mahatab said that in a Parliamentary Democracy a coalition Ministry should resign sometime before the General Election so that the groups forming the coalition rnight be free to work in further move of their party interests.[13] The Governor sounded the leaders of the opposition parties, especially the Gantantra Parishad, about the formation of an alternative Ministry. They all expressed their inability to do so. Hence, Orissa was ripe for Article 356. On 25 February,1961 President's rule was imposed on the state, the sixth one to have come under direct central dispensation. The Legislative Assembly too stood dissolved. Furthermore, the speaker of the Assembly was also removed from his office. The last event is no less significant. It was for the first time an independent Indian's history that this functionary was dismissed from his when the Assembly was dissolved.[14]

Kerala

The Election in Kerak following a 206 days spell of President's rule after the dismissal of Namboodripad Ministry in 1959, led to a situation of political instability as no party emerged with a clear majority in the state Assembly. A coalition Government under the Chief Ministership of PSP's Pattom Thanu Pillai consisting of the congress and the PSP was consequently formed in February, 1960. It was no before long that an astonishing even occurred in the state. In September, 1962 Pattom Thanu Pillai who was the leader of the PSP resigned his Chief Ministership to take up the Governorship offer of Punjab, an event which visibly shook the Praja Socialist Party and was interpreted by it as well as by many others as a political trick on the other part of the Congress to lure other to its ranks. R. Sanker, the leader to the Congress Legislature Party and the Deputy Chief Minister in the Congress-PSP coalition immediately stepped into Pillai's shoes angered by such a manoeuvre on the part of the Congress. The PSP-left the Coalition Government in October, 1962, thus bringing an end to the thirty one months collaboration between the Congress and PSP, though the Congress Party continued to be the Ruling Party under the Chief Ministership of R. Sanker, it was itself river by deep internal factions and feuds. In, 1964 fifteen dissident members under the leadership of K.M. George left the Congress later to form a separate party called the Kerala Congress. On 7 September, 1964 no confidence motion against the Sanker Ministry was moved in the Assembly and the following day the Government fell before the combined onslaught of

Opposition Parties and the breakaway Congress Legislatures. Immediately after his defeat, Sanker submitted to V.V.Giri the Governor the resignation of his Ministry. The Governor's attempts to form an alternative Ministry having and inability to form a Government on 8 September he recommended President's rule and the following day the necessary Presidential proclamation was issued from New Delhi. The State Assembly was also dissolved. It was due to the fierce factional fight within the Kerala Congress over charges of corruption levelled against Mr. Sanker had gravely affected the efficiency of the state administration for quite sometime before the overthrow of the Sanker Ministry. In these circumstances the people of Kerala have every reason to welcome the introduction of President's rule since they can henceforth expect the administration to be run with a fair degrees of efficiency.[15]

The President's rule in Kerala was followed by election to the Legislative Assembly. The polling which was held on 4 March 1965, however, did little to clear the political confusion in Kerala. The party position in the 134 members State Assembly after the announcement of the election results stood as follows:

Communists (Marxists) 40, Congress 6, Kerala Congress (led by K.M. George) 23, Swatantra 1, who aligned with Kerala Congress SSP13, Muslim League 6, Communists Party of India 3, Independents 10, Karshaka Thozhilali Party 1.

Thus no single party as in the past managed to secure an absolute majority and was not by itself in a position to form a Government. The Government got in touch view to ascertain the possibility of formation of a stable government in the State. He summed up his discussions with term thus. The position that emerged from these consultations briefly was that although Mr. Namboodripad, Communist Party of India Marxist (CPI-M) felt it possible for him to negotiate with the various groups and individual legislators and evolve the basis on which a non-Congress Government could be formed, the leaders of the Kerala Congress and the Muslim League made it clear to the Governor that they would not join or support any ministry that might be formed or sponsored by the Communists. The attitude of the Congress was that it would act as a constitutions opposition whatever government might be formed supporting it to the extend its policies were in line with those of the Congress, but not otherwise. The leaders of the Samyukta Socialist Party (SSP) while desiring that the leader of the largest party should be called upon the form a government said that they would not agree to be in a Ministry formed by the CPI-M and would function as opposition taking however, a responsive attitude to wards such a Ministry. Thus except for the SSP which was not opposed to a Ministry formed or sponsored by the CPI-M the parties were clear that they would neither lend support to nor seek the support of that party in forming a government. In the circumstances the Governor found no possibility of the CPM commanding a working majority even if those of their members, who were in detention were free to function as members of the Assembly. The Governor did not therefore, call upon the leader of that Party to form a government.[16]

The Governor recommended President's rule and the Vice President, Zakir Hussain, discharging at this time the function of the President, signed the proclamation taking over the state Government and also dissolving the freshly elected Legislative Assembly.

The denial of an opportunity to the leader of the single largest party to try to form a government became an issue of intense political controversy in the country. It would have been a more prudent course of action if the leader of the single largest party was formally invited to form a ministry and face the Assembly for a vote of confidence at an earliest possible date commencing on the eve. It is undoubtedly unfortunate that for the fourth time in nine years, Presidential rule should offer the only way out of a constitutional deadlock. The regret will be all the greater because over eighty members who had been elected to the Assembly for the first time are denied the fruits of their victory by dissolving of the Assembly even before it could hold its first meeting.[17]

Punjab

It was under the directive of the central organisation of the Congress Party that the Gopichand Bhargava Ministry in 1951 had to resign. Ironically, history repeated itself in 1966 when Ram Kishan, the Chief Minister heading the Congress Government in the state, was induced to resign under the advice of the Party's central leadership. But the circumstances immediately attending the event on 1966 were dramatic, if not somewhat melodramatic. The Chief Minister Ram Kishan was addressing a crowded conference in Chandigarh when Mr.Gulzarilal Nanda's (the then Home Minister) phone came. All correspondents were asked to leave the room soon after, the Chief Minister called his Cabinet colleagues who were present in Chandigarh. It is learnt that all of them favoured acceptance of Mr. Nanda's advice. A little later Mr. Ram Kishan got in touch with the Governor on the telephone and informed him decision to resign. The Governor counselled patience and said that the resignation could be submitted to him on his return to Chandigarh on Thursday (following day). The Chief Minister, however preferred to send a special messenger with his letter of resignation. The Chief Minister told newsmen that he had tendered his Ministry's resignation in the interest of the smooth reorganisation of Punjab and the welfare of its people. Asked whether he had resigned voluntarily or at the instance of central leaders, Mr. Ram Kishan said that he had been in touch with central leaders for some weeks and knew their mind.[18]

Ram Kishan, who succeeded the controversial Pratap Singh Kairon on 6 July, 1964, could not succeeded in curing his party of internal factional politics which, indeed were rampant. The states in India had been reorganised on linguistic basis in 1956 but Punjab and Bombay until 1961 remained bilingual. In view of the mounting popular agitation for bifurcation of Punjab into Hindi Haryana and Punjabi speaking Punjab, the Central Government set up in September, 1965 a Parliamentary Committee of Members of both Houses of Parliament to examine the question of formation of a Punjabi speaking State. Reporting in March, 1966 the Committee recommended that the present state of Punjab he reorganised on the linguistic basis. On 10 June, 1966 the Central Government announced the formation of the two States of Haryana and Punjab with Chandigarh to remain as a Union Territory under the direct administration of New Delhi as the State was at this passing through the inevitable agony of division, passion in both parts of Punjab had been running high and the factions within the Ruling Party itself were making rather menacing noises.[19]

The unseemly haste in tendering resignation was matched by an ungainly delay in making the necessary Presidential proclamation. Although Ram Kishan submitted the resignation of his Ministry on 22 June 1966 itself within minutes of the feteful telephonic call from New Delhi. It was not until 5 July that President's rule in Punjab could be imposed. The delay was apparently caused by New Delhi's sudden resolve to install a new Governor in Punjab to administer the President's rule. On the afternoon of 22 June soon after Ram Kishan's resignation, the Central Government announced the appointment of Dharam Vira, Cabinet Secretary at the Centre, as Governor of Punjab in place of Ujjal Singh who was placed as he himself put it under order of transfer to Madras as its officiating Governor. The Central Government apparently wanted, the Governor's Report from Dharam Vira's hands. The latter assumed office on 27 June, 1966 and his report on 29 June, 1966 recommending President's rule in Punjab, on 6 July, 1966 Punjab was formally placed under President's rule. It was the first time in the history of President's rule in India that the state assembly was not dissolved but instead kept in suspended animation. As some doubts had been raised about the legality of this step the matter was referred to the Attorney General and the law Ministry. Both had advised that President's rule could be imposed in any state without dissolving the Legislature. Dharam Vira's first major task under President's rule was to facilitate the smooth division of assets and liabilities between the two new states. An advisory committee consisting of the outgoing Chief Minister and senior leaders from the two regions were immediately constituted to assist in the task. It was left to Dharam Vira to decide whether to have adviser or not. As President's rule Punjab was calculated to help in dividing it into two separate states of Punjab and Haryana, it was designed as but a short term measure to be lifted on 2 October as soon as the two states were ushered into existence. However, as subsequent events proved, it was not possible to revoke the rule until 1 November 1966.[20]

SECTION-B

[1967-1971]

Rajasthan

In Rajasthan, the Congress failed to obtain an absolute majority after the Fourth General Election in 1967 winning 89 seats in the 184 members Assembly. The position of other political parties stood as follows:

Swantantra 49, Jana Sangh 22, Samyukta Socialist Party 8, Communist Party of India 1, Independents 15 (including of the Janata Party, a break away party of the Congress) the effective strength of the Congress was 88 as one of its members was returned from two constituencies. The Swatantra, the S.S.P. the Jana Sangh and the Janata Party got together to form the United Front in the State. As four Independent legislators declared their support to the Congress, each side claimed ninety one members, the minimum strength for forming the thereby, being ninety two. Soon the solitary Communist Legislators threw his lot with the United Front thus giving the letter majority of one.

On 4 March 1967, the Governor, invited the Leader of the Congress legislature party, Mohanlal Sukhadia to form Ministry defending this step. Governor said that the Congress had got eighty seats while all the Opposition combined had only eighty Legislators. According to him the parties had fought the election on the basis of their policies which was not the case with the Independent as the people do not know their policies.[21]

That is why, he explained, he had not counted them while coming to his conclusion, he recalled a similar situation which occurred in Madras in 1952 when C. Rajgopalachari headed the Congress government even though the Congress Party did not command a majority and T. Prakasam, leader of the Opposition in that state had brought together all Opposition parties and rendered the Congress a minority party.

The Governor's decision to invite Sukhadia was completely denounced by the local opposition as unconstitutional, undemocratic and one sided.[22] On the following day (5 March) to make their protest, the United Front leaders led a demonstration to the Governor's residence. A clash with police resulted in the arrest of all the Opposition leaders which caused rioting. Jaipur continued to be the scene of disturbances, resulting in repeated police firing and many deaths. However, as a result of an intervention by Maharani Gayatri, Member of Parliament, the Home Minister Y.B. Chavan agreed to convene the first session of the State Legislature on 14 March, instead of on 20 March as earlier fixed. Just a day earlier i.e. on 13 March, Sukhadia informed the Governor that in view of the deterioration of the law and order situation due to the agitation by the Opposition he did not want to take up the responsibility of forming the Government.[23]

Plainly the Congress was not prepared to face the Assembly. On Sukhadia's refusal however, the Governor did not call upon the United Front led by Maharawal Laxman Singh to form the Ministry, observing, strengthly, that I cannot for a moment expect such persons to follow democratic methods and procedures in administration. On 13 March the Governor sent his report to the President recommending the latter's rule in Rajasthan. The same day the Central Cabinet decided to put Rajasthan under Article 356 and the necessary Presidential Proclamation was issued immediately. The State Legislature was not dissolved though this was the Governor's recommendation, but only kept suspended. As if to punish the Legislators, their allowances and other facilities were completely withdrawn giving reasons for introduction of President's rule in Rajasthan, the Home Minister observed that the local Opposition had planned a march on the Legislature and this could have caused riots and bloodshed.

The imposition of President's rule in Rajasthan was viewed by the Opposition as a dishonorable device to enable the Congress, which had forfeited its majority in the Legislature, to gain time and cleverly manage by inducing defections in the ranks of the Opposition parties Maharani Gayatri Devi termed it as absolutely wrong. S.A. Dange, Chairman of the CPI branded it as unconstitutional and unprincipled, while SM Joshi, Chairman of the SSP called it as cold blooded murder of democracy.[24]

The United Front thereupon, provided a physical demonstration of its majority by parading before S.Radhakrishnan, the President all its members now totalling ninety three.

A Memorandam, signed by the ninety three Legislators was submitted to the President urging, among other immediate redressal of wrongs done to them. This however proved to be unavailing.

As time passed, political horse trading began, the ranks of the United Front began to shrink, one of its members died and two defected to the Congress. Meanwhile, the Governor completed his five year terms of office and Hukam Singh (the former Speaker of the Lok Sabha) succeeded him on 21 April. Sukhadia submitted to the Governor a list of ninety three members and Maharawal Laxman Singh the leader of the United Front, a list of 109 names. The Governor interviewed all the legislators personally to verify their party allegiance and he found that the Congress had ninety four supporters and the United Front eight. The verdict was clear, and the 26 April he invited the Congress to form the Government in Rajasthan. The President's rule this lasted a total of forty four days. Many viewed it as serving an immediate political purpose, in the sense that the Congress which in the beginning was not in a position to form the Ministry was enabled to muster the necessary majority and to come to power. The Central Government did not seek Parliamentary approval of the President's proclamation which was placed before the two Houses soon after they met, which implied that it would cease to have any force two months after its have its promulgation. The President's rule was of a shorter duration.

The Rajasthan case, the first of its kind was not to go unrepeatable in the future. The political situation characterised by neither the Congress nor the Opposition parties initially commanding an absolute majority was to be faced time and again was the largest single party to be invited to form the Ministry. This doctrine could perhaps work where there was not party or coalition of parties commanding an absolute majority of seats in the Legislature. If however, a group claiming a majority emerges it ought to be given an opportunity. In such a situation it is scarcely open to a Governor to act as if that group did not exist. Likewise, the Governor's stand on the position of the Independent become highly controversial.

Above all, the Rajasthan episode underlined the need for a code to guide Governors on the question of formation of Ministries.[25]

Haryana

Unlike Rajasthan and many other States, Haryana did not reflect the general political fluidity prevalent soon after the Fourth General Election though ridden with deep caste cleavages the Congress succeeded in securing an absolute majority the State Legislature and was installed in power on 10 March, 1960. It was however, hardly ten days old when it fell a prey to its internal strife which climaxed into the defection of thirteen members from its fold thus ruling its strength from forty eight in the state. Assembly of eighty one to a minority. The immediate occasion was the election of Rao Birender Singh, a dissident Congress Legislator, as Speaker of the Legislature which was made possible by a group of Congress Legislatures voting for him and not for the official Congress nominee. This was the clear case of floor crossing on their part a phenomenon which, though by no means confined to it alone, was soon to give Haryana the dubious distinction of being its most avid practitioner. On 22 March, 1967 the Congress Ministry resigned and on the same day Rao Birender Singh was sent for by the Governor to form the Ministry. Samyukta Dal led by Rao Birender Singh came into office on 24 March, 1967. The Samyukta Dal was a coalition of many parties and groups including not a few defectors from the Congress, which hardly augured well political stability in a State singularly marked for its caste and faction strife. Before long the Ministry began wobbling. It drew sustenance from the changing loyalties of Legislators and its majority was a matter of almost daily fluctuations.

In no State did floor crossing assume such a virulent form as it did in Haryana. From March till November 1967, when the President's rule was imposed in Haryana, the score card of floor crossing in this state showed that in the eighty one member Assembly, thirty one defected one way or another each two other thrice, four two times and the remaining twenty three one. Obviously, the Samyukta Dal Government could not have stability as a result of defection and counter defections. It remained permanently instable until November, 1967. On 6 November, 1967 Hiranand Arya a member of the opposition Haryana Congress (led by Devilal) defected to the Samyuta Dal and immediately appointed as Minister of Agriculture. On 8 November a Congress Legislature defected and was appointed a Minister. On 11 November Arya redefected to the fold of Devilal's Haryana Congress and thus kicked it (ministership) away to exposed the Chief Minister's (Rao Birandra Singh's corrupt practies.[26] Further alleging that the Chief Minister had offered him a bag of money to change side which he promptly refused. Thus merrily continued the see-saw game of defections and counter-defections Rao Birender Singh still commanded a majority of forty legislators in an effective House of seventy eight.

On 17 November the Governor B.N. Chakravaty, sent a report to the President indicting the Rao Birender Singh Ministry, high-lighting the need for a clean and efficient administration and a fresh election after the administration had been toned up by a brief dip into President's rule. The governor observed in his report that political defections became the chief feature of Haryana polities. The State Congress Party led by Pandit Bhagwat Dayal Sharma could not forget or forgive Rao Birender Singh for having started the game of defection from the party. Efforts were made almost continuously to topple the Ministry in cooperation with Devi Lal by expanding his Ministry. The Ministry couth to maintain itself precariously in power by creating too many Ministers which is an abuse of constitutional powers, such large members of Ministers and Parliamentary Secretaries numbering at one stage twentythree out of Ruling Party's strength of Forty one and twenty two now out of total strength of forty cannot be justified on any grounds of administrative requirement the position is even worse if it is remembered that the ten Jana Sangh in the Samyukta Dal have not accepted any office as Ministers so that in reality twenty two out of the thirty remaining MLA's are holding office. The Government, being preoccupied with the problem of its own survival was not able to do much for the people with such a then majority the individual MLS's were making demands which, even if they were unreasonable could hardly be resisted by the Chief Minister on account of the constant threat of defections. Administration was thus paralysed. Every Legislators wanted to be Minister or a Parliamentary Secretary and political support was sought by offering ministerial offices at cost of the tax payer.[27]

Since the loyalty of its followers is so flexible the exact majority of the Ruling Party is not of any consequence allegations have been made by the opposition that the Ministry is continuing the power through corruption, bribery political victimisation and distribution of offices but than the opposition is also apparently securing detections through no better means or through no cleaner methods. Allegations are being made openly by both sides that money is being paid to defectors, while it is difficult to pay how far these are true, there are good reasons to believe that the defections are being secured by none too honorable means, Opportunist Legislatures whose members is fairly large, can wild tremendous power by threat of transferring their loyalties. They can do, and are doing, in calculable be damage by transferring in administration. Too frequent transfers at their instance is demoralizing the services, Since premature transfers causes a lot of inconvenience ^ junior officials often tend to succumb to such threats. The governor further added, if the Assembly is convened and either the Ruling Party or the opposition can establish its majority even then there will be up peace or stability in the present circumstances. Defection would continued and majority on the one day might be reduced to a minority the next day what would be more unfortunate is that as soon as one party establishes its majority in a trail of strength in the Assembly, it would like to get the Assembly prorogue. Even during the intercession period, attempts would be made, as are now being made, to win over members from the rival group. Administration will continue to be paralysed since the ministry will be kept busy only in maintaining itself in power. I do not recommend a mere suspension of the Legislature because in that case, the see saw game of defections and counter directions will be resumed and one party or the other would insisted on being allowed to form a Ministry on the basis of a lounges majority which will not last since he next government can as surely be made ineffective if not toppled over by malcontents crossing and re-crossing the floor.[28]

On 21 November the President issued the proclamation dismissing the Samyukta Dal Ministry dissolving the State Legislature and imposing his rule on Haryana. A copy of the proclamation was placed before Parliament the same day.

The Home Minister, Y.B. Chavan, while seeking Parliamentary endorsement of the Presidential proclamation, contended that organised defections had become a new phenomenon in Indian Politics with Legislators crossing and re-crossing the floor as many as four or five times, In this process, the people who had elected them had been cheated, democracy had been made a force and the administration was at a standstill. The principal complaint of some of the opposition leaders was that the centre was not applying one yardstick everywhere.

Atal Bihari Bajpai and Bakshi Ghulam Mohammed favoured legally enforced prevention of defections and provision for the recall of Legislators who changed their party loyalties after election. The resolution was passed by the Lok Sabha on 21, November. The Rajya Sabha approved it on 27 November, 1967.

Rao Birendra Singh filed a writ petition challenging the Presidential proclamation which however, was dismissed by the High Court.[29]

The proclamation of Article 356 in Haryana added an altogether new and novel dimension to the theory and practice of President's rule. Hitherto, the President's rule followed either the defect of a Ministry or the unability of any party or coalition to form a Government, the only exceptions being Kerala (1959) justifying the Central takeover of the Namboodripad Ministry of Kerala (1959), which it may be recalled, continued to command a majority. Jawarharlal Nehru told Lok Sabha that the mal-administration of this Ministry had untested a man up surge' assuming the character and proportion of a civil war which it was plainly beyond its power to control and, more particularly, the struggle acquired a communal turn inasmuch as the Christian had been definitely alleviated by certain measures adopted by the Ministry. In the case of Haryana (1967) the Central action did not follow any 'mass upsurge' or civil war in the state. The theory propounded in the case of Haryana was that the political defection had polluted the politics of Haryana from which it need to rescued through the device of President's rule in the state. This Rule was lifted on 21 May, 1968.[30]

West Bengal

The Left wing political parties supported by some Independents had a membership of 151 in the 280 Members State Legislative Assembly after the fourth General Election. On 25 February, 1967 they formed a coalition of thirteen political parties known as the United Front under the leadership of Ajoy Mukharji, the leader of the Bangla Congress, a splinter party formed by the dissident Congressmen. The members of the United Front were Bangla Congress, a C.P.I., C.P.I.M Forward bloc, Workers'

Party, Revolutionary Socialist Party Centre. SSP, Gorkha League, Praja Socialist Party, Lok Sewak Sangh, Swatantra, Jana Sangh and some Independents, on 2 March, 1967 the United Front formed the Ministry, though committed to a commonly agreed minimum programme the United Front consisting as it did of disparated members was based evil by acute internal dissensions. The differences between constituents related primary to the manner or handling industrial and agrarian disputes and to questions of law and order. The United Front Ministry was dominated by the Leftists and under its regime the industrial disputes in West Bengal rose steeply affecting the industrial and commercial activities all over the state and law and order deteriorating in an alarming way.

On 2 November, 1967 the fateful split in the United Front occurred. PC. Ghosh, a Minister in the Ajoy Mukherji Ministry and the first Chief Minister of West Bengal, after independence, resigned his ministership and along with 17 other legislators withdrew their support from the Ministry thus reducing it to a minority. Giving reason for his resignation P.C. Ghosh anticipated an upheaval in the State if the United Front continued to be informed in checking the activities of the violent elements of party workers. Soon after 15 of the defectors informed the Governor, Dharam Vira, about the decision to support the ministry headed by P.C. Ghosh, and at the same time the Leader of the Congress Legislature Party (which had 130 members in the 284 Legislatures) communicated a similar decision to the Governor P.C. Ghosh and his followers soon formed the Progressive Democratic Front (P.D.F.) from now on, political events began moving fast. On 6 November, Dharam Vira asked the Chief Minister to convince the Assembly as soon as possible.[31] So that the majority of his Ministry could be ascertained. The following day Ajoy Mukherji informed him that 18 December was the earliest passible date for the purpose. Giving reasons for not holding the Assembly earlier than 18 December he pointed out that the Cabinet and the Legislators were busy in the Government's paddy procurement drive and further, the cabinet would be very busy for the few weeks in finalising the following years Budget.[32] He denied that his Ministry had lost the majority. The Governor considered Mukherji's decision that the Assembly be summoned on 18 December as a prolongation of the present uncertainty and did not feet convinced that it could not be convened earlier. On 15 November he requested Mukherji to summon the Assembly not later than 23 November but the Ministry rejected this suggestion two days later. At the same time the latter decided to request the President to seek the advice of the Supreme Court on the following constitutional points, (i) whether the Governor has authority to dismiss the Council of Ministers without taking the verdict of the Legislature under Articles 163 and 164 of the Constitutions? (ii) If the Governor, on the basis of information available to him, entertains a doubt that the Council of Ministers does not enjoy the confidence of the Legislature can be, in his individual discretion, dismiss the Ministry? (iii) As the Governor is found to act on the advice of the Council of Ministers in the matter of cummoning the Legislature is it open to him to disregard the advice of the Chief Minister? (iv) can the Governor advice or insist that the Chief Minister should summon the Legislature on any other date ? (v) If the Chief Minister fails or disagrees to comply with Governor's advice, can be dismiss the Council of Ministers on the ground that non-compliance with the advice amounts to violation of the Constitution? (vi) If the Chief Minister fails or disagrees to comply with the advice of the Governor in the matter of summoning of the Assembly, can the Governor on that ground make a report to the President under Article 356? (vii) Is it open to the governor to disregard the advice of the Council of Ministers to dissolve the Assembly on the ground that in his personal opinion, the Council of Ministers do not have support of the majority in the Assembly?[33]

The President declined to refer the Ajoy Mukherji Ministry's request to the Supreme Court. Y.B. Chavan, the Home Minister told the Rajya Sabha on 20 November that the issue of the discretionary power of Governors could not be referred to the Supreme Court because such powers were not justiciable.

Earlier, the Governors Conference, Meeting in Delhi on 9 and 10 November, 1967 came to the view that the Governors were not to be guided solely by the advice of the Chief Ministers in regard to the summoning and dissolution of Legislative.

The Governor later (15 November) suggested to the Chief Minister that even if the Minister was not able to convince the Assembly by 23 November it could recommended a date not much later.[34]

This too was rejected the Ministry mean while sought the opinion of the States Advocate General on the question whether it could be dismissed for its refusal to convene the Assembly at an early date in spite of repeated suggestions by the Governor. The Advocate General was reported to have told the Cabinet that the Ministry could be dismissed if the Governor was satisfied it was not being run in accordance with the Constitution.[35]

Meanwhile, the Ministry contented to be intransigent on the issue of the date of the Assembly meeting. On 21 November 1967 the Governor acted, dismissing the Ajoy Mukherji Ministry installing P.C. Ghosh as Chief Minister and in consultation with the new Chief Minister fixing 29 November as the date for summoning the Assembly, Ghosh's was the Assembly at an early date in spite of repeated suggestions by the governor. The Advocate General was reported to have told the Cabinet that the Ministry could be dismissed if the Governor was satisfied that it was not being run in accordance with the Constitution.

On 29 November as the date for summoning the Assembly Ghosh's was a minority Ministry rejoin the support of the Congress Legislative Party having 130 Legislators. It was not very proper for the Ajoy Mukherji Ministry not to advance the date of summoning of the Legislature. The reasons given for fixing the date of meeting after nearly one and a half months were simply irrelevant when what was precisely at issue was whether the government commanded the majority in the Legislature or not. The Chief Minister's right to advise the governor emanates from his having a majority in the Legislature. When this itself is open to doubt he must himself take the earliest opportunity to convene the Assembly and have his majority demonstrated. It was, therefore, unwise constitutionally no less than morally, for Ajoy Mukharji to precipitate a crisis over a matter hardly capable for arguing. The Ajoy Mukherji Ministry apparently lost its majority consequent upon the defection of P.C. Ghosh and his seventeen followers. It was fully aware of its imminent defeat on the floor of the legislature. It had before it three choices, to resign forth with, to have a trial of strength in the legislature and then to bow out of power, and thirdly, to seek confrontation with the Governor and face dismissal by him the Chief Minister was all the time under serve pressure from his Communist (Marxist) colleagues and the cabinet was most unwilling to openly acknowledge the loss of its majority. Ultimately, dismissal by the Governor was preferred as such an action was bound to make it in popular eyes a wronged party and thus to generate goodwill and sympathy for it which it needed rather desperately in view of its nearly completely unimpressive record of work since its inception. Dismissal was viewed as an imparting halo to the United Front Ministry.

Between the dismissal of the Ajoy Mukherji Ministry and the imposition of President's rule another event was to intervene. As soon as the Assembly met on 29 November the Speaker, Bjoy Kumar Banerjee, ruled that the dissolution of the United Front Ministry by the Governor, the appointment of P.C. Ghosh as Chief Minister and the summoning of the Assembly on his advice were unconstitutional and invalid since it has been effected behind the back of this House.[36] And he immediately adjourned the house sine die without giving a chance to the P.C. Ghosh ministry to prove its majority. *The* central issue ever since P.C. Ghosh left the United Front was, who was the Legislative majority and how best this could be ascertained? And this became impossible to assess under the Speaker's ruling. This was a most bizarre situation created in the constitutional system of the State. While a popularly elected Ministry is subject to removal by the Governor under certain circumstances, the Speaker cannot be unseated except by a vote of the Assembly. But the Legislature must first meet before such a Resolution can be taken up for consideration. The Speaker's ruling consequently had the effect of completely paralysing the constitutional machinery in the State. The Assembly was prorogued by the Governor. It was again convened on 14 February 1968. Meanwhile, on 15 January there was a split in the State Congress Party as a result of which 31 Congress and P.D.F. Legislators wrote to the governor asserting that they had withdrawn their support from the Ghosh Ministry.

When the Assembly met on 14 February the Speaker announced that he had found no reason to change the ruling of 29 November, and again adjourned the Assembly sine die. As a result, there was no way left except to bring West Bengal under the President's rule. Dharam Vira sent a report to the President on 15 February 1968 recommending such an action. On 20 February, the Chief Minister P.C. Ghosh, submitted the resignation of his Ministry recommending that the Assembly be dissolved, the Speaker removed and President's rule imposed in West Bengal. The same day 20 February, 1968 the President issued a proclamation introducing President's rule in West Bengal, dissolving the Assembly. It was the second important and year mark occasion in the history of President's rule in the country that the Speaker was removed from office simultaneously with the dissolution of the Ministry and the Assembly, the first instance of this kind occurred in Orissa in 1961.[37]

Uttar Pradesh

Regarding in the case of Uttar Pradesh the Congress emerged as the victorious party in U.P. as in Haryana after the Fourth General Election. Its trouble however, started immediately after it formed the government under the Chief Ministership of Chandra Bhanu Gupta. Soon after its installation in power a number of Congress Legislators led by Charan Singh defected, culminating in the collapse of the Congress Ministry. The defectors launched a new party, called the Janata Congress which later became the Bhartiya Kranti Dal, which immediately joined hands with the non-Congress parties which had earlier formed Samukta Vidhayak Dal (SVD) of which Charan Singh was elected as the new leader. With the downfall of the Congress Ministry, Charan Singh was invited by the Governor Bezawade Gopala Reddy, to form the Ministry. The SVD, thus, immerged as a six party coalition government consisting of BKD, Jana Sangha, Socialist Party, PSP,CPI, Republican Party and some Independents. The SVD had originally formulated a nineteen point common minium programme for implementation in case it came into power in the State. This had been chalked out before the BKD joined SVD. The BKD later adopted the position that it was not necessarily bound by this common programme to which it was not an original signatory. Any way, the SVD Government consisted of such ideologically dissimilar constituents that its functioning became progressively difficult. It remained incessantly torn by grave dissensions which manifested themselves in the open. Not able to cope up with such a spectacle Charan Singh, who had barely completed ten and a half months in office, resigned from the Chief Ministership on 17 February 1968 though he continued to be the leader of the SVD whose majority in the Legislature was intact. While tendering his resignation he advised the governor to send for a new leader of the SVD with a view to forming the government, in case the Governor did not consider it advisable to do so, or the (SVD) failed to elect a Leader, he might dissolve the Legislature and hold a midterm election. Giving reasons for his resignation, Charan Singh told a Press conference that there could be no further compromise while his conscience and the with the dictates of democracy. The SVD failed to elect a new leader even after six days. The Governor reported to the President that there was no possibility at present of a stable Ministry being formed in the State either by the SVD or Congress. In his report to the President, the Governor said that the Leader of the State Congress Legislature Party C.B Gupta was not able to command a comfortable majority in the Assembly that would enable him to form a stable government. He explained why it was not possible for him to accept the recommendation of the outgoing Chief Minister that in case he (the Governor) did not consider it advisable to invite the new leader of the SVD to form the government or the SVD not being able to elect a new Leader, he should dissolve the assembly and order midterm elections. The Governor said that Charan Singh had not asked him straightway for the dissolution of the legislature but he had expressed a desire that the governor should wait and see whether the SVD was in a position to elect a leader and if one was elected he should be given a chance to form the Government. This was Charan Singh's first recommendation, and the subsequent recommendation was conditional on this recommendation not being found to be either acceptable or capable of implementation. Hence, the recommendation for dissolving the Assembly was only a secondary one and had been watered down by the earlier recommendation. The governor felt that the dissolution of the Assembly was to be ordered only when it was absolutely clear that no possibility of constituting a stable government existed. His assessment was that such an extreme situation had not yet arisen and given a reasonable time a reorientation of political affiliations might emerge facilitating the formation of a stable Ministry without the necessity of the state going through the turmoil and expenses of midterm elections. Another, perhaps equally if not more weighty consideration for recommending suspension, not dissolution of the Assembly was that 12 members of the Rajya Sabha were soon retiring and the State Legislature was to elect new members in their place.

The elections could not have been possible if the Assembly had been dissolved. On 25 February, 1968 the President's rule was imposed in Uttar Pradesh thus ending the eight day political stalemate in the largest State of the Indian Union. As the Assembly remained suspended, the efforts by both the SVD and the Congress to form the government continued each claiming majority support in the Assembly. Explaining the dilemma facing him, the Governor asked them whether he could install a ministry without verifying the bonafide of the claims of majority should that Government continue without lasting the House till July as the four-month vote on account had already been passed by Parliament. Will it be fair to all concerned, specially when I am confronted with some written evidence which is placed before me. The only issue before me is whether I should verify the claims of majority or not.[39]

Both the SVD and the Congress held diametrically opposed views on the question of ascertaining which party held the majority. The SVD advocated the floor theory, i.e. it should first be called to form the government and its majority be tested on the floor of the Assembly. The Congress was firm on the verification theory which implied that governor should adopt any procedure he considered to be appropriate for confirming the change of loyalties of those legislators who had written to him and to the Speaker. The governor was reluctant to take the odium of deciding which party had a majority in the absence of agreement between them on how to test the majority. Reluctantly, he veered round the opinion that it would do the political parties a lot of good if they had a 'holy dip in the Ganga of popular poll'.[40]

Thus, he recommended to the President on 10 April, 1968. The President signed the necessary proclamation on the same day dissolving the Assembly and ordering new elections.

The President proclamation was approved by both the Lok Sabha and the Rajya Sabha on 25 March and 1 8 April, 1968 respectively despite the Oppositions's criticism that the question of majority must always be decided in the Legislature and not in the Raj Bhavan. The Uttar Pradesh State Legislature Act was also passed in March, 1968 as the proclamation is constitutionally operative for not more than six months at a time the central government unwilling to revoke it by 18 October, 1968 approached the Parliament for its approval for the extension of President 's rule for a further period of six months. The Lok Sabha and the Rajya Sabha passed the necessary resolution on 19 and 27 August, 1968 respectively although some members regarded the demand for extension for President's rule as politically motivated. Midterms election were held in Uttar Pradesh in February, 1 969. On 26 February, 1 969 A President's rule was terminated.[41]

Bihar

No party emerged with an absolute majority in the State Assembly after the Fourth General Election. In the 318 Members Legislature the Congress had 128 Members, SSP 67, Jana Sangh 26, CPI 24, Jan Kranti Dal 24, FSP 18, Swantantra 4, CPI-M 4, Republican Party 1 and Independents 22. In bid to form the government the eight non-Congress Parties formed an alliance called Samyukta Vidhayak Dal (United Front) committed to a common programme, and the former BKD President Mahamaya Prasad Sinha was elected as its leader. On 5 March 1966. The SVD formed the coalition government in Bihar. The motivating force behind this alliance was not any integrated sit of belief but expediency. The coalition was not ideologically compatible and was based on anti-Congress feeling quite early in its life the SVD Government had to lace serious differences over a proposal to make Urdu the second official language of the state. While feelings were running high in the State over this issue communal riots broke out in Ranchi in August 1967. On 25 August, BP Mandal of the SSP resigned from the government and formed the Soshit Dal claiming 25 Legislators as his followers. The SVD government resigned following its defeat in the Assembly on 25 January 1968. This was the fall of Bihar's first coalition and was followed by its several reshuffled versions in quick succession. B.P. Mandal of the Soshit Dal just nominated to the upper House of the State Legislature formed a minority Ministry on 1 February, 1968, with the support of the Congress. The Soshit Dal Ministry fell on 18 March, 1968 when 1-5 Congress Legislatures voted with the SVD in support of a vote of no-confidence, four days later (22 March) Bhola Paswan Shastri, one of the fifteen dissident Congress Legislators who formed a separate party, called the Lok Tantrik Congress Dal (Democratic Congress Party) and now elected as the Leader of the SVD was invited to take the reins of government in his hands.[42]

As the Assembly was debating the Appropriation Bill on 25 June 1968, Paswan Shastri abruptly resigned on getting a hint that one of his supporters, the Raja of Ramgarh, was planning to defect and immediately more a no-confidence vote against the Ministry Paswan Shastri advised the governor to dissolve the Assembly, introduce President's rule and hold midterm elections in the State, the Governor however, invited the Leader of the Congress Legislature Party to form the Government. The latter sought lime to consult the Central leaders of his party. The governor wanted a new Government immediately so that the State Assembly could without delay sanction expenditure after 30 June 1968 (it had passed a vote on account for three months). Having failed in his efforts on 27 June he recommended President's rule as well as the dissolution of the Assembly in Bihar. The President issued the necessary proclamation on June, 1968, and also an order authorising expenditure from the consolidated fund of India for two months pending sanction of it by Parliament. It is worth recalling that 85 out of the total member of 318 Legislators in Bihar had changed sides since the last election of 1967 and the state had three Ministers and four chief Ministers during this period. The President's proclamation was approved by the two Houses of Parliament on 25 July, 1968. The approval for its continuance for a further period up to six months was given by the Lok Sabha and the Rayja Sabha on 10 and 19 December, 1968 respectively. The extension of President's rule became essential as the Chief Election Commissioner had fixed the date of the midterm poll in Bihar in February, 1969. On 26 February. 1969 President's rule was revoked and a popular Ministry came into power.[43]

The Midterm Election held in early 1969 did little to remove the political instability troubling Bihar since 1968. The first Ministry under the Chief Ministership of Sardar Harihar Singh fell on 20 June, 1969, consequent on its defeat in the Assembly, installed on 26 February, 1969, it was a coalition consisting of the Congress, the Janata Party, the Soshit Dal, the Swatantra, the Jharkhand and some Independents. The Bhola Paswan Shastri Ministry, which came in to power on 22 June and supported by the SSP, the PSP the CPI the Jana Sangh, the Soshit Dal, the Hul Jarkhand, the BKD, the Lok Tantrik Dal and some Independents lasted just for ten days and resigned on 1

July, 1969. Thereupon, the Governor Nityanand Kanungo, recommended imposition of President's rule in Bihar. In his report to the President sent on 2 June, 1969 he explained the developments which led to the fall of Paswan Ministry. He also referred to the claim made by Harihar Singh, leader of the Congress Legislature Party, that he was in a position to form an alternative government, the Governor, however came to the conclusion that under the circumstances obtaining in Bihar no Ministry could be stable. He attributed this to the constant defections and shifting loyalties of MLA's. Governor, however, suggested that the State Legislature should kept in suspended animation for two months.[44]

The political situation in Bihar was unlikely to improve in two months to facilitate the formation of a stable Ministry. The real reason for the governor asking for the suspension of the Assembly lay in the forth coming Presidential Election, due in August 1969. On 4 July, 1969 Bihar was formally placed under President's rule. This was for the second time in Bihar since 1967, and within five months of the midterm election. The proclamation was approved by the Rajya Sabha and the Lok Sabha on 21 August and 30 August 1969 respectively. It was revoked on 16 February 1970 on receipt of a report from the Governor that Daroga Prashad Rai of the Congress was in a position to form the Government.[45]

Punjab

In Punjab again no political party secured an absolute majority in the 104 members state legislature after Fourth General Election, the largest party was the Congress which fell 5 short of an absolute majority. The party wise position in the Legislature stood as follows:

Congress 47, Akali Dal (Sant Patch Singh Group) 24, Akali Dal (Master Tara Singh Group) 2, Jana Sangh 9. CPI 5, CPI (M) 3, Republican 3, SSP 1 and Independent 10. On 4 March, 1967 the Akali Dal (Sant Group), the Jana Sangh, the CPI, the CPI-M the political party, the SSP and six Independents formed a coalition, known as the United front, commanding 53 seats in the 104 members Assembly under the leadership of (Sant) Akali Dal's Gurnam Singh. On 8 March the United Front Ministry headed by Gurnam Singh was installed in office in Punjab within a month, it suffered an adverse vote on the Governor's address in the Assembly, but it did not resign, its argument was that (1) the substance of the amendment to the Governor's address has been conceded by the Government, (ii) none crossed the floor and the Ministry continued to enjoy the support of the majority in the Assembly, and (iii) the vote was free one as no party whip had been issued by the united Front, Soon started the unidentifying game of defections, three legislator of the Congress joined the United Front, and were immediately made ministers. Defections and counter defections continued. On 22 November 1967 when the Assembly met for its winter session Lachhman Singh Gill, the Education Minister and 15 other legislators resigned from the United Front and formed a new party, the United Punjab Janata Party, Gurnam the Chief Minister of the United Front, resigned on the same day, adivicing the Governor to dissolve the Assembly and hold hew election, Meanwhile the Congress promise support to Gill, the Governor did not accept the outgoing Chief Minister's advice about dissolution of the Assembly arguing that as long as it is possible to form a government, it should be formed.[46]

On 27 November, L.S. Gills formed minority Government, exclusively of defectors, made possible by the Congress support but without the latter's participation on it. The Gill Ministry never enjoyed any measure of popular esteem and was propped up by the assistance of the Congress which held 43 of the 104 seats in the Assembly, Gills Janata Party having but 20 seats. The Governments attempt to remove the Speaker Jogender Singh Mann, apparently to give a job to a Congress Legislator, Mann's repeated adjournments of the Assembly and the subsequent legal battles are not directly related to the theme of the present work and are therefore not discussed here. The Congress support to it was more forced that spontaneous being in pursuance of the decision of the Party's national leadership.

On 21 August, 1968 the President of the Congress Party announced the withdrawal of his party's cooperation to the Gill Ministry which at once sounded the death knell of the defectors Ministry L.S. Gill tendered his resignation on the same day. The Governor. D.C. Pavate recommended introduction of President's rule in his report to Zakir Hussain, the President. In his report sent on 21 August he regarded the minority Government as ab-initio fraught with instability as the Gill Ministry consisted of and was led by Legislators who were drawn together not by an ideological affinity but by a desire to gain political power. The relationship between the Ministry and the Congress Legislature Party, its main supporter, did not continue to be smooth as was originally hoped for by both parties. The inevitable outcome of lack of report was the use of the Government machinery by the Ministry to raise its own following. The use of Government authority for political purposes affected not only the Congress Legislator Party but has had a deleterious effect on the services also. The President issued the necessary proclamation on 23 August 1968. The Assembly was also dissolved. The proclamation was approved by the Rajya Sabha and the Lok Sabha on 27 and 29 August respectively.

The whole episode could be said to have conveyed two political messages. A minority Government, more so of the size of Gills, is most unlikely to succeed in a country like ours; secondly, post-election alliances not hinged on common minimum programme are apt to proved politically fragile.

The President's rule was revoked on 17 February 1969. A popular Ministry came into power following the midterm poll in the State.[27]

West Bengal

The President's rule in West Bengal continued until after the midterm election of February 1969, when coalition Government consisting of 14 non-Congress political parties including the CPM came in to power again under the Chief Ministership of Ajoy Mukherji. The United Front Government included such desperate elements that it hardly enjoyed any internal harmony. Progressively, internal differences within it grew so acute that on 16 March 1970, one year and 3 weeks after remaining in power the Chief Minister resigned swearing that in future he would never be in a front which includes the CPI-M. While submitting his resignation to the Governor, he made no definite recommendation on the future course of action by the latter. The Governor, S. Dhavan, thereupon invited Jyoti Basu, Leader of the CPI-M largest single party in the Legislature (80 members in a House of 280) to form the Ministry. The CPI-M leader was ready to do so but demanded that his majority be tested in the Assembly and in this regard he cited the precedents in Kerala and Bihar. The CPI-M claim in Calcutta today that it could form a government made little impact on the Union Government's assessment that there is no alternative to President's rule in the State. Although, the Union Government would like the Government to go through the fell constitutional drill by calling the CPI- M leader, Jyoti Basu, to justly his claim there were sufficient indication to strengthen the belief that Central Government is not going to be a party to allow Basu to form a Government on the assumption that the strength of the new Government could be tested in the Legislative Assembly."[48]

The Governor reported to the President, V.V. Giri that Jyoti Basu had told him that he had the support of a majority of the legislatures in advance of a total of strength in the legislature since the other parties had also declined to take the responsibility. On 19 March, 1970 West Bengal found itself placed under President's forming a Government, the Governor recommended President's rule in the State rule again. The State Assembly was suspended. This was intended apparently to give time for the political situation to stabilise in the hope of new alignments emerging leading to the formation of an alternative government but in reality to allow election to the Rajya Sabha, which are shortly due to completed. S. Dhawan came from the field of law lacking any previous administrative experience. Appointment of advisors was therefore one his earliest tasks under President's rule. In the beginning, the appointment of only two advisors was considered. Ultimately five were appointed, K. Sen M.M. Basu A.K. Ghosh, B.B. Ghosh and A.N. Kidwai. Although President's rule so as imposed in the State on 19 March 1970 the Advisors could be appointed only on 6 April, 1970, and even after that it took them some time to get going primarily because of an internal wrong over the allocation of work among them two days after his appointment B.B. Ghosh resigned his advisorship arguing that his portfolios were not good enough for him.[29] He even had meetings with the Prime Minister and the Home Minister explaining his stand ultimately, he accepted the advisors post but the frame work of administration of the state was somewhat reside under the new arrangement. The Governor was returned of executive responsibility which came to be vested in the advisors. One of the advisors, designated as the Principal Adviser, was put in charge of coordinating in work of the different portfolios.

This was a kind of climb down for the Governor. It is reported that both the Prime Minister and the Home Minister whom Dharam met after the imposition of President's rule in the State told him in very clear terms that he was to be guided by the Centre's advice in the selection of his advisors or allocation of portfolio among them. Official sources, maintained that the administration in the state must be carried on in accordance with the Centre's wishes. Very soon, the rules of business were amended primarily to provide for regular meetings of the advisors, under the new arrangement the Governor and his advisors were to function as a Council of Ministers and the Governor used to provide over the meeting of the advisor.[50] While seeking Parliament's approval of the promulgation of President's rule in West Bengal, the Minister of State for home affairs confessed that the Central Government could not cure all the ills of West Bengal under President's rule. But the Centre, he said, would try its best to give a positive and dynamic direction besides a clear administration in the state. The President's rule was revoked on 2 April, 1971.[51]

Kerala

In 1970 Kerala's United Front Ministry was a coalition consisting of the CPI, the India Muslim League, the Indian Socialist Party (ISP) and the Kerala Congress and supported by the revolutionary Socialist Party, its Chief Minister, C. Achuta Menon, belonged to the CPI. In April 1970 the (ISP) one of the Constituent parties faced a split. On 2 April following this party's request the Chief Minister asked NK Seshan the Finance Minister who had broken away from the ISP and joined the dissident group to resign. On 26 April this group consisting of 3 Legislators retaliated and merged with the Praja Socialist Party (PSP) which encouraged by its increased membership at once demanded membership of the co-ordination Committee of the United Front. Meanwhile, a battle between the (ISP) and (PSP) ensued the former party threatened to wreck the coalition if the PSP were included in the co-ordination Committee, but if it were not included the PSP swore the Ministry of its majority. Achuta Menon's dilemma was apparent.

It was barely five weeks since the Government had demonstrated its majority in the Legislative Assembly on 23 March the Achuta Menon Ministry had received a vote of confidence from the Assembly by a majority of 66 votes to 58. The Government would have lost its majority if the ISP had withdrawn its support Anxious to avert this danger. Achuta Menon on his won advised the Governor, Y. Viswanathan, to dissolve the Assembly which the latter did on 26 June, 1970. It was only after the Governor had dissolved the Assembly that he informed the Assembly that he had himself asked for dissolution of the Legislators. As he later explained to the press, Achuta Menon advise dissolution to get a clear mandate from the people so that the political uncertainty could be ended and there could be a stronger Government.[52]

On 1 August, after the date of election which was 17 September, 1974 was announced, he tendered the resignation of his Ministry declaring that he had done so in view of the criticism that the continuance of the his Ministry would have hindered free and fair elections in the State. Accordingly on 4 August President's rule was imposed in Kerala for a period of two months. As the period did not exceed two months the Parliament remained out of the picture. President's rule was lifted on 3 October, 1970 and a popular Ministry took over the reins of Government.

Uttar Pradesh

The elections to the Assembly held in February 1969 gave the Congress 209 seats in the 425 Members Legislature. On 25 February, the Governor recommended revocation of President's proclamation which was done the following day under the Chief Ministership of CB Gupta, the Congress formed the Government. Though it won the electoral war, it could not enjoy for long the fruits of its victory, what the electorate gave in no uncertain terms the party set out to decimate before it even completed one year of it's tenure in office the fateful split which occurred in the Congress a year later, which reduced the Chief Minister's followers now in Congress (O) into a minority still claiming the support of majority of the Legislators, CB Gupta did not, however, stepdown from the Chief Ministership immediately after the break up of the Congress into Congress (O) and the Congress (R). It was only on the eve of the Budget session that he resigned.

On 17 February, 1970 Charan Singh stepped again into Gupta's shoes, this time with the support of the Congress Legislators on 19 April the Congress formally joined the Ministry. Before long however internal difference marred the harmony of the coalitional partners BKD and Congress (R) so much that the coalition was seen hurthing inevitably to wards its collapse. On 25 September, 1970, Charan Singh demanded dismissal of all the 26 Congress Ministers, though more than two days elapsed after Charan Singh urged the Governor to dismiss the Ministers the Governor did not responds to the Ministers refusing to resign at Charan Singh's instance and the Governor resisting the Congress suggestions to remove Charan Singh, the State found itself plunged into an unprecedented constitutional crisis.

The Ministers were too busy trying to save a sink the Ministry to attend to official work, and administration virtually stood paralysed.

When the Governor did not act the Chief Minister wrote to him on 27 September 1970 that under Rule 3 of the UP allocation of Business Rules, he was advising him that the department held by the Congress Ministers will with immediate effect also be held by me.[53]

The Governor accepted the advice and informed the 13 Cabinet Ministers belonging to the Congress, the Ministers of State and Deputy Minister of the Congress stood automatically divested of their work when the portfolios of the Cabinet Ministers to whom they were attached were taken away, since the Governor did not accept to Chief Minister's advice to dismiss the Congress (R) Ministers they remained as Ministers without portfolio.

Later, the Governor, acting on the advice of the Attorney General, refused to dismiss the ministers sacked by Charan Singh and asked, instead, the Chief Minister himself to resign. "You are heading a coalition in which the major partner was Congress (R) the coalition no longer exists as is apparent from various letters which I have received from you and Shri Kamlapati Tripathi. Under these circumstances, the doubt naturally arose about the constitutionality of your functioning as Chief Minister and whether I could act on your advice about the removal of the Ministers. I therefore, obtained the opinion of the Attorney General, I am now satisfied that in the existing circumstances, your functioning as Chief Minister is not in accordance with the Constitution.[54]

B. Gopala Reddy, the Governor recommended imposition of President's rule in Uttar Pradesh. In his report, the Governor said that there had been breakdown of the constitutional machinery following the withdrawal of support by the Congress to the Charan Singh Ministry. He recommended imposition of President's rule for a short period as no stable Ministry could be formed either by Kamlapati Tripathi or by BKD, the alliance of Congress and the Jana Sangh. He was convinced that even if an alternative

Ministry was formed it would not last long. In view of the fickle loyalties of Legislators and other factors President's rule was the only out of the impose, the Governor concluded.

"In nut shell, the situation today is that 27 Ministers have refused to resign at the suggestion of the Chief Minister. He has asked me to dismiss them. When I requested the Chief Minister to resign he was asked for clarification and is prevaricating, which it is true that the philosophy underlying the functioning of the coalition Government has not yet crystallised the power of the Chief Minister of such Governments. Laws to be viewed vis-a-vis the constitutional obligations of the Governor taking into account the due realities of the situation. In order words, the Chief Minister of a coalition Government cannot be treated as par with the Chief Minister of a single party majority government in the matter of removal of Minister or reconstitution of Council of Ministers which involves a fundamental change in the complexion of the government. When an occasion for such reconstitution of the government arises, the spirit of the constitution demands that the Chief Minister should first tender his resignation and then reconstitute the Government. In defence of the Constitution, the Governor cannot permit any other course to be taken.[55]

The Governor's Report was first discussed in the Political Affairs Committee of the Cabinet which was unanimous on the question of accepting the Governor's recommendation. Soon after this, the Cabinet met to give its formal approval to the decision of the Political Affairs Committee.

It need to be noted that as is obligating with such reports, the Governor's Report was addressed to the President, V.V. Giri who at this time was on a state visit to the Soviet Union. The Report although addressed to the President was immediately forwarded to the Ministry of Home Affairs by the President's Secretariat. Indeed, the opposition parties had questioned the property of the Cabinet deciding on the Governor's Report before it had been so much less studied by the President to whom it was addressed. The report went to the President for his approval after the cabinet had already taken a decision on it. A courier flew to Russia on 30 September, 1970 to secure V.V. Gir's signature on the proclamation. V.V. Giri's signed it at Kiev (in the Soviet Union) on 1 October, 1970. The courier returned to India with the signed papers and on 2 October, 1970 Uttar Pradesh was brought under President's rule, this being the second occasion in its political life.

The President's rule proved to be a very brief duration indeed, it was the shortest ever spell in the history of President's rule in India just 18 day in all. On 18 October TN Singh, leader of the Samyukta Dal SVD was invited by the Governor to form the Government.[56]

Orissa

In 1970 a coalition ministry was formed by the Swatantra Party and Jana Congress (a splinter party which left the Congress in 1966 in protest against the Biju Patanaik Ministry) under the Chief Ministership of R.N. Singh Deo the Swatantra Leader. In May, 1970 the Congress Party suffered large scale defections from its ranks and the defectors floater a new party the Utkal Congress under the leadership of Biju Patnaik with the old foe (Biju Patnaik) gone the reason for the separate existence of the Congress and the Jana Congress, too had substantially disappeared. Accordingly, there two parties initiated a dialogue for a possible reunion. But the Congress wanted the other party first to delink its association with the Swatantra Party, a partner in the coalition. Events began moving swiftly and finally on 5 January, 1971 the Jana Congress severed its relation with the Swatantra-led coalition and requested the Governor Angari to dismiss the Ministry and hold a midterm poll in the state. As the Chief Minister continued to claim the majority in the Assembly, the Governor, on 7 January 1971 asked him to prove it by seeking a vote of confidence. On realising that this would not be possible, R.N. Singh Deo resigned on 9 January, 1971 recommending at the same time the dissolution of the Assembly. The Governor did not accept the Chief Minister's advice as he was of the view that question would be considered only after he had explored the possibility of an alternate government. Since no party was capable of forming the Government he recommended on 11 January, 1971 the imposition of President's rule in Orissa. On the same day the President put Orissa under Article 356 as no alternative Ministry could be formed, the Assembly was dissolved on 23 January, 1971. On the same say as announcement was made to hold the election to the State Assembly on 5 March, 1971, simultaneously with the Parliamentary Election. As the President's rule was not intended to last for more than two months Parliamentary endorsement was not taken the Presidential proclamation lapsed on 22 March 1971 and another proclamation was issued on 23 March 1971, President's rule was revoked on 3 April 1971 and a non-Congress coalition Ministry under Biswanath Das was inducted into office.[57]

SECTION-C

[1972-1976]

Mysore

Mysore came under President's rule on 27 March, 1971, and remained so administered until 30 March 1972. This was Mysore's first taste of President's rule. The split of 1969 did not perceptible alter the Ruling Congress Party in the State as only twelve of its Legislators joined the Congress(R), the great majority remaining with the Congress(O). The Congress Ministry under the Chief Ministership of Veerendra Patil was in power in Mysore, when the State was called upon to elect 27 Members of Parliament in the 1971 Lok Sabha Election. Contrary to all expectations the Congress(R) (presently referred to as Congress) scored spectacular electoral success, bagging all the 27 Lok Sabha seats and completely routed the Congress(O). The ruling Party in Mysore stunned by the Lok Sabha Election result found 20 of its Legislators including 3 Ministers defected to the Congress(R).

The complete rout of the Congress (O) in the Lok Sabha election had already shaken its moral authority to continue in power. The large scale defections from the party clinched the issue by stripping it of its majority. On March, 1971 within a week of the announcement of Parliamentary election results Veerendra Patil submitted resignation of his Ministry to the Governor, Dharam Vira, although he did not face an adverse vote in the Assembly.

The Governor, thereupon called the leader of the Congress (R) to form the Government, no sooner than Patil resigned, that his Party's Legislators began lying with each other in joining the Congress almost in a kind of gold rush.[58]

Its strength swelled from 57 on 15 March to 120 on 22 March, with many applications still under consideration. The Praja Socialist Party, having 11 Legislatures in the Assembly was not to be left behind and joined the stamped by altogether merging with the Congress Party on 19 March. The leader of the Congress would have formed the Ministry with the support of the ever swelling number of defectors but for the ferny directive of the Central Party leadership forbidding Ministry making. On 26 March the Central Party leadership decided to have a temporary spell of President's rule in the state. It was proclaimed on 27 March but the Assembly was Dept under suspension. President's rule did not altogether still political activity in Mysore for the suspension of the Assembly indicated a hopeful sign of a popular Government being revived. The Legislators on general and the defections in particular were most loath to go into wilderness and desperately tried to put any party into power therefore the Congress party's decision not to take office became known at least 20 of the defectors re-defected to the Congress (O). The last ray of hope vanished when Veerendra Patil whom the Governor invited on 13 April to form the Ministry, declined to do so stating that the Ministry dependent on the support of the defectors could not expect to be stable. On 14 April, 1971 the Assembly was also dissolved.

The Lok Sabha and the Rajya Sabha approved the proclamation on 24 May and 25 May, 1971 respectively. K.C. Pant who moved the resolution for the adoption by Parliament referred to the impact on defections caused by the President's rule. Another Member of Parliament M.K. Krishnan countered this argument by observing the ruling party does not want any other party to be in power in any state and if there is any state where any other party is in power the ruling party at the Centre does everything to topple it. In June, the Mysore State Legislators (delegation of Power Act) conferring on the President, the powers of the State Legislature was enacted.

As President's rule was contend beyond six months Parliamentary approval for its extension was obligatory. The two Houses of Parliament gave this approval on 18 November and 22 November, 1971 respectively. The President's rule lasted until 20 March, 1972. Midterm poll held early 1 March led to the formation of a popular Ministry in the State.[59]

Gujarat

Like Mysore, Gujarat was another stronghold of Congress (O) which continued to be Ruling Party under the Chief Ministership of Hitendra Desai even after the split. But the Parliamentary Election of 1971 left no one in doubt even in Gujarat about the parliamentarians of the Congress and panicked the opposition parties everywhere. Gujarat being no exception claiming that the Congress (R) was the real Congress, 17 legislators including a Minister left the Congress(O) on 29 March 1971 and joined the former party. Having lost its majority the Congress(O) became dependent upon the 21 Swatantra Legislators. 11 of whom however withdraw their support to the ruling Party on 30 March. The writing on the wall became clear as a result of this action and on 31 March, 1971 Hitendra Desai tendered his resignation to the Governor. As in Mysore Minister only served to unmask the sordid state of affairs in the country's political system. The next week saw wholesale defections as in both directions but ultimately the Congress(O) succeeded in mustering majority in its favour and again assumed office on 8 April under the Chief Ministership of Hitendra Dasai. Ironically, the Congress (O) won office but no stability for on 10 May began an exodus from its ranks to the real Congress. On 12 May the Congress (O) stood with its majority reduced to 68 in a house of 168 members. Sensing the snow balling effect of defections on 11 May the

Chief Minister advised the Governor to dissolve the Legislature and hold fresh election while his Ministry was to remain in office on a caretaker basis. Shriman Narayan rejected this demand and recommended the imposition of Article 356 in Gujarat which was done by the President on 13 May 1971. It may to be mentioned that on 29 March the Assembly had passed a note on account for expenditure for only the first four months of the year 1971 -72 and the budget for the remaining part of the year was to be passed before 31 July, 1971. The Governor explained to Hitendra Desai that if the Assembly was dissolved as suggested by him, it would not be possible to pass the budget by 31 July and the state administration would come to a standstill. Hence, the inevitability of President's rule in the State. The President's proclamation was approved by the Lok Sabha and the Rajya Sabha on 21 June and 31 May 1971 respectively. As President's rule continued for more than six months another Parliamentary approval was secured during the Winter Session of 1971. It was revoked on 13 March 1972, when a Ministry came into office following the midterm poll.[60]

Punjab

The midterm poll held in Punjab in February 1969 did not give absolute majority way single political party in the State. In the Assembly of 104 Akali Dal had 43 seats, Congress 38, Jana Sangh 8, CPI-M 2, Swatantra 1, Janata Party 1, and Independents 4, as Akalis and Jana Sangh already had forged a pre-election alliance a coalition ministry consisting of both these parties came to office on 17 February, 1969 with Akali Dal's Gurnam Singh as the Chief Minister. However, the two parties did not see eye to eye on many a matter especially on the question of language policy for the state. Moreover, the Akali Dal itself was ridden by internal dissensions which soon led to the emergence of two separate groups led respectively by Sant Patch Singh and Gurnam Singh and ultimately climaxed in the our throw of Gurnam Singh. On 25 March, 1970 the coalition suffered a defeat in the Assembly. After a measure of initial hesitation Gurnam Singh resigned on the following day. On 27 March, 1970 the Gurnam is installed Prakash Singh Badal as the Chief

Minister heading a coalition Ministry consisting of the same old partners i.e., Akali Dal and Jana Sangh. But the two parties could not get along for very long. The immediate reason for the estrangement was the refusal of the Akalis to honour their commitment to the setting up of the Dayanand University at Jallunder or to restricting the jurisdiction of the newly set up Guru Nanak University at Amritsar. Irked by such a volte face on the part of the senior partner, the Jana Sangh walked out of the coalition on 1 July. Also the Akali Dal suffered a reduction in its strength as a result of defection from its ranks, consequently, the party position in the Assembly had become extremely fluid. To test the support of the ruling party the Assembly was convened on 24 July 1970. In the trail of strength that took place in the legislature the Badal Ministry survived, thanks to the neutral posture adopted by the Congress at the crucial time of voting. But this was significant in heralding the emergence of an understanding between the ruling Akali Dal (Sant Patch Singh Group) and Congress.

The Akali Dal though minority party, now continued to be in power on account of the support assured by the Congress,. But the party was torn by acute internal decisions. Many of its members demanded reduction in the size of the Ministry and an inquiry into allegations of corruption against some of the ministers. In a dramatic move on 1 June 1971, all the ministers submitted their resignations to the Chief Minister to enable him to reconstitute the Ministry. In the meantime a secret move to topple the Badal Ministry was also afloat. The Congress reached an understanding with Gurnam Singh, Badal's predecessor and political advisor and was contriving defections from the ruling Akali Dal. The plan was either to instal Gurnam Singh as the Chief Minister with the support of the Congress or to form a coalition of the Congress and the defectors from the Akali Dal. On 12 June one of the ministers resigned from the Government alleging that the Ministry was sinking with corruption.[61]

Immediately on receipt of the resignation Prakash Singh Badal rushed to the Raj Bhawan to advise the Governor to dissolve the Assembly, accusing the Congress of encouraging defections. On 13 June 1977 D.C. Pavate, the Governor ordered the dissolution of the Assembly but asked Badal to continue till alternative arrangement were made. Meanwhile, the Akali Dal was further wrecked by defection, as a result it was left with a following but 39 in the Legislators of 104 members. The defectors formed new party called the Shiromani Akali Dal demanded that the Assembly should not be dissolved the appeal proved to be unavailing as the Governor had already ordered its dissolution and there was no question of going back. Prakash Singh Badal tendered his resignation the same day and President's rule was proclaimed in Punjab on 15 June 1971.

As the Punjab Assembly had passed a vote on account for the first three months the budget for the remaining part of the new financial year needed to be passed. This the Parliament did on 17 June, 1971. On 2 August the Lok Sabha began considering two resolutions simultaneously, in relation to the President's proclamation and another on the Punjab State Legislature (Delegation of Power) Bill. The resolution and the Bill were passed on 5 August, 1971 after a discussion lasting slightly less than three hours. The Speakers participating in the discussion generally accused the Badal Ministry of rampant corruption and the Ruling Party at the centre for showing sign of impatience and intolerance immediately after the Government even in a State by an Opposition Party. Following Midterm poll the President's rule was withdrawn on 17 March, 1972.[62]

West Bengal

As discussed earlier, West Bengal had come under President's rule for the second time in March 1970. The State was torn by violence during this period, the Central Minister of State for Home Affairs stated on 9 December, 1970 that 226 political murders were committed in the state in the first 10 months of 1970 compared with 95 in 1969. An unprecedented wave of terror was sweeping this western state and understandably the foremost attention of the State Government under President's rule was to strike out terrorism from its land. The Central

Government, too was determined not to left President's rule until law and order was reasonably restored in the state this continued to be the central stand until the end of December even after the Lok Sabha had been dissolved on 27 December to seek fresh mandate from the people. But suddenly, on 7 January 1971 an announcement was made to hold election to the West Bengal Assembly on 10 March 1972 simultaneously with the Lok Sabha poll. The election campaign which was geared to a high pitch was marked by widespread violence but the voters turnout was impressive and the electoral verdict unclear.

The election was fought by two party alliances or Fronts. The United Left Front (ULF) consisted of CPI-M Revolutionary Communist Party Forward Bloc (Marxist) workers party and Biplab Bangala Congress. The United Left Democratic Front (ULDF) included CPI Socialist Unity Centre, Forward Bloc and Gurkha League.

The Congress(O) and the Bangala Congress contested the election independently. The party position in the 280 member Legislative Assembly stood as follows:

1.	United Left Front:		
	Communist Party (Marxist)	–	111
	Other	–	12
2.	United Left Democratic Front:		
	Communist Party	–	13
	Other	–	12
3.	Other Parties:		
	Congress	–	105
	Muslim League	–	7
	Bangala Congress	–	5
	Congress (O)	–	2
	Other	–	10
		Total-	277

(3 seats were vacant)

As would be evident from the above results, the politics of West Bengal became greatly polarised, the two chief contenders for power being the CPI-M and the Congress, the former having emerged as the single largest party in the state. The United Left Front (which had become into existence before the election) commanded 123 seats in a house of 277. As the ULF had the single largest block of Legislators, Jyoti Busu, the CPI-M Leader stated his claim for invitation to form the Government. But the Governor S.S. Dhavan wanted Basu to first prove that he had an absolute majority in the Assembly. In the meantime, the ULDF (except the Socialist Unity Centre having 7 Legislators) decided to support a coalition Ministry including the Congress. Accordingly, the Democratic Coalition was formed on 23 March, 1971 consisting of all the parties in the Assembly except the ILF parties, the Socialist Unity Centre, Revolutionary Socialist Party and Jharkhand Party, and having a combined strength of 142 in the house of 277 (3 seats vacant).

On 2 April, 1971 Ajoy Mukherji the Bangla Congress leader, assumed the office of Chief Minister of West Bengal this time heading the Democratic Coalition and the President's rule was revoked. Slender was the majority behind the Ajoy Mukherji Ministry and it was to receive further setback within weeks of its formation two results in the three byelections held in June of that year went in favour of the CPI(M) and one in favour of Congress. Further, on 6 June three of the five Bangla Congress legislators led by Sushil Dhara, the party's General Secretary broke away and formed an independent group. Despite this, on 14 June, 1971 Ajoy Mukherji expressed confidence in the stability of his Ministry saving that even if Dhara's group voted with the opposition, the Assembly would stand evenly divided with 140 members supporting him and 140 voting with the Opposition.

Meanwhile, terrorism did not abate in West Bengal not even to the slightest degree and the Government is task became much more difficult with the unceasing flow of refugees from East Pakistan (at present Bangladesh). On 25 June, 1971 Ajoy Mukherji advised the Governor to dissolve the Assembly three days later he tendered the resignation of his Ministry and President's rule was introduced on 29 June 1971. The reason put forward by Ajoy Mukherji for asking the resolution of Assembly was that the refugees problem had become serious and required strong majority.

Departing from the general practice under which the Parliament gets three separate opportunities for approving the President's proclamation enacting the Bill authorising delegation of Legislative Power and passing the State Budget all the three formalities were taken up together on 23 July 1971 and were disposed of in six and a half hours quite understanding the discussion in the House rigidly followed party lines, the Speaker belonging to the Ruling Congress Party stoutly proclamation was approved by the President's rule and the Opposition members vehemently censuring it. Many speakers from the Opposition criticised the Governor for not inviting the Opposition to form the Ministry and further demanded immediate election in the State. The proclamation was approved by the Lok Sabha on 26 July 1971 and the Rajya Sabha on 22 July 1971. The resolutions for the continuance of President's rule for a further period of six months were passed by the two houses in 1971 Winter Session. The elections to the Assembly were held on 11 March 1972. On 20 March 1972 the President's rule was revoked and the popular ministry belonging to the Congress Party took office.[63]

Bihar

President's rule for the second time in Bihar lasted for 229 days from July 1969 till February 1970. It came to an end with the coming into office on 16 February 1970 of the Daroga Prasad Rai Ministry which was a coalition consisting of the Congress, the Jharkhand Party the Soshit Dal and independent. It fell on 18 December 1970 as a result of defections of some supporting Legislators. Four days later Karpoori Thakur, the SSP leader formed the Samyukta Vidhayak Dal (SVD) Government which comprised of the SSP, the Congress(O), the Jana Sangh, the Swatantra Party, the BKD, the Janata Party, the Soshit Dal and a group of PSP. This ministry did not last long either having been outvoted on 18 December 1971. From now on the Bihar politics began a turn in favour of the Congress and a beginning in this direction was signified by the coming into power on 22 December, 1971 of the coalition Ministry led by Bhola Paswan Shastri and independent member of the Assembly. This Ministry which assumed the name of Progressive Vidhayak Dal consisted of the Congress, the CPI, the FPSP, the Jharkhand Party and Soshit Dal. In other words major parties, mini-parties and defectors. No one expected such an assortment of parties to have a longer life.

Meanwhile, the political environment in Bihar as in the rest of the country was undergoing a perceptible change the spectacular Congress success in the Parliamentary Poll held in February, 1971 confirmed that the wind was blowing in its favour everywhere, furthermore the liberation of Bangladesh in 1971 and the defect inflicted on Pakistan engendered euphoria among the Congressmen. The time was clearly auspicious for this party to go to the poll and thus cash its popularity with the masses.

Accordingly, in January 1972 the Central leadership of the Congress decided to hold elections along with several other States in March and immediately instructed Bhola Paswan Sastri to resign and recommend midterm poll in Bihar. As Assembly did not have any Party commanding a majority an early election was expected to go in favour of the Congress. On 27 December, 1971 the Ruling PVD resigned and the Governor D.K. Barooah recommended the imposition of President's rule in Bihar. At that time a President proclamation could not be issued immediately because of a constitutional hitch and so Mr. Barooah dissolved the Assembly under Art. 174 on December 29. On 9 January, 1972 President's rule was proclaimed in Bihar, this being its third experience since the General Election of 1967. As Parliamentary rectification of President's rule was not possible this body not being in session its validity expired on 8 March. But a fresh proclamation was issued by the President on 9 March, 1972. The midterm poll was held early in March. The President's rule was revoked on 19 March, 1972 with the Congress which gained absolute majority in the Assembly coming into office.[64]

Manipur

Manipur, a Union Territory was under President's rule since 16 October, 1969 as provided for under the Government of Union Territories Act, 1963. It gained the status of a full-fledged state of the Indian Union on 21 January 1972 and was immediately put under President's rule by invoking Article 356. A state must have a Council of Ministers with the Chief Minister at the head to aid and advise the Governor. As such a political institution was non existent at the time and could be expected to come up only through the process of an election which, too needed sometime to be organised. The formality of President's rule alone could ensure the constitutionality of the prevalent governmental arrangement in Manipur. Election to the Manipur Legislative Assembly was held in March and popular Ministry assumed office on 20 March 1972. On the same day President's rule was revoked. Thus the effective date of birth of Manipur as a state is 20 March 1972.[65]

Tripura

There is generic likeness between Manipur and Tripura. A Union Territory, Tripura had been under President's rule since 1 November, 1972. It acquired the status of full-fledged state on 21 January 1976 and President's rule had to be imposed on the same day to rationalise the absence of popular Ministry in it. Election to the Tripura Legislative Assembly was held in March. President's rule was revoked on March 1972 and a popular Government took office, thus both the State of Manipur and Tripura were born while in sleep.[66]

Andhra Pradesh

President's rule in Andhra Pradesh was for an altogether different reason. It attracted the provisions of Article 356 not on account of the all too familiar fickleness of the Legislators loyalty but because of the regional cult to which both its people and a segment of its political leadership have remained committed with varying range of intensity, ever since the formation of this State in 1956.

The threat of bifurcation of the state into two separate one of Andhra and Telengana has been met ever since it became openly intensified in January 1969, by internal adjustment and reshuffling within the Ruling Congress Party and by administrative devices, to appease the separationists, Brahmnand Reddy, the Chief Minister of Andhra Pradesh since 1964 was made to resign from his office in 1970 at the insistence of the Congress High command. P.V. Narasimha Rao who succeeded him could not however succeed in snuffing out the separatist agitation in the two regions and was finally asked by the party's high command to submit the resignation of his Ministry and thus pave way for President's rule in the state. Interesting as it may appear, the decision to ask Narasimha Rao to step down was first taken by the Political Affairs Committee of the central Cabinet.

In India on many occasions the roles of a purely party organ like the Congress High command and of the Political executive become in practice indistinguishable, in the process either of them gets reduced to the level of merely ratifying body. Constitutionally speaking the Central Cabinet cannot issue any directive of this kind to any political party in the land, but this happens because of single party dominance in the country and an unwillingness to keep the roles of governmental and purely party organs distinct and separate. Coming however, to the present theme Narasimha Rao resigned on 17 January 1973 altogether his Congress Party continued to command a majority in the State.[67]

The Governor sent his Report to the President the same day and President's rule was imposed in Andhra Pradesh on 18 January 1973. In accordance with the Governor's recommendation, the State Assembly was kept in suspended animation to be reactivated after normal conditions had been restored in the State.

The resolution seeking Parliament's approval of the President's rule came for discussion in the Lok Sabha on 28 February and was voted the following day. In the course of discussion BN Reddy observed, "I would like to ask this house as to why the situation has been created that 4.5 crore forty five million people of Andhra Pradesh have been made to suffer this President's rule. The government there is supposed to be the most stable of all the government in the South. It was also a Congress Government with an absolute majority today President's rule is proclaimed because it is stated that the separated proportions, this President's rule is not a political solution of the various problems that are being faced by the state. To put it in a nutshell, it is only a continuation of the CRP and Military Government that had been perpetrated by the Government of Shri Narasimha Rao which is completely unconnected and unaware of the problems of the people. The Parliament was again approached for continuance of President's rule for second term of up to six months. In December 1973 the central leadership of the Congress party decided in favour of forming the Government in Andhra Pradesh with this done all the necessary rituals were very completely very swiftly. Accordingly, on 8 December, 1973 J. Vengal Rao was elected as leader of the Congress Legislative Party, the Governor sent his report to the President recommending revocation of latter's rule. On 10 December, 1973 the Congress Ministry formally returned to the state after an absence of nearly eleven months.[68]

Orissa

The party position in the 140 members Orissa Assembly resulting from the election held in March, 1971 stood as follows:

Congress 51, Swatantra Party 36, Utkal Congress 32, Praja Socialist Party 4, CPI 4, Jharkhand 4, CPI-M 2, Congress(C), Janna Congress 1 and Independents 4. As is amply confirmed by this figure Orissa continued to be in love with coalitions. As soon as the election result were out the Governor initiated the constitutional process by inviting the Congress, the single largest party in the Assembly to form the Ministry. Unwilling to have a coalition Ministry, the Congress was anxious to secure a complete merger of the Utkal Congress with it in order to obtain the necessary majority and then assume office. This demand was unacceptable to the Utkal Congress.

Meanwhile, the Utkal Congress formed a United Front with the Swantantra Party and the Jharkand headed by Biswanath Das who at that time was not a member of the Assembly and did not belong to any headed by Biswanth Das who at that time was not a Member of the Assembly and did not belong to any party. On 3 April, 1971 United Front having a majority support of 72 (three Independent supporting it) in the 140 member Assembly formed the Government. This Ministry fell in June as a result of floor crossing by some foot loose legislators and the Congress led Ministry came into power, its Chief Minister being Nandini Satpathy who at the moment was not a member of the Assembly. Having come from the Centre Satpathy's induction into the State Level Congress was regarded by many Congressmen as an imposition on the State Party by the high command. Moreover, the Congress could come into power only by encouraging floor crossing and admitting the defectors from the Swatantra and the Utkal Congress.

In January 1972 Harekrishna Mahatab and four of his supporters broke away from the Congress to form a separate group thereby reducing the Party's strength to 78 in a House of 140 members. The Utkal Congress dissolved earlier was revived on 12 November and commanded group of 18 Legislators under the leadership of Biju Patnaik. On 29 January, 1973 the Utkal Congress, Swatantra Party and Harekrishna Matab's group formed an alliance called the Orissa Paragati Legislative Party, which consisted of 47 members. On 29 June 1973, a desperate bid to stall defection from the Party of the Chief Minister of the Utkal Congress MLAs. But they could not bring themselves to excuse Mr Patnaik's role in the recent byelection in the Cuttack Constituency.[69]

Any such compromise, however, was not acceptable to Mr. Routray and Mrs. Stpathy seems to have only anticipated his walk over to the opposition by dismissing him from her Cabinet within a few hours of tendering its resignation to the Governor and asking him to dissolve the State Assembly.

On 1 March, the Chief Minister resigned and advised the Governor B.D Jatti to dissolve the Assembly because she wanted to get a clear verdict from the electorate for her progressive measures. Explaining why she choose to resign, she alleged that intrigues by her collegues made it impossible for us to give undivide attention to the problems of the State. The Governor immediately prolonged the Assembly which was then in session.

Meanwhile the opposition leader, Biju Patnaik stated his claim to be invited to form the Ministry, asserting that he was in a position to form a stable Ministry. He alleged that the Chief Minister had denied an opportunity to the opposition to defect her in the Assembly by resigning when it was in session.

The Governor sent two reports to the President, the Preliminary report and the final one both dated 1 March. He recommended dissolution of the Assembly and imposition of President's rule. At 12:30 P.M. on 3 March, 1973, the President signed the necessary proclamation to this effect.[70]

Manipur

The election to the Manipur Legislaure held in March, 1972 did not give decision majority to any single party. In the 60 members Assembly the congress (R) had 17 seats, Manipur People's Party 15, CPI 5, Socialist Party 3, United Naga Integration Committee 3, Congress (O) 1 and Independents 16. Soon after the announcement of the results, the Manipur People's Party, the Socialist Party, the United Naga Integration Committee, the Congress (O) and 10 out of 16 Independents formed the United Legislative Party with Manipur People's Party Mahamad Alimuddin as its leaders. Having a majority of 32 in the House of 60 the Alimuddin Ministry took office on 20 March, 1972. In the Twelfth month of its career however the Ministry faced rough weather as a result of defection by nine of its supporters including two Cabinet Colleagues. On 26 March, 1972 when no confidence motion was being debated in the Assembly. The Chief Minister unwilling to face an adverse vote in the Legislature, went straight to the Governor to tender his resignation and demand of dissolution of the Assembly. Explaining the reason for his demand of dissolution of the Legislature, he said no stable Government could be formed in Manipur as there were many professional defectors among the Legislators as many 10 Legislators had crossed the floor in one year and 6 of them had defected an redefected some six times.

Immediately, after the resignation of the Alimuddin Ministry, A Diaho the leader of the Progressive Democratic Alliance (Opposition) staked his claim to form an alternative Government. The Governor in his report to the President recommended the imposition of Article 356 in Manipur but favoured that the Legislature should be suspended not dissolved as it would not be possible to held election before the end of the year.

The Central Government did not agree with the Governor's recommendation for suspension of the Assembly its reason being that as both Orissa and Manipur had fallen under more or less similar circumstances. It was invidious to make a distinction between them. Accordingly, on 28 March 1973 the President imposed Article 356 in Manipur and dissolved its Assembly. This was the second occasion in the annals of President's rule in India when the Centre acted contrary to the Governor's formal recommendation.

The Lok Sabha and the Rajya Sabha approved the President's rule in the State on 14 May and 13 March, 1973 respectively. Approval for further continuance of the rule was accorded by the two Houses in August 1973, Mid-term elections were held in Manipur in February, 1974 and the Manipur People's Party led coalition Ministry having majority of 35 members in the Assembly of 60 into office in March 1974. Thus President's rule was revoked on the same day.[71]

Uttar Pradesh

The T.N. Singh Ministry could not last beyond March 1971. Early in 1971 U.P went to the polls to elect its Legislature. The electoral verdict was overwhelmingly in favour of the Congress, Kamlapati Tripathi formed the Ministry on 4 April 1971. Secure behind its massive legislative majority, the Tripathi Ministry was in a position to take up bold measures to ameliorate the many grievances of the people in the state. This however was not happened. The Government showed little evidence of activity and vigour in the management of State affairs. The administration did not indicate many signs of life. Then broke out May 1973, the revolt by a section of the Provincial Armed Constabulary (PAC). The State Government swiftly suppressed it, displaying in the process rather excessive ruthlessness and severity. But neither success nor excess proved to be of much help in rehabilitating its image. Above all, Kamlapati Tripathi even seemed to lost the confidence of the Prime Minister, Indira Gandhi who had emerged after the election of 1971, as the most powerful leader of the Congress. A month after the occurrence of the PAC revolt, it appears that she made up her mind to jettison Tripathi to be sure alternative suggestions had been considered change of leadership in the State reconstitution of the Council of Ministers by dropping those Ministers whose reputation were suspect etc. Kamalapathi Tripathy was reluctant to make any drastic changes in his crew, observing that he could not sack any of his senior colleagues who had stood by him through thick and thin. Ultimately, the preference went in favour of President's rule in Uttar Pradesh.[72]

On 13 June 1973 Tripathi bowed out of office and he rationalised his exit in terms of the revolt. In his letter to the Governor, Akbar Ali Khan, Kamlapati Tripathi referred to the PAC revolt which had wider repercussion, coming as it did in midst of a period of unprecedented strain through which the state had been passing. Mostly because of drought resulting in scarcity of essential commodities and in the shortage of electricity. He continued, you (the Governor) would agree that it would be in the paramount interest of the state and the country that the civil and armed wings of the police are now recognised in such a manners that the force becomes a more effective and disciplined instrument for serving the people. Such a reorganization will have to be in future with the overall national requirements of maintaining law and order from the point of view of national security and integrity.

No doubt, this exercise could be done by us as we have been already doing, but, we feel that the requirement of the situation would be better served if this responsibility is undertaken by the Centre which can achieve the desired results more quickly and effectively with its resources and expertise. The sharp psychological which direct central involvement should bring out about will help in the speedy cleansing of the remaining cobwebs of indiscipline. This premise is based on our understanding of the basic interest of the people of our state and the country at large at the present crucial juncture.[73] Reminding the Governor about his comfortable majority in the Legislature, he recommended a speel of President's rule in U.P with the Legislatore kept under suspension. The Governor reported straightaway to the President's recommending application of Article 356 in U.P. At the time Tripathi stapped down, the ruling party commanded a strength of 272 members in the House of 421. President's rule was introduced in U.P on 13 June, 1973. In August, 1973 the Uttar Pradesh State Legislative (Delegation of Power) Act was put on the statute book.

The Presidential proclamation was approved by the Lok Sabha on 9 August after three days discussion. Jyotirmoy Basu was penchant in his criticism of the imposition of President's rule in U.P. saying there are many standards. In Orissa, there was one standard and the Assembly was dissolved actually with greast hurry, in unseeming hurry. In U.P there is a design to prevent a sure defeat and that is why they (Centre) have kept the Assembly alive paying 425 MLA their salaries and perquisites at the cost of the people.[74]

Apparently no one mourned to exit of the Kamlapati Tripathi Ministry. Public administration of the states was put to most serve strains during the period of his Government. Allegations of corruption including charges of nepotism flew thick and fast. The political interference with the day-to-day working of the administration acquired scandalous proportions.

The same evening i.e. (13 June 1973) the Governor, Akbar Ali Khan, asserted that it would be his endevour to discharge the new responsibilities of running the administration of the state with sincerely devotional and that he would expect the same from all officials of the Government. The following day he convened a press conference, appealing to the press to function as a link between the Government and the people in the absence of the people's representatives, to see to it that the food distribution system which was the most critical problem confronting the state at the moment served the people well. He proposed to introduce the major administrative changes in the state details of which he promised to work out with his advisors. Earlier, addressing a meeting of Secretaries to the Government he pledge to take drastic action against corrupt and inefficient civil servants.[75]

The Presidential rule in U.P was followed by a despatch from Delhi of a team of three Advisors, all senior members of the ICS who had served in U.P. earlier in different capacities. The public administration of the state when the Advisors took over, it had not recovered from the trauma of the PAC revolt. Moreover, the state was in the grip of a severe drought. The foremost problem before the Advisors was to tackle these problems, besides many other concerning administrative reforms. The power engineers were restive because of non-implementation of the assurances given to them by the popular regime and so was the case with students and teachers. The Advisors drew a plan of action and listed their priorities. 'By and large', wrote the *Hindustan Standard,* the performance of the Advisors during all these months has been quite good. They worked silently, cautiously without much fuss or fanfare and without causing controversies. Even then the Advisors Government came under pointed criticism by politicians as well as legislators to whom a popular regime was much more profitable in every sense.

The first task of the state Government under the Presidential rule was to tone up efficiency in public administration. The Advisors Council finalised measures to ensure clean and efficient administration by weeding out corrupt and incompetent officials. There were transfers of civil servants having dubious reputation. The Advisors addressed themselves to the task of preparing scheme for decentralistion of administration by delegating power to the divisional commissioners and the district collectors. It was proposed to strengthen the office of the divisional commissioners as effective instrument of administrations as against their earlier position of that a post box between the district and the Secretariat. They were now proposed to be clothed with both administrations and financial powers so that the work got disposed of quickly and Secretariat, was relieved of the unnecessary volume of work.

The President's rule in U.P. was revoked on 8 November, 1973 on the receipt of the Governor's report and H.N Bahuguna was sworn in as the Chief Minister.[76]

Gujarat

The election to the Gujarat Assembly held in 1971 gave overwhelming majority to the Congress with a strength of 137 members in a House of 167 and it assumed office under the Chief Ministership of Ghanshambhai Oza. Though victorious at the hustings, the party was not at peace with itself, being riven with internal dissensions in the middle of 1973. Oza was replaced by Chimanbhai Patel. Meanwhile, the food situation in the state was deteriorating and so grave because the problem that rioting occured in Gujarat in January 1947. The disturbances began with a protest by the students against increased college food bills and their demands initially were very modest and sectional. As the Government did not take any action on them the protest progressively acquired the aggressive range and scale of mass movement with began demanding the resignation of the Chief Minister himself whose alleged corrupt practices had directly contributed to the rise in the food process as well as the dissolution of the State Legislature. The popular movement became widespread and was supported by student organisations, Trade Unions, Opposition parties and even a section of the rulling Congress. Rioting began on many towns in Gujarat and grain shops were being looted and set fire to by agitators. To prevent such occurances, the police repeatedly opened fire on the rioters which further aggravated the situation in the state. In short, Gujarat was convulsced into a massive movement of unprecedented scale and nature, demanding resignation of the Ministry and dissolution of the Assembly.

Meanwhile, a section of the ruling party including some Ministers and demanding the chief Minister resigantion. On the latter's refusal some ministers even resigned from the Ministry. [20] Forced by Party dissidents as well as by progressively worsening circumstances, Chimanbhai Patel tendered the resignation of his Ministry to the Government on 9 February, 1974. On the same evening the President imposed Article 356 on Gujarat but kept the Assembly under suspension without it is alleged waiting for the customary Governor's report. The protest which began as an anti-price stir and grew into anti Chimanbhai Patel agitation was to climax into an anti-Assembly movement. New Delhi's decision to keep the Assembly in a state of suspended animation served only to raise the people's doubt about the credibility of its action.

For the popular upsurge, especially in its advanced stage, was directed not only against the Chimanbhai Patel Ministry but also against the entire system which made possible the coming into Chimanbhai Patel Ministry but also against the entire system which made possible the coining into power of such a discredited regime. The Centre however decided to resist such a demanded, its stand being not to give into mob violence. But the State Legislator's clearly realising that the Assembly was beyond retrive were resigning their seat. It is significant that as many as 95 Legislative in a House of 168 which include 68 Congressmen tendered their resignation. Even Chimanbhai Patel who was in the meantime asked by the party's Central leadership to quit as the leader of the Congress Legislature Party, resigned from the assembly as long with 12 his supporter, thereby smashing any hope of revival of the Assembly.[78]

On 11 March, 1974 the Lok Sabha discussed and passed the resolution regarding the proclamation of President's rule in Gujarat. The Home Minister Uma Shanker Dikshit told the House that the dissolution of the Assembly would be considered only after normalcy was restored and intimidation and violence stopped. The entire opposition staged a walk out from the Lok Sabha as the Home Minister moved the resolution for approval of the President's proclamation.

The resolution was passed, as expected but the internal situation in Gujarat was not to be regulated by it in any way. On the same day in Ahmedabad Morarji Desai began an indefinite dissolution of the Legislators. On 15 March 1974 the Centre dissolved the Gujarat Assembly, ultimately bowing to the enevitable.

This, however, was not the end of the Gujarat's travail. The President's rule was twice extended first on the ground that the fresh delimitation of constituencies on the basis of 1971 Census had to be completed before the election was held, and second time on the plea that the state was in the grip of an unprecedented drought and election at this stage would interfere with the relief operation. Safe behind its majority, the Parliamentary approval of extension of President's rule was not difficult for the ruling party. But the reasons advanced by the Government were hardly convincing. These plainly looked like delatory tactics on the part of the ruling parties and appeared to be an illustration of how constitutional duties were on occasions getting subordinated to political considerations. The delay in the return of democratic rule again revived a popular agitation in Gujarat. On 1 April, 1975 Morarji Desai threatened to go on 'a fast unto death' from 7 April if by then New Delhi failed to announce a time table for holding elections to the State assembly. As the plan for election was not announced, he began his fast from the announced date.

On 13 April the Prime Minister announced to hold election to the Gujarat Assembly around 7 June 1975. On 18 June 1975 the President's rule was revoked and a popular Ministry under Babubhai Patel became into power in Gujarat.[79]

Nagaland

The party-wise position in the 60 members State Assembly after the election held in February, 1974 was as follows:

The United Front (UDF) 25, Nagaland Nationalist Organisation (NNO) 23 and Independents 2. Supported by 32 Legislator, the United Democratic Front formed the Government under the Chief Minister of Vizol, on 10 March 1975 the government lost its majority as a result of defections by some of its supporter and consequently it resigned. The NNO strengthened by the defectors, formed the Ministry headed by John Bosco Jasokie. Consequent upon the defectors redefecting it too lost its majority within ten days of its coming into power. The Assembly which met on 20 March 1975 was adjourned amidst confusion and a trial of strength could not take place. The Governor L.P. Singh recommended to the President's proclaim his rule in the state but to keep the Assembly suspended. According to him 8 Legislators had defected twice, another eight crossed the floor once, while two other switched their loyalties thrice. On 22 March 1975 the President issued the necessary proclamation. As result Nagaland came under Article 356 and the State Assembly was kept under suspension. On 20 May 1975, the Assembly was also dissolved.

The President's rule in Nagaland was extended for a further period of six months from 26 March 1976. The necessary resolution was passed by the Rajya Sabha on 9 March and Lok Sabha on 11 March 1976. Justifying the extension, the Home Minister said the time not yet ripe for holding elections in Nagaland. The implementation of the accord between the underground Nagas and the Central Government signed on

November, 1975 had reached a crucial stage, the modalities to deposit arms by the underground were being worked out and holding of election might hamper the process. A situation which prevailed in Nagaland for the last 20 years was coming to end and we should not do anything to vitiate the atmosphere by holding early elections. Peace and tranquility in the area should continue. Nor were the two major parties of Nagaland the UDF and the NNO were anxious for early elections. Some Opposition members however, criticised the move and favoured an early return on popular government in the state.

Uttar Pradesh

Uttar Pradesh came under a brief spell of President's rule for the fourth time in the winter of 1975-76 this step being precipitated by purely factional polities within the ruling state congress party. H.N Bahuguna, the Chief Minister was under constant attack from the dissident party members but continued in office as he enjoyed the confidence of the Central Party leadership especially the Prime Minister. But on 29 November 1975 the Prime Minister apparently wished him to step down and so on the same day he resigned.[80]

The Governor, M. Chenna Reddy recommended the introduction of President's rule in the State as the Congress Party did not elect Bahuguna's successor. On 20 November, 1974 the President's rule was introduced in U.P but the Assembly was kept under suspension. On 21 January, 1976 the Central leadership of the Congress Party sponsored Narain Dutt Tiwari Finance Minister in Bahuguna's Cabinet for the Chief Ministership of Uttar Pradesh and on the following day the President's rule was thus revoked.[81]

Tamil Nadu

Tamil Nadu, which had the Dravida Munnetra Kazhagam (DMK) as the ruling party since 1967 came under President's rule on 31 January, 1975 exactly fifty days before the normal five year term of the State Assembly was due to expire. The

DMK commanded majority support in the assembly but the decision to dissolve the DMK Government and introduce President's rule was taken by the Central Government on the ground of widespread political corruption in the state. On 31 January K.K Shah, the Governor sent a report on the Tamil Nadu situation to the President who forwarded it to the Prime Minister for advice. The Cabinet endorsed the move to impose Article 356 on Tamil Nadu and immediately thereafter the President issued the proclamation dissolving the Assembly. The five year term of the Assembly would have automatically expired on 21 March, 1976 but the Central Government did not wish to wait for 50 days more because of the serious situation in Tamil Nadu in terms of the Governor's Report.

The Governor reported that the DMK had indulged in serious acts of maladministration, corruption and misuse of power for partisan ends, setting at naught all canons of justice and equity. He complained that it had disregarded the instruction of the Centre in relation to the emergency while misusing the emergency power for its own purposes and moreover, under the guise of greater State autonomy it held out 'vested threats of secession'. Finally, he called for the appointment of high power commissioner to inquire into allegation of corruption and misuse of power made against the DMK ministers. It was for the first time that Central Government ordained for itself the role of some kind of the nation's concience keeper and took a State Ministry to task by summarily dismissing it on the ground of corruption and secessionist ambition.

On 3 February 1976 the Centre appointed a one man Commission consisting of R.S Sarkaria, a Judge of the Supreme Court under the Commission of Inquiry Act, 1952 to inquire into and report by 1 February, 1977 the allegation against M.K Krunanidhi, the former Chief Minister of Tamil Nadu and some members of the DMK Ministry removed from office. This was the first time in the history of President's rule that Governor made such a recommendation and also that the Centre ordered such an inquiry.

The Lok Sabha and Rajya Sabha approved President's rule in Tamil Nadu on 8 March and 10 March 1976 respectively. Some Members of Parliament belonging to Congress(O), CPI-M, DMK and Socialist Party protested against the President's rule. Era Sezhian the DMK leader in the Lok Sabha was critical of the resolution and was opposed in principle to the Central Government appointing a Commission of inquiry against State Government in a federal setup.[82]

Gujarat

Closely following Tamil Nadu on its heel was a Gujarat which had gone to the polls only nine months ago to elect its State Legislature. As a result of the mid-term elections held in June 1975 a coalition of non-Congress parties, the Janata Front under the Chief Ministership of Babubhai Patel assumed power on 18 June 1975 a week before the proclamation of emergency in the country. In the 179 members Assembly the Janata Front had 86 members drawn from its five constituents—the Congress(O), the Jana Sangh, the Bhartiya Lok Dal, the Socialist Party and the Rashtriya Mazdoor Paksha and was supported by the 12 members of Kisan Mazdoor Lok Paksha.

Despite the common programme of action agreed to by all the constituent units of the Congress (O) led Ministry were following diverse ideologies and nursing conflicting interests that the coalition was bound to disintegrate before long. And it did began tottering when the Kisan Mazdoor Lok Paksha withdrew its support to it in February, 1976. On 21 February, the Chief Minister felt it necessary to withdrew a vital tax proposal which was an indication of the vulney of the coalition regime. The Janata Front Ministry headed by Babubhai Patil suffered a defect on 12 March 1976 when its budgets was not passed in the Assembly. Following his defeat, the Chief Minister resigned Recommending imposition of Article 356 in the state, and keeping the Assembly suspended, the Governor pointed out in his report to the President. To my mind the position is fluid and no party or combination of parties is in a position at present, or in the immediate future to form a stable Government. President's rule was imposed on Gujarat in 12 March 1976, this being the third time in less than five years when Gujarat came under Article 356. The State was under the President's rule for nearly 10 months in 1971 -72 and again for about 12 months in 1974-75.[83]

REFERENCES

1. *The Statesman,* 21 June, 1951.
2. *Parliamentary Debates,* Part II, Vol. XIV, No.4,9 August, 1951, col 195.
3. *Parliamentary Debates,* Vol, D, No.4, 12 March, 1953, col 1893-94.
4. *The Hindustan Times,* 12 March, 1953.
5. *The Hindustan Times,* 5 November, 1954.
6. *The Hindustan Times, S* November, 1954.
7. *Lok Sabha Debates,* Part II, Vol,VII, No, 5, 19 November, 1954, col 418.
8. *The Times of India,* 24 March, 1956.
9. *Lok Sabha Debates,* Part II, Vol, III, No.31, 29 March, 1956, col 3778.
10. *The Statesman,* 13 September, 1958.
11. *The Times of India,* 12 June, 1959.
12. *Lok Sabha Debates,* Second Series, Vol, H, No.19,8 March, 1961, col 3657.
13. *The Times of India, 22* February 1961.
14. *Lok Sabha Debates,* Second Series, Vol, IV, No.SSj 25 April, 1951, col 13609.
15. *The Times of India,* 10 September, 1964.
16. *The Hindustan Times, 26* March, 1965.
17. *The Times of India,* 23 June, 1966.
18. *Report of Parliamentary Committee on the Demand for Punjabi Suba,* New Delhi, Lok Sabha Secretariat, 1966, p. 2.
19. *The Times of India,* 5 July, 1966.
20. *The Hindustan Times,* 14 November, 1966.
21. *The Hindustan Times,* 5 March, 1967.

22. *The Statesman,* 5 March, 1967.
23. *The Hindustan Times,* 14 March, 1967.
24. *The Hindustan Times,* 25 April, 1967.
25. President's Rule in States and Union Territories, Lok Sabha Secretariat, 2New Delhi, 1989, p. 53.
26. *The Times of India,* 12 November, 1967,
27. *The Statesman,* 22 March, 1967
28. President's Rule in the States and Union Territories, Lok Sabha Secretariat, New Delhi, 1989, p.29.
29. *Ibid.*, p. 3l.
30. *The Tribune,* 2 March, 1968.
31. *The Times of India,* 7 November, 1967.
32. *The Statesman,* 8 November, 1967.
33. *The Hindustan Times,* 20 November, 1967.
34. *The Hindustan Times,* 11 November, 1967.
35. *The Times of India,* 16 November, 1967.
36. *The Tribune,* 30 November, 1967.
37. President's Rule in the States and Union Territories, Lok Sabha Secretariat, New Delhi, 1989, p. 54.
38. *The Times of India,* 18 February, 1967.
39. *The National Herald,* 8 April, 1968.
40. *Ibid.*
41. Lok Sabha Debates, Fourth Series, Vol. XVl, No. 45, col. 1440-48.
42. *President's Rule in State and Union Territories,* Lok Sabha Secretariat, New Delhi, 1989, p. 27.
43. *Lok Sabha Debates,* Fourth Series, Vol. XX, No. 25 August, 1 968, col . 2266,69.
44. *The Times of India,* 4 July, 1969.
45. *President's Rule in states and Union Territories,* Lok Sabha Secretariat, New Delhi, 1989, p. 76.
46. *The Hindustan Times, 26* November, 1968.
47. *The Hidustan Times,* 23 August, 1968.
48. *The Hindustan Times,* 18 March, 1970.
49. *Times of India,* 9 April, 1970.
50. *The Times of India,* 17 April, 1970.
51. *Rajya Sabha Debates,* 31 March, 1970.

52. *The Times of India,* 27 June, 1970.
53. *The Time of India,* 28 September 1970.
54. *The Hindustan Time,* 29 September, 1970.
55. *The Times of India,* 3 October, 1970.
56. *Lok Sabha Debates,* Fourth Series, Vol. XVI, No. 45, col 1440-48.
57. *The Statemen,* 22 March, 1971.
58. *The Statesman,* 23 March, 1971.
59. *Lok Sabha Debates,* Fifth Series, Vol. II, No. 1, 24 May, 1971
60. *Lok Sabha Debates, op, cit,* col 200.
61. *The Tribune,* 13 June, 1971.
62. *Lok Sabha Debates,* Fifth Series, Vol. VII, No. 55, 5 August, 1971, col 224.
63. *President's Rule in the States and Union Territories,* Lok Sabha Secretariat, New Delhi, 1989, p. 67.
64. *The Hindustan Times,* 10 January, 1972.
65. *President's Rule is States and Union Territories,* Lok Sabha Secretariat, New Delhi, 1989, p. 24.
66. *Ibid.* p. 25.
67. *The Indian Journal of Public Administration* Vol. IV, No. 4. Oct-Dec. 1973, pp. 441-71.
68. *Lok Sabha Debates,* Fifth Series, Vol. XXIII, No. 8, col. 233-35.
69. *The Times of India,* 2 March, 1973.
70. *Ibid.*
71. *The Times of India,* 27 March, 1973.
72. *The Times of India,* 14 June, 1973.
73. *Lok Sabha Debates, Fifth Series,* Vol. XX, No. 13, 8 August, 1973, col. 298.
74. *The Times of India,* 15, June, 1973.
75. *The Times of India,* 16 June, 1973.
76. *The Hindustan Standard,* 19 October, 1973.
77. *The Tribune,* 8 April, 1974.
78. *Lok Sabha Debates,* Fifth Series, Vol. XIV, No. 37, 7 September, 1974, col. 99.
79. *The Hindustan Times,* 23, March, 1975.
80. *The Hindustan Times,* 23 March, 1975.

81. *The Hindustan Times*, 10 January, 1976.
82. *Lok Sabha Debates*, Fifth Series, Vol. XIV, No. 32, 14 March, 1976 col. 104.
83. *Ibid.*, p. 224.

3

The Position and Role of the Governor During the President's Rule in the State

Article 154 of the Constitution of India vests the executive power of the state in the Governor who exercises his power directly or through officers subordinate to him. He is appointed by the President under his hand and seal. The President selects a person for governorship on the advice of council of ministers. This is a clear departure from the practice in the United States where the governor is directly elected by the people of the State. In this respect, the Constitution of India has followed the Canadian practices.

According to the provisions of the constitution, the Governor possesses immense powers—executive, legislative, financial and judicial. However, he is to exercise the powers on the advice of the State Council of Ministers. As is the practice of the Parliamentary government the Governor cannot act except in accordance with the advice of the Council of Ministers. Under the Act of 1935 the Governor had vast discretionary powers but the present constitution has taken away all such power and made him the constitutional head of the State. The fact of his appointment by the President also speaks for his nominal role in the State. The constitution makers rejected the proposal of the election of the Governor and instead decided for his appointment. His significance is ornamental rather than functional. His position is that of influence rather than of authority.

There is, however, another aspect of the governor's position which may be noted. In discharge of his several functions he acts as the agent of the President, while so action he may discharge the advice of his Council of Ministers. The Constitution provides many occasions wherein the Governor acts as the agent of the President and has to carry his instructions, irrespective of whatever advice his Minister's tender to him. If the governor on such occasions does not act according to the instructions of the President the latter may remove him. Thus, his responsibility to the President is not only moral but constitutional. In such situations when the governor acts as the agent of the President, his position becomes difficult one. He has to serve two—Ministers who represent the voice of the people, and the President whose nominee he is. This can embarrass his position. The Governor in such cases is to act widely and with fact.

The Governor has an important role to play in the State when the State Governments refuse to abide by the directions of the centre which it is empowered to issue. The exercise of discretionary powers become a matter of practical importance. The Governor cannot be regarded a puppet controlled by the Chief Minister. He has an important role to play and a great contribution to make for the stability of Government in the State. It may not be out of place to point out that governor who generally danced to the tune of the Chief Minister had become a tool in the hands of the central Government to outst the non-Congress Ministries after 1967 general election. He could find an excuse to advise the President of India to proclaim emergency in the State. In Haryana he got the ministry dissolved as horse trading had made the State politics fluid. In the Punjab, the directions in-chief was made the Chief Minister and the other party was made to vacate the ministerial seats. During 1976 March, ministries were dissolved in Tamil Nadu and Gujarat through Governor's intervention and the matter was reported to the President regarding constitutional breakdown in the State. Thus the Governor in non-Congress States played havoc with the ministries or got them dissolved. Similarly, history was once again repeated by the Janata Government at centre which dissolved ministries in certain Southern States. Guidelines on the manner in which discretionary powers were exercised by the inter State Council and on acceptance by the Union were issued in the name of the President. They should be placed before both Houses of Parliament.[1]

A public controversy has recently arisen in the field of Centre-State relations over the appointment of Governors and their powers and functions. For the first two decades after Independence, the office of the Governor did not give room to controversy, the main reason being that a single party was in power, both at centre and in almost all the States and its dominating leadership the centre facilitated smooth management of affairs involving Centre-State relations. This picture of political homogeneity underwent a radical change in the wake of the general Elections of 1967. The heterogeneous political spectrum that emerged ranged from the Communist parties at the one end to the Swatantra and Jan Sangh parties at the other. At the centre, the Congress Party, though depleted in strength, has continued to be in power in different States of India. The differences in the ideologies and objectives of the political parties in power have become a source of friction in the Centre-State relationships in various matters including the appointment and the role of the Governor.

The Governor is the Constitutional head of the State acting on the advice of his Ministry. He does not himself directly discharge executive functions. He is, however, required to exercise his discretion in certain circumstances which are either explicitly stated in the Constitution or can be inferred therefrom. Till recently in view of the existence of political harmony between the Centre and the State governments there was hardly any occasion for him to play an active role by exercising these discretionary powers. He was concerned mostly with the discharge of formal functions like the swearing in of Ministers, addressing the legislature at the commencement of sessions, and gracing official functions with his presence. This predominance of the ceremonial and the formal functions discharged by him has promoted some people even to question the need of the institutions of governor, which appeared to them to be a costly superfluity.[2]

The above position has, as already stated, changed since 1967. Buffing problems of a nature hitherto unforeseen arose in the working of the constitutional provisions relating to the role of the Governor and the functioning of legislatures. A figure head role for the Governor could hardly be feasible in the situations created by the problems. The difficult situations that arose in some of the States are briefly described below.

In case of West Bengal, the Governor was confronted with the question as to whether or not the Chief Minister enjoyed the confidence of the Assembly. The Chief Minister would neither resign nor seek a vote of confidence, nor would he agree to the advice to the Assembly to have the support enjoyed by the Ministry ascertained beyond doubt. The Ministry was, therefore, dismissed and a new one sworn in, the Governor summoned the Assembly on the advice of the new Chief Minister. When the Assembly met, the speaker took the extraordinary step of adjuring the Assembly sine-die on the ground that the action of the Governor in dismissing the previous Ministry and swearing in of the new Ministry and the summoning of the Assembly was unconstitutional. The Calcutta High Court, however, upheld the action of the Governor. When the Assembly was summoned the speaker again adjourned the Assembly without allowing it to transact any business.

Again in the context of Bihar, the Council of Ministers openly expressed its unwillingness to accept the person appointed by the President as Governor. A controversy arose as to the extent to which the Chief Minister should be associated with the choice of a person to be appointed as Governor. Further, the political situation in Bihar underwent many changes calling for the exercise of the judgement of the governor repeatedly in regard to the appointment of the Chief Minister and the functioning Ministries.

As regards Punjab, in the course of a discussion during the Budget session of a motion expressing lack of confidence in the speaker the Assembly was adjourned by him for two months with the result that the Budget could not be discussed and the

Appropriation Bill could not be put to vote. This resulted in the commencing month of the next financial year being left without provision for expenditure. An embarrassing deadlock was thus created. The Governor of Punjab thereupon promulgated an ordinance to enable the Assembly to meet and to consider the Appropriation Bill. When the Assembly was summoned by the Governor, the speaker created a further deadlock by ruling that the summoning of the House was illegal, and reaffirmed his earlier decision adjourning it for two months. When he left the House, which was in a state of pandemonium the Deputy Speaker occupied the chair, put to vote the Appropriation Bill and declared it as passed. This was subsequently declared ultra virse by the High Court, creating further administrative and constitutional problems. The matter went in appeal before the Supreme Court, which upheld the action of the Governor.

The Governor after the 1967 General Elections in the State of Rajasthan was faced with in question as to which political party or group in the legislature enjoyed majority and should be called upon to form the Ministry. Neither party nor group would concede the position of majority to the other. After his own assessment of the position, the Governor invited the leader of the Congress Party in the legislation to form the Ministry. But when this leader declined the invitation President's rule was imposed but the Assembly was not dissolved. The combined opposition of all non-Congress parties paraded their member before the President to establish their claim of majority, this method of parading MLA's before the President was adopted for the first time in India. But, when the list of MLAs of respective groups were called for by the governor, it was found there were 21 names common to both of them. The Governor then arranged to meet the MLAs, whose allegiance was uncertain to find out their party affliction. He ultimately found the Congress Party in a majority and, on his advice, President's rule was withdrawn and the leader of the Congress Party who was invited formed the Ministry.

In Madhya Pradesh, the Chief Minister had to resign on

account of political defections. He advised the Governor to dissolve the Assembly. The Governor did not accept the advice and called upon the person who in his judgment commanded the majority support of the Assembly to form the Ministry. Later another Chief Minister, appointed by the Governor, held office only for 13 days and submitted his resignation as he did not command the majority in the Assembly. He also advised the Governor to dissolve the Assembly, though it had not been summoned to meet. This advice was not accepted by the Governor. In this case also the Governor who again appointed another person as Chief Minister who had in his opinion, the majority support in that Assembly. In some States the law and order situation was adversely affected by the deliberate acts of omission and commission of ministries concerned. Thus, in the changed context the Governors office ceases to be merely ornamental and ceremonial. The governor has to face situation's in which he will have to take decisions, in keeping with his oath of office to preserve protect and defend the constitution and the law. His character, calibre and experience must be of a high order, so that the may be able to stand up to the needs of a new situation with confidence. His discretion and Judgment should be exercised in such a way that a happy relationship between the centre and the State is insured. As head of the State he should free from political and party, by his impartiality and sense of fair play, in the Constitutional setup and the democratic institutions. He should necessary have rich experience in public life and administration such are the requirement to be looked for in a person who is to be appointed as a Governor.

No institution can be correctly studied by a mere perusals for the concerned provisions of the constitution, and this is particularly true with the office of the Governor. He is appointed by the president for a term of few years and is under an oath to faithfully execute the office of Governor, to prefect and defend the constitution and the law and to devote himself to the service and wellbeing of the people of his State. The Governor is equipped with a Council of Ministers with the Chief Minister at its head to aid and advise him. In accordance with the well-known convention of the parliamentary democracy, however the Governor is ordinarily a constitutional head acting on the advice of the Council of Ministers. At the same time the Constitution visualizes situations where he is to act in his discretion and not on the advice of the Council of Ministers and moreover, what is his discretionary field of activities is also left to his discretion. In the initial period of about fifteen years during which the Constitution was functioning within the framework of a single party dominance the only matter in which he could act in his discretion was one of inviting the leader of a political party commanding a majority in the Legislature to form the Government. Here again the Governor was left with hardly any discretionary choice as he had no option but to summon the leader of the majority party if as was generally the case its majority was clear. It was only when the party position in the Legislature became fluid as it happened in several States. Following the general election of 1967, the Governor was called upon to exercise his discretion and in the process his role in this matter became real and complex what was more, his discretion in the selection of the Chief Minister continued to be final. Dharam Vira's action in inviting P.C. Ghosh to form the Government in West Bengal after the dismissal of the Ajoy Mukherjee Ministry was challenged in the Calcuta High Court. The verdict supported the gubernatorial action. In appointing a Chief Minister the Governor must act in his own discretion. It is for him to make such enquiries as he thinks proper, to ascertain who among the members of the Legislature ought to be appointed the Chief Minister and would be in a position to enjoy the confidence of the majority in the Legislative Assembly of the State. The exercise of this discretion by the governor cannot be called in question in writ proceeding in this court.

Right to summon the legislature under the existing constitutional arrangements the Governor summons the legislature on the advice of the Chief Minister. As the constitution permits an interval of as many as six months between two sessions of the Legislature some Chief Ministers have lent themselves to the charge of taking unfair advantage of such long intermission by not convening the legislature and thus continue in power even though they in the meantime, lost their support. At present a governor is left with no alternative but to persuade his Chief Minister to convene the State Assembly, if the latter does not agree, he has only one weapon, admittedly of an ultimate category, available to him that of dismissing the Ministry. But by so behaving he exposes himself to a criticism of being arbitrary in his action if not acting under instructions from the centre. Far better way, therefore, is formally to clothe the governor with the power to summon the Assembly at his discretion even vetoing the negative advice, if any of the Chief Minister, and thus have the latter majority verified. The Administrative Reforms Commission also made a similar recommendation. It observed, if a doubt arises whether a Ministry has the confidence of majority in the Assembly the wisest course would be to have it settled by summoning the Assembly and to leave to the Assembly the verification of the support claimed by the Ministry.[4]

We suggest that the governor should try to persuade the Chief Minister to agree to the Assembly being summoned as early as possible and to face it. If the Chief Minister still refuses to agree to advise the summoning of the Assembly, the Governor should summon the Assembly for the purpose of obtaining its verdict on the question as to whether the council of Ministers enjoys the confidence of the Assembly.

Governor's Interpretation of Article 356

A situation of political flux in a State may give rise to a complex of events in which, according to the gubernatorial analysis, the government of the State cannot be carried on in accordance with the provisions of the Constitution. This culminates in the invoking by the President of Article 356 of the Constitution on receipt of the Governor's Report and other information received by him. Governor's interpretation of such an occasion warranting the imposition of Article 356 ambries a fairly wide range of circumstances as is borne out from the following few illustrations.

In Andhra Pradesh, in 1954 after the defeat of the coalition Government headed by T. Prakasam, the Communist Party, the second largest Party in the Assembly, pressed its claim to be invited by the governor to form the Government. The Governor did not explore the possibility of forming an alternative Government in the State and instead immediately recommended the dissolution of the Assembly and imposition of President's rule.

In Kerala, in 1959 the ruling party, the Communist Party of India, enjoyed a clear majority in the Legislature but there was fairly widespread popular agitation against the Government. The governor recommended President's rule on the ground that there was virtual abrogation of rule of law by the Communist Government.

Again in Kerala in 1965, no single party secured majority in the legislature after the election while the Governor consulted various parties on the question of formation of a Government he did not formally invite the single largest party the Communist Party to form the Government. Guided by his assessment that no party was in a position to form a Ministry, he recommended President's rule.

In case of Haryana, in 1967 the Samyukta Vidhayak Dal continued to command majority in the Legislatures. The governor recommended dismissal of the SVD Ministry and Promulgated of the President's rule on the Ground that defections in the Assembly become in order of the day, administration stood paralysed and the Ministry was interested only in maintaining itself in power.

In Tamil Nadu, in 1976 the ruling DMK continued to enjoy unwavering majority in the Assembly but the Governor recommended President's rule in the State, charging the Ministry with corruption, abuse of powers and secessionist activities.[5]

The governor has thus recommended President's rule in the event of a mere defeat of a party or a coalition in the Assembly without any attempt at any Ministry making. Voting out of power of a party in the Assembly and explicit inability of other parties to form an alternative Government in the State, frequent floor crossing of legislators and alleged corruption of the Ministry. The Governor's discretion is thus wide enough and the Tamil Nadu episode has definitely widened the scope and freedom of Governor's actions. Indeed the Governor's office is much more open ended than is generally surmised. As a Member of Parliament put it. There is a very serious lacuna in the Constitution in the sense that it allows a Governor to function according to his whims and fancies. He can decide on anything as he likes. There is no forum for testing his action. They do not allow the Assembly to meet to test whether this party or that party got majority or minority. It is being decided by the Governor.

So undefined and unstructured is the discretionary power of the Governor that the manner of its exercise has become a subject of public controversy on many occasions, and a demand has been made to set bounds to his discretion. In this regard, suggestions made by the Administrative Reforms Commission (1966-70) are worthy of our notice. The Constitution lays down that the Governor is the sole judge in determining what does and does not fall under his discretion. In the light of the new development and complicated situations a clear annexation as to the method and manner of exercise of discretionary power of the Governor affect some of the vital issue in the functioning of democratic Governments in the States. Some guidelines should be evolved to enable exercise of these discretionary powers by the governor for the purpose of preserving and protecting democratic values.[6] But no Governor should interfere with the democratic process when the Chief Minister of the day is prepared to face the Assembly without delay. Where a Chief Minister drags his feet in summoning the Assembly, it would be desirable to arm the Governor with the discretion to fix a date for the Assembly session rather than with the power to send the Government and the Assembly packing even temporarily. It goes without saying. However, that the discretion to summon the Assembly, like any other discretion allowed to Governors under the Constitution, should not only be exercised fairly and impartially but also seen to be exercised fairly and impartially.[7]

No such measure by way of ground rules for Governors has been completed or even contemplated. But in 1970 the President wrote to all the Governors suggesting a course of action by way of help to them in their decision-making process. The President's circular to Governors dated 30 March 1970 said, "The Governor of the State may occasionally consider it advisable to obtain the opinion of the Attorney General of India on matters involving the interpretation of the provisions of the constitution relating to the powers and duties of the Governor except those involving Centre-State relationship. In future the Govern may, if he should consider it advisable to seek the opinion of the Attorney General on such a matter involving interpretation of the constitution refer the matter to the President's Secretary for taking action to obtain the opinion of the Attorney General through the Law Secretary." This also brings to the fore the question of proper appointment of Governors. No longer should this office he regarded as a sinecure or a nursing home. As Governors are increasingly called upon to exercise their own judgment and take decisions of the highest importance, they should be persons having reputation for independence and integrity. So that the requisite degree of impartiality and objectivity which are expected of this office do no get umpired.[8]

The office of the Governor has some considerable ambivalence. Appointed by the President, he has to search constantly for a working reconciliation between his loyalty to his sector and to the Constitution which he is supposed to defend. Even when Article 356 is imposed on a State the power of governance gets vested in the President and that of legislation in the Parliament. It is only through on order, of course issued simultaneously with the President's proclamation that the newly vested powers in the President are exercisable also by the Governor subject to the superintendence, direction and control of the President. But Parliament's authority remains intact, in the sense that it is not delegated to the Governor. It ought to be noted that at the time Punjab fell under President's rule in 1951 there was serious thinking in some quarters that the President could discharge the responsibility of administering the state through the Central Cabinet but had no authority to delegate it to the Governor. This course, however, was not pursued and Governor comes into the picture directly, prominently and pervasively. As the President is only a nominal head, and stands for the Central Government which is a party Government, the Governor's office is apt to remain subject to political pressures, direction, even control from above, more so under times of stress such as President's rule. The Governor's discretion has on occasions turned into the centre's discretion especially in the context of Article 356, and in the process this office has become more politicized tending, more to subshrub narrow ends of the political party at the centre than the purposes visualized by the framers of the Constitution. A Governor anxious to remain loyal to his oath seeks an honorable balance between central accommodation and Constitutional duties of his office. The true remedy lies in the Governor not succumbing to central pressures and in the central Government not becoming too much demanding in its relationship with the Governor but instead helping in evolving sound conventions, practices, customs and protocol in this field. It is not without significance that he is appointed by the President by warrant under the latter's hand and seal.[9]

The Governor's Report to the President was until 1962 treated as a secret document, and thus was not made public while seeking parliamentary endorsement of the President's rule, the Home Minister used to give an account of the factors and circumstances leading to the promulgation of President's rule in the State. Most often, the Home Ministers Statement was itself a summary of the Governor's report but as a rule the latter was not placed in parliament. Defending this practice in the face of opposition demand to make available the Andhra Pradesh Governor's report. KN. Katju the Home Minister, told the Parliament in 1954. The report of the Governor to the President is a document of a very secret and confidential nature, and it will not be in the public interest to produce it. This appears to be an untenable position. As it is a Constitutional obligation of Parliaments to accord its approval to the President's rule in a State, it must have access to the Governor's report before it makes up its mind whether it should give its endorcement to that action or not. The opposition has consistently demanded the publication of the Governor's Report. Since the sixties the Government has been tabling in each House of Parliament the full text of the Governor's report along with the Presidential proclamation when it seeks parliamentary approval. The Governor emerges as a functioning or executive Governor, without the ordinance making powers. When Article 356 is imposed on a State, all powers of governance as already mentioned get vested in the President but the latter delegates the executive authority to the Governor and therefore what is constitutionally called President's rule get vested in its day-to-day functioning into the hands of the Governor. This confront him with a situation of potential role conflict President's rule being centre's rule, the Governor may be and indeed a being increasingly looked upon as New Delhi's agent and mouthpiece.

But the constitution and his oath commit him to a particular course of action. There is no inherent hostility between these two roles but where politics is not sufficiently enlivened with understanding and adjustment, his dilemma becomes indeed deep. He ought to shun what A.P. Jain, the Governor of Kerala, did in 1966 when that state was under President's rule. When the then Prime Minister Lal Bahadur Shastri suddenly passed away the battle of succession between Indira Gandhi and Morarji Desai ensued, and A.P. Jain oblivious of his gubernatorial responsibilities rushed to Delhi actively to campaign on behalf of one of the contenders for the office of the Prime Minister. His view that he should be treated like an American Governor was an instance of misreading of the Indian Constitution. Dharam Vira, who as functioning Governor of West Bengal and Mysore went through the mill, has the following to say in this regard, "My personal view is that there is no reason at all for the Governor to act during the president's rule as if he was subordinate to the Ministries at the centre. In matter requiring legislation the position is clear. Such proposal have to be sent to the centre for appropriate action.

"In day to day administration, however, the Governor should be free to act independently and on his own. It is another matter to keep the centre informed in regard to all important developments and decisions. This is a must. But in dealing with these developments or in taking decisions the normal rules and procedures of the states are to be followed and central directions have no place there. If for all important administrative acts central directions and approval were necessary and impossible situation involving fatal delays might develop besides embarrassing the governor constitutionally. In actual practice, however with goodwill on both sides, no difficulties need arise and the work should proceed smoothly without any friction or irritations on either side."[10]

With the Council of Ministers gone, the rules business in the Government are suitably amended and issued. In short the Governor assumes the place of the council of Ministers. He begins attending conferences such as the National Development Council and the Chief Ministers conference. The official papers being coming to him for his decisions and he directly issues instructions to the personnel in the administrative hierarchy on the manner of transacting the eloquency prove by his attending the office regularly in the secretariat something which is normal times he never does.

The Nature of Functioning of Governor during the President's Rule in the State

But there is no single modes of functioning Governors under the President's rule. Indeed, one may construct two typologies of this office as it has evolved since 1950. Some Governors especially those drawn from the administrative cadres have functioned without advisors, and they have directly exercised the effective authority. The first President's rule in Punjab passed off without any advisors to the Governor. C.M. Trivedi Dharam

Vira did not have any advisors in both West Bengal and Mysore. Shriman Narain Agrawal, the Governor of Gujarat, did not ask for any advisors for the first few months. In all such instances the official papers come to the Governor directly from the Chief Secretary, and he functions as the Chief Minister and the Council of Ministers rolled in to one. The second typology is of the Governor having advisors. Historically speaking, Governors having background of public life belonged to this typology. But of late the installation of advisors has apparently become an integral part of the exercise of President's rule. The Governor of Nagaland (1975) is a retired civil servant but is assisted by advisors. The appointment of advisors is accompanied by a formal distribution of portfolios among them and they in effect stake the place of the Ministers getting official papers directly from the secretaries to the Government. They thus become an effective level in the regular administrative hierarchy and only such categories of papers as are enumerated in the Rules of Business get referred to the Governor for his decisions. If however there is a principal Advisor, as was the case in West Bangal with SS Dhawan as governor, he virtually functions as the Chief Minister and the Governor is in practice little more than the Constitutional head although constitutionally speaking he can overrule the advisers just as the President has the authority to set aside any action of the Governor. Some Governors have convened regular meetings of the advisors in which they used to preside very much like the meeting of the cabinet thus attempting to evolve the ministerial style of decisions-making. The exact position of the Governor in the resultant Governor in Advisor form of Government depends, however, upon the allocation of work under the Rules of Business, his position nevertheless is not the same as of his counterpart of the first typology discussed above. But effectiveness is not exclusively institutional it also depends upon the personality of the Governor himself, his rapport with the Central political leadership etc.

Apropos of the typology, the prestige and power of this office have suffered erosion over a period of time. The emerging impression is that the Governor visits and consults New Delhi before he sends in his report and gains the tacit approval of the centre. As early as 1967, K. Santhanam referred to the practice of practically instructing the Governor, if not ordering him to send such a report recommending President's rule. On three or four occasions we have had instances of Governor's report following the imposition of President's rule. Even the earlier convention of governor intending his advisers has become rusty and the centre has bow of its own accord been appointing them.[11]

Scope of Article 356

President's rule should be imposed only in the last resort and that too under only two circumstances. One being a situation of near complete breakdown of law and order in the state and another one when no Political Party or coalition of parties including Independents is able to form a Government, even if not very stable. The latter circumstance needs elaboration. In case a ruling party apparently loses its majority in the Assembly and wants to convene the Assembly on a date later than what the governor thinks appropriate it is always desirable to prefer this to an abrupt imposition of Presiden s rule.

Indeed, the Governor needs to be armed with the power to summon the Assembly in his discretion in case when the majority of the ruling party is in doubt. Similarly when a Ministry falls the Governor should give an opportunity to the opposition to form the government. That BD Jatti the then Governor of Orissa, did not invite the opposition when the Nandini Satpatht Ministry was voted out of power in 1973 rightly incurred judicial strictures. In the case called Bijayananda Patnaik and 73 others Versus President of India and others the High Court of Orissa observed on 22 October 1973. The Governor examined the claim of the Pargati Party of heaving 72 members on withdrawal of 25 members from the ruling party. He noticed that the figure 72 had been reduced by two within a few hours.

After taking in to consideration various aspects he came to the conclusion that there is no guarantee that the present majority claimed by Shri Biju Patnaik and his supporters will remain stable and if a ministry is allowed to be formed under the leadership of Shri Patnaik, the said ministry might not remain for a long time. Thus, the governor did not called the leader of the opposition to form the ministry not because they had no majority but because he express that the majority might fall at any moment and their would be no stable ministry. In arriving at this conclusion the governor did not honour the convention prevalent in Great Britain in the matter of formation of the Ministry. The breach was in the following way on the resignation of the Ministry of Nandini Satpathy having lost its majority support in the Assembly, the Governor should have called the leader of the Opposition to *form* the Ministry. It was for the latter to say whether he would be able to form a Ministry or not? The leader of the Opposition asserted that he had a majority support and that is confirmed by the Governor's own finding that he had support of 70 members. Even assuming that the Governor wanted to test the exact support he should have called upon the leader of the Opposition to test his strength in House *itself,* which was in session. This was exactly what the Governor of West Bengal did when he dismissed the Ministry of Ajoy Mukherjee in November 1967. The Governor is not concerned whether the Ministry could be stable in future. If the Ministry which would have been formed by the leader of the Opposition would have been justified to recommend for the President's rule if that have no other person was in a position to form an alternative Ministry by having majority support.[12]

While the Governor should take a generous view of the second factor he should not be liberal in interpreting the situation relating to breakdown of law and order. For, it permits a wide measure of subjectivity and moreover is prone to political interpretation when the state level ruling party is different from the one at the centre. Indeed a wise Governor is he who reposes trust in the wisdom of the political parties and the elections. Democracy is a self correcting, self purifying experience, and Raj Bhawans are by no account its quality control rooms.

Thus viewed, a political party must continue in power so long as it commands majority in the legislature and in case of fall of this Ministry, another party which could ensure majority legislature support should be invited to form the Government. It implies that to dismiss a Ministry having legislative support on any ground such as corruption or attempt veiled or other wise at secession is an act of over interpretation of his role by the Governor.[13]

The Appointment of Governor's Advisors during the period of President's Rule in the State

In the exercise of functions and power, while Article 356 is in the force, the Governor may appoint Advisors to assist him. This practice dates back to the period of the British Raj. In Mumbai (Bombay), under the provisions of section 93 (during the second World War) the governor had three Advisers, namely, Sir Henery Knight, Sir Charles Bristow and Sir Godfry Collins all being members of the ICS (Indian Civil Service). The institution of advisers which has progressively come to constitute the kingpin of President's rule owes neither to the constitution nor to any stature, it being purely executive in its origin and design. Obviously, there can be no fixed rule or formula regarding the number of advisers or even organization of work among them. Nor are they obligatory at all, being meant for a Governor who needs advice.

The number of advisers has ranged from nil to five. Punjab, the first State to have succumbed to the President's rule in 1951, did not have any adviser although at one time this proposal seems to have been considered. Y.N. Suthankar, the Governor of Orissa functioned without Advisers when that state was placed under Article 356 in 1961. Dharam Vira did not appoint any advisers in West Bengal and Mysore when he was the Governor. On the other hand, S.S. Dhavan, the Governor of West Bengal, had as many as five Advisers in 1970, when an M.P. showed an inquisitiveness about the logic being such a number, the Home Minister replied, "One has to make an assessment about it. There cannot be any rigid rule in this matter. One has to go according to the conditions prevalent there. The present Governor thinks that possibly he could do justice and ensure more efficient administration with the help of five people."

Nevertheless, a State under Article 356 must guard itself against too many advisers. A very large number puts a heavy strain on the quality of administration which can be best ensured by a small and compact team of officers. Likewise, how exactly do advisers function is also not laid down in strict terms. The style of their functioning gets to be determined in each State in the light of its own political and administrative compulsions.[14] The need for advisers is to be articulated by the Governor but in practice he may not be like with any choice both in regard to the necessity of their services and in the matter of final selection. The ultimate decision in all such matters really rest with the Prime Minister who is advised in this respect by the Home Minister. All senior appointments are as a rule made by the Appointments Committee of the cabinet, but advisers appointment is kept out of its purview, for they fall in the category of constitutional appointments. Although it is the Governor who formally appoints them the preparatory work is done in the Home Ministry and the Prime Minister's orders are obligatory. The name of persons for advisorship are as a rule initiated by the Home Ministry. Simultaneously with the appointment of advisors the Rules of Business of the state government concerned are amended to delete the provisions relating to ministers and to include certain provisions about the powers and functions of the advisers.

Advisor's role broadly corresponds with that of ministers and as such the departments of the state government are formally distributed among them. All papers which used to be disposed of by ministers ordinarily come to them for their decisions. They put up the more important cases to 'Rajyapalji' which is the customary nomenclature employed. The Governor is thus, relieved of routine administrative matters which would otherwise have shifted to him. In addition, the advisers advise the Governor on important matters. The pattern of functioning of the advisers has not been uniform, determined in practice, by the personality of the governor and the style of his own working. In certain states each advisor has disposed of work individually but in others there have also been regular advisors meeting presided over by the Governors.

In such cases matters which were required to be submitted to the cabinet are ordinarily put up for cllective decision making. In West Bengal when S.S Dhavan was the Governor, the Rules of Business provided for regular meeting among advisors every week. In effect, the advisors functioned almost as a Cabinet and their meetings resembled the Cabinet meetings. It was customary for the Governor to preside over the meeting of the advisers almost on the same lines as a Cabinet meeting. Constitutionally speaking, the Governor can overrule his advisers and the gubernatorial assertiveness has manifested itself on a few occasions. The advisory meeting with Governor during the President's rule is more better and smoother than the normal popular ministry in the state, because, there may be not more than five advisers who could take the best decision without any party or personal influence. Whereas, in the popular ministry hampering are often arises from party levels, favouritism, nepotism in particular decisions. So Cabinet ministers could not take any major decision in the Cabinet meeting. As advisers have been regular civil servants, their services conditions are as a general rule, governed by appropriate service rules. The salary of an adviser is determined according to the rank of the person.

The number of advisers have totalled up to 44 till 1976. But it has been increased up till now, advisers have all been civil servants and retired Indian Civil Service and Indian Police Service personnel. Such a composition need not be surprising in view of the administrative role of the advisers.[15]

Governor and Advisors

Although the practice is to appoint advisors in a State placed under President's rule except where it is intended for a very short speed as in the 1975 case of Uttar Pradesh the merit of the advisory arrangement must not be exaggerated or accepted at its face value. Strictly speaking, there is hardly any need for advisers, for the Governor has at his back and call the centre state administration headed by the Chief Secretary to assist him in tasks of administration. But a Governor lacking previous experience of administration may perhaps require the advice of advisers. But in such cases absolutely front-ranking civil servants who may also get along with the Governor need alone be appointed. Indeed, advisers shine only when Governor have been non-professionals nor wanting in administrations orientation. The case of H.C. Sarin, who functioned as an Adviser to Khandubhai K. Desai in Andhra Pradesh in 1973 as well as in Gujarat in 1974 is deeply educated. While Sarin stalked in state of Andhra Pradesh having a less imposing Governor his presence in Gujarat remained only barely noticed with a words, the advisers function's cannot be studied in isolation from the Governor's. The part which the Governor plays under President's rule comes to depend essentially upon his own measure of experience in administration and his personality. A person like Dharam Vira, well-versed in administration may and does in solve himself more actively in the sphere of administration so much no that he may not stand in need of any advisers. In the case of Governors not so endowed or oriented, advisors become necessary and what is more they may come to be actually guided by the latter. It is significant to note that the Andhra Pradesh Governor, Khandubhai K. Desai, attracted some adverse judicial observations for what he did was virtually abdication not delegation to his advisors.[16]

Qualities of Advisors

There is also the question of whether advisers should be drawn from outside the state or from within. The foremost qualities of the highest order—Objectivity, political sensibility and, last but not the least, acceptability by the Governor. The above question thus does not seem to be directly very relevant. Yet, its importance cannot be brushed aside for local roots do breed subjectivity, which becomes more marked in the single-party dominance system of India.

The advisor sent to Uttar Pradesh in 1973 after the fall of Kamlapati Tripathi, belonged to the Uttar Pradesh cadre, had earlier served Uttar Pradesh in various capacities and the officials whom they were expected to pull up or punish for inefficiency or other irregularities or neglect had been their junior colleagues for long years. It is not without significance that no senior police officer was removed after PAC revolt although it was well revealed that this so called mutiny itself was the result of tax control by the officers and their failure to built up rapport with the men that commanded. Still another reason for lack of improvement in administration was the disinterestedness in bringing about change in administration. Some of them were too deeply associated with some political leaders of the state to be able to look at the challenges objectively and act decisively. It is further discuss that, the story of an advisor who made his first call on reaching Lucknow at the residence of former Chief Minister. It may not therefore be a sound administrative policy to send as advisors the civil servants who belong to the same state except when President's rule is intended for a brief period or when possession of the knowledge of local affairs is considered to be of overriding importance.

Relationship between Advisers and State Government Personnel

A word about the status of the Chief Secretary and other Secretaries under President's rule is necessary here. Surprising as it may sound, the advisors as a class are not very much welcome to the Secretaries to State Government. In the first place, a distinct mental status characterises the relationship between the secretaries and the advisors, both coming as they do from the same profession. Secondly the minister and the secretary play complementary roles in the system of Government as involved in India but the induction of advisors duplicates the already available administrative skills with the consequence that the secretaries position in available gets devalued and they begin functioning more like joint secretaries under the advisory regime. Thirdly, most ministers, dependence on secretaries is deep and continues, and their voice virtually prevails in a large numbers of matters. No longer do the secretaries derive this feeling of indispensability and this measure of authority when they are called upon to work under advisers. Finally, the psychological inhibition becomes conspicuously marked in the case of advisers belonging to the same state and thus having unwillingly crystallized biases and prejudices characterising their relationship with the secretaries who had in the past functioned as their junior colleagues. On the other hand, the secretaries in general and the Chief Secretary in particular generally get clothed with enhanced power when no advisers are appointed in the state.[17]

During the President's rule in Kerala in 1970, which was necessitated by the resignation of the popular Ministry to seek fresh election, the Chief Secretary was conferred the power of the ministers for all the departments and the Governor preferred to act as Chief Minister.

The main grievance against the Centre's interference in the affairs of the States has been in regard to the office of Governor and his power. Instances of dismissal of Governors by the Centre has caused great dissatisfaction and apprehension among the States having the non-Congress Government in power. The Constitution gives an absolute authority to the centre in the matter of appointment of state Governor. A Governor is appointed by the President and holds office during the pleasure of the President. Besides being the Head of the State, he is the agent or representative of the centre in the State. For such purpose, it has been realised that with a view to increasing the smooth functioning of the Constitutional machinery in the State it would be best to consult the state Chief Minister while appointing the Governor, and convention has thus grown accordingly. There was no such difficulty and controversy in the matter of appointment of Governor till 1967. From 1967, the appointment of Governor has become a somewhat controversial matter, particularly in those states where the political party in power differs in hue from that of the centre. Recent trend is that the 'yes man' shall be appointed as Governor by the centre to act only as an agent ignoring the very principle that for a smooth working of federal structure it is necessary that the person to be appointed as the Governor should be such as to inspire confidence from both, the Centre and the State concerned and be independent of party affiliations. It is seen that in a situation where there arises a conflict between the Governor's role as the representative of the centre and that as the constitutional head in the state, then undoubtedly, the former obligation is taking precedence over the latter. The Governor is bound to submit to the dictates of centre and the same is highly objectionable, the practice being contrary to the philosophy of administrative autonomy to the states.

Being a centre's representative the Governor of a State in discharging his duties shall have to see as to whether the State is functioning according to the provisions of the Constitution. If not he shall inform such non-compliance to the Centre and the President shall attract immediately Article 356 for its remedy. It needs no elaboration as to how many times President rule has been imposed on this plea from the commencement of the constitution. North-Eastern Region (NER) specially Assam has already experienced much of it.

On the other hand Article 356 is giving a clear way for imposition of President's rule in States for simple and trifle reasons. Article 356 provides that where a states has failed to comply with or to give effect to any direction of the Union under any of the provisions of the Constitution, it shall be lawful for the President to hold that a situation has arisen in which the State Government could not be carried on. Such a finding on the part of the President could provide for a takeover of all administration of the states on any pretext which takes away the federal character of the Constitution forcing it to work in a unitary system.

The policy of one party dominance both in the center and state is the policy and politrict played by the central leaders, as a matter of fact, the elected members from the multiparties are also desires for holding the power, otherwise, their aims for next winning in the election could be failed. So defection and change of party when elected has been often happening particularly in the states politics. Taking the chance of such political unstable and misbehaviour of the elected members the central political leaders insisted to the governor and called the administrative reports of the particular state and thus, the Governor acts as the pure role of an agent. Suddenly the Governor made the report as pursue and desire by the Union Government. Here, I am presenting sample of reports sent by the Governor to the central Government in various cases of different states for different steps. Moreover Governor played partisan role in the state administrative affairs in appointing and dismissing the state ministries summoning, proroguing and dissolving the assemblies, reserving large number of bill for the consideration of the President under Articles 200 and 201 and issuing ordinances. There are instances of the misuse of constitutional emergency powers under Article 356 by dismissing the state ministries having majority in the Assembly on untenable grounds and suspending and dissolving the Assemblies keeping in view the interests, of the ruling party at the centre, discriminatory attitude of the Center towards states in appointment and transfer of Governors, appointment of Enquiry Commission against Chief Ministers and financial devolution in general and loans and grants-in-aid in particular, the use of central Reserve Police by the centre in states without consulting them, refusal or resentment by certain state Governments to carry out centres direction issued under Article 257 and 356 of the constitution not being in the interest of the ruling party in the States. Sociocultural and regional pressures of state politics, etc.[18] The texts of the reports of the Governors of Bihar and Uttar Pradesh sent to the President of India are referenced below. So as to reflect different type of the role of the Governor during the President's rule in the state.

Text of the Bihar Governor's Report to the President, dated 26 June, 1968

Do. No 141 GB.

Bihar Governor's Camp
Patna
26 June, 1968

Dear Sir,

Shri Bhola Paswan Shastri submitted the resignation of his council of Ministers at 3.15 P.M. on 25.6. 68 and was requested by me to continue in office till alternative arrangements were made. In his letter of resignation the Chief Minister advised the dissolution of Assembly and holding of midterm election. I invited Shri Mahesh Sinha, leader of the Congress party (which is numerically the largest group in the Assembly) on 26.6.68 and met him twice. I asked him if he was in a position to form stable Government. He wanted four days or more time intimate his decision, to which I declined four reasons stated below. He expressed his inability to form a Government. Shri Bhola Paswan Shastri who had submitted his resignation yesterday was written to me today that he is in a position to form a government, presumably with the support of defectors from other Parties. I cannot accept his claim.

On 25.6.68 the Appropriation Bill was under discussion when the Government resigned and the House has been adjourned sine die by the speaker unless the Appropriation bill is passed by the Assembly before the 30th June 1968 no expenditure from the consolidated Fund would be possible and working of the Government will come to stand still. Voting on the budget in March 1968 was for a period of three months which expires on 30th June 1968.

There have been three successive Ministries inducted into office since the general elections held in 1967. Each of the Ministries has been defeated when it faced the legislative Assembly on the very first occasion, except the Ministry headed by Shri Mahamaya Prasad Sinha, which defeated on the second occasion when it faced the Assembly.

The Bihar Assembly has a strength of 318 (with one vacancy) members out of whom 85 members have changed parties at least once, some having done so twice, thrice and four times within a period of one year. No party or group is free from erosion. When my predecessor invited the leader of the Congress party, which had the largest following, to form the Government in March 1967 immediately after the general elections 35 members of the Congress Party submitted a signed memorandum to the Governor expressing their opposition to the formation of Government, the possibility of which their leader was exploring. Out of these 35 members 20 have, later on, defected from the Congress party and formed the Lok Tantrik party, of which the present Chief Ministers is the leader. The remaining 15 signatories are still members of the Congress party and according to my information some of them as well as others of Congress party may desert from their party if and when occasion arise.

Shri Kamakhya Narayan Singh (Raja of Ramgarh) leader of the Janata Party, while claims the strength of 18 members, has changed his mind thrice in 24 hours by his public statements starting with a letter to me on the 24th instant withdrawing his support from the present Ministry of which he still continue to be a member. This phenomenon is not confined to Congress party alone but applies to all parties or groups in the Assemblies. It is my considered view that it is not possible to form a Government which can be stable in any sense, and therefore, I recommend that action may be taken under Article 356 of the Constitution of India urgently so that consequential steps may be taken to enable drawals from the consolidated fund before the 1st July 1968.

I recommend that the Assembly should be dissolved forth with.

Dr. Zakir Hussain
President of India
Rastrapati Bhavan
New Delhi

Yours Sincerly
Nityanand Kanungo

Text of Uttar Pradesh Governor's Report to the President, dated 5 November, 1973, Recommending Revocation of President's Rule

Governor
Uttar Pradesh

Raj Bhavan
Lucknow

My dear respected Rashtrapatiji,

You had been pleased to assume to yourself all the functions of the Government of the State of Uttar Pradesh, vide Proclamation No G.S.R. 316 (E) dated 13th June 1973 under Article 356 of the constitution. This was done after considering my report dated 12th June 1973 in which I had intimated to you that the Chief Minister, Shri Kamlapati Tripathi had submitted his resignation to me in the wake of certain developments particularly, certain incidents of grand indiscipline of the part of subordinate ranks in some companies of the Pradeshik Armed constabulary. This resignation was submitted by him in spite of the fact that his leadership of the majority party in the Legislative Assembly (which had the strength of 272 in a House of 426 members out of which 5 seats were vacant) was virtually unchallenged. He and his colleagues felt, and I had agreed with them, that direct involvement of the central Government for a short period in the administration of the state would be helpful in safeguarding the security of the state ensuring the well being of the people. I had at that time recommended that the legislative Assembly may for the time being remain in suspended animation so that after the situation in the State had stabilised, it might be possible for the leader of the majority party in the Legislative Assembly to form a new Government. You were pleased to agree with me in this assessment and accordingly, the proclamation provided only for the suspension of the powers of the state legislative and not for the dissolution of legislative Assembly.

2. Since than I have been running the administration of the state government under your kind supervision. During this time the Pradeshik Armed constabulary has been reorganised while recalcitrant elements have been punished, the grievances of the subordinate ranks of the force have by and large been removed, their pay scales improved and certain other facilities given to them. This has given satisfaction to the men and created confidence among them. The

Pradeshik Armed constabulary will I am sure again be a fine force which the Government can rely on in times of need. Steps are also under way to reorganise the Intelligence department of the Police.

3. During the period of President's rule public order was well-maintained. There were virtually no cases of communal trouble or of atrocities on Harijans. The crime figures also showed a decline and there was general improvement in the law and order situation in the state. Peaceful conditions obtained in the Universities and other educational institutions.

4. A drive was launched to clean the administration and chop off the deadwood. A number of public servants were after careful screening compulsorily retired from service or reverted to their substantive ranks. In order to revitalise the administration and create confidence among the technical services, promotion prospects in the engineering services and the medical and health services were enlarged. At the same time, financial and administration delegations have been made to the Heads of Departments.

5. Unfortunately, the four months or so, during which I have had to look after the administration personally with the able assistance provided by my Advisers have been a period of great stress and strain owning to the shortage of essential commodities and particularly of power. The state had an acute drought in the beginning and later, there were heavy floods in some of the areas. These were effectively tackled and the people were held to the extent possible. Prospects of kharif crop are quite good and the process of food grains have shown a tendency to decline.

6. Shri Kamlapati Tripathi has now intimated to me by his letter dated the 3rd November 1973 that he is resigning from the leadership of his party and that the election of the new leader shall take place on the 7th November 1973. He also met me in this connection on the 4th November 1973 and I had a detailed discussion with him. He clearly feels that in the light of the overall improvement in the situation brought about under President's rule, the new leader of the majority party should immediately after his election be called upon to shoulder the responsibility of forming the Government. The party position in the state legislative Assembly, as intimated in my report dated 12th June 1973 has remained

substantially unchanged (the Congress party now has the strength of 271 instead of 272 intimated earlier). In these circumstances, 1 agree with Shri Tripati's assessment of the situation and feel confidence that the new leader of the majority party should be able to carry the legislature and the people of the state with him in running the administration.

7. In view of the above, I feel that the purpose for which the provision of Articles 356 of the constitution were invoked have been fully served and the time has come when the Government of the state can once again be carried on in accordance with the provisions of the constitution. I recommend accordingly that the proclamation referred to above may kindly be revoked with effect from 8th November 1973.

With kindness regards

Shri V.V. Giri — Yours sincerly
President of India — Akbar Ali Khan.
Rashtrapati Bhavan
New Delhi.

The above correspondences indicate that Governor has certain role in imposition or revocation of President's rule in the State. The exercise of emergency powers by the president and the controversy and misgivings which surround it are closely linked with the position and role of the Governor. For it is on the basis of his report that the President has always acted although the constitution also enables him to act on his own. In the actual working of the political system neither the President nor the Governor is a mere figurehead. Apart from being the head of the state the President has the responsibility of functioning as an umpire, standing outside political conflicts and the struggle for power. Like the British monarch the President has to maintain stability and balance among the competing forces in politics but his role is more complicated because of the character of federal politics. There is a gap between the law of the constitution and the conventions according to which the office of the President has evolved. Although he has discretionary power he has generally acted on the advice of the central cabinet. This is inevitable, given to logic of the parliamentary system. Yet this very convention makes him a party to the political decisions of the central Government. Moreover, the choice of the President and the Process of election by the electoral college of members of parliament and those of state Assemblies affect his image as an impartial umpire in federal politics.

The Governor like the President functions as a nominal executive in the state and has his ceremonial functions to perform. Like the President he has to stand outside the conflicts of politics within the state but he too is no ornamental figurehead. He has a delicate and difficult role to perform within the state as the representative of the President. He is appointed by the President and holds office during his pleasure. In practice, this means that he is appointed on the advice of the Union cabinet, specially the Prime Minister. During an emergency, it is on his report that the President would act and he would do so on the advice of the Union Cabinet. The Governor, therefore, functions all the time in the midst of politics and it is in such a position that he has to strive to acquire an image of impartiality.[19]

As constitutional head of the state Government he has a role to play in the formation of the ministry and has the right to summon, prorogue and dissolve the Assembly. The uncertainties of politics in several states which were widely prevalent after the Fourth General Election of 1967 and the practice of wholesale defections from one party to another made it difficult for the Governor to ascertain which party had a majority in the state legislature. There have been times when the situation has changed from day to day. A chief Minister may request the Governor to dissolve the Assembly

In order to secure a fresh mandate, the Governor evidently has room for the use of discretionary power but his actions have come under attack by state politicians and it has been suggested that there ought to be guidelines for the exercise of discretionary power evidently a contradiction in terms. Finally, the Governor has also the power to reserve bills for the consideration of the

President. This is a power which can be exercised only in exceptional circumstances.

The fact that the Governor like the President, has frequently been a politician who returns to politics when he was ceased to be a Governor has been detrimental to the image of impartiality so essential to the office. The report of the Rajanner Committee mentioned, not without justification, that since the central Government has the power to appoint and remove the Governor he cannot but look to the central Government for advice in the discharge of his duties. This part played by several governors has contributed to tensions in Indias federal politics and the office itself has been an important channel for federal centralization.[20]

When any state is placed under the President's rule, the position of the Governor undergoes a change. The President in exercise of the powers conferred on him by Article 356 of the constitution first assumes to himself all the functions of the state and all powers vested in or exercisable by the Governor. And then by a separate order he directs that the powers which have been assumed by him shall subject to the superintendence, direction and control of the President be exercisable also by the Governor of the state. In other words, during President's rule the Governor loses his independence status and functions by virtues of the authority delegated to him by the President and is subject to the latter's superintendence direction and control.

Regarding the use of Article 356 it may be mentioned here that India is no more a single party dominated polity but the misuse of Article 356 still remain. Allies of BJP who want an inconvenient state regine removed seem to overlook that. Article 356 is the ultimate two edged sword. A future government could as well use it against them should the opportunity arise. Such extreme views on centre-state Relations fly in the face of India federalised nature.

The see saw battle in Uttar Pradesh epitomises how complex and prove to misuse Article 356 of the Indian constitution providing for the imposition of President's rule has become in today volatile politics. Indian democracy has survived many crises. But the recent development in Uttar Pradesh involving the recommendation of President's rule by Governor Vishu Kant Shastri and later promulgated by President K.R. Narayanan has proved to some extent that the President of India is just not a mere titular head. After dethroning Indira Gandhi's emergency regime in 1977, the Janata Party government misused the provision with impurity to bring down the Congress led state Governments similarly, the Congress Government also unabashedly misused Article 356 to scrap many legitimately elected state Governments led by other parties on the pretext of deteriorating law and order situation in the state. But for deep rooted personal animosity between the leaders of some of the political parties, by now a Government would have been in place in Lucknow. The Governor would have also been save the embarrassment of emulating. Romesh Bhandari who in 1996, chose to ignore the claim of the then single largest party, Bharatiya Janata Party (BJP) with 174 seats to form a Government. Like Shastri too has cited the inability of political combines to provide a stable Government as the reason for recommending central rule. True, the Assembly elections result have left the state in a predicament. The badly fractured mandate was clearly not in favoured of any party although the Mulayam Singh Yadav-led Samajwadi Party did emerge as the single largest party with 145 seats. But the 57 seats need for a majority proved to be a tall order for the wrestler from Etawah. In a way Yadav has only himself to blame. His past behaviour has that he does not have too many political friends. Indeed, the Congress saw in the UP developments an opportunity to settle scores with Mulayam for the earlier humiliation he had heaped on Sonia Gandhi when she refused to such her claim to form a Government at the centre. Six months of President's rule will give ample time for various parties to buy defections. The auction will in due course produce a collision that can be sworn in.

Clearly, we need some radical surgery. One way would be to amend the Representation of the people Act to nullify any election where a legislator defeats or disobeys the party whip in a vote of confidence. Another would be to amend the constitution to provide for a chief executive who cannot be toppled by election Americans style democracy with fixed terms and a directly elected President and State Governor, in one such possibility that will be no means eliminate corruption or horse-trading on individual Bills, but will mean greater representation of the people's will than defection led politics.

A responsible Government is an immediate necessity in Uttar Pradesh given the fragmentation of its society. This brings to the fore the need for the political establishment cutting across the spectrum in Uttar Pradesh as well as those at the helm in the Union Government to acknowledge the gravity of the situation and agree to put on hold them partisan considerations. The civil administration needs a firm signal from the political establishment that the rule of law will be meticulously upheld in the state in the days ahead.[21]

The developments in Uttar Pradesh since February 24, particularly after the emergence of the BSP (Bahujan Samajwadi Party) as the second largest party in the Assembly, have implications that go beyond the immediate contact of Government formation. It will be in order to make a set of qualifications before delving further into the subject. To begin with, even if it was accepted that the B.S.P would emerge as a major player in the post poll situation, hardly any one expected Mayawati to emerge as the leader of a 97 member Legislature party 30 seats more than in 1996 After all, the consolidation of Dalits behind the BSP was complete even in 1996 and there was no scope for further consolidation on this front and hence there was little basis to expect such an increase in the number of BSP seats. Second, after the impressive performance there were many who felt that the BSP was vulnerable to poaching. It seemed that Mulayam Singh Yadav, who emerged leader of the single largest party, could land up at the Lucknow Raj Bhavan and hand over a list of 202 MLAs which could include 35 from the BSP, apart from

26 from the congress (I) and at least a dozen from Ajit singh's party. This too did not happen.

While it is simple to explain the reasons why the BSP did not split, the factors behind the impressive gains it registered are contained in the complex mosaic that the Uttar Pradesh socio-political discourse is made of. To break the BSP (and manage the numbers with Congress-I support), the Samajwadi Party needed to promise ministerial berths (or positions in the state Government corporation) as was done by Kalyan Singh in 1996 this would have been possible only if Mr. Yadav was invited by the Governor to be sworn in and prove his majority within a reasonable time. In a sense, the Governor Vishnu Kant Shastri, helped Mr. Mayawati keep her flock together by refusing to accept the single largest party be invited precedent set by Sankar Dayal Sharma, the President of India in 1996.

Having made these qualifications it will be pertinent to look at and place in context the meaning of the BSPs rise and consolidation its strength is higher than the BJPs in the Assembly now placed under suspended animation. It is necessary to understand the factors that went in the BSPs favour in the elections to make sense of their implications for the political discourse in the state in the next couple of years. While the BSP was expected even by those who criticise Mayawati's dalit exclusive agenda to retain the same number of seats it won in the 1996 elections (67), the additional 30 came as a surprise even to those who emphasis with the agenda. In addition to the Dalits (whose consolidation behind the BSP since 1987 when Kanshi Ram founded the party was more or less complete), a substantial section of the forward caste voters had favoured the BSP. It was this shift that helped the party notes up close to 30 seats more. It may be true that in some of the cases the BSP victory was possible because its nominees were men (invariably from the forward castes) who strike terror in their constituencies. Amarmani Tripathi, Uday Singh Doctor etc. There is another explanation now doing the rounds that the BSP manage to perform so well because Miss Mayawati managed to shed the image of her party being a Dalit exclusivity plate form and she could do this by striking the right social balance while choosing the party nominees. Such explanation however, are based only on the factors in the apparent. It would make better sense to look at the 2002 poll verdict from the overall contest of the social dynamics in Uttar Pradesh since the first general elections.

A key factor that guided the political discourses of the Gangetic plains since 1952, a determining among the forward castes to unite against any kind of assertion by the members of the Backward castes continued to influence the voting pattern this time too. It was this unity against the many avatars of the socialist platform that kept the Congress (I) going in Uttar Pradesh in the three decades after Independence. The Congress (I) after all, was able to valley around it the Dalits and the Muslim (along side the members of the forward castes) during this phase.

It was the same dynamics that helped the BJP after 1990 but then the party could hardly enlarge its social base beyond the forward castes: As over time it became impossible for the forward castes to decide which way the dalits voted, (a non violent way of rigging elections was in vogue in this region for long), it made ample since for them to look for a plate form led by some one who shared with them an antipathy to all forms of Backward caste assertion. In other words, the forwards castes found in Mayawati a leader who was as much opposed to the Samajwadi Party (SP) as they were.

It is this dynamics, rooted in the complex social chemistry of the Genetic plains that helped the BSP gain at least 30 seats more this time. The BSP, in this sense, has taken over the Congress (I)'s place among the Dalits and the forward dates in Uttar Pradesh. For this very reason. The Congress (I)'s revival in the state looks a distant dream.

But for the BSP to ensure further gains in the state and to emerge as the number one party it needs to expand its appeal to the third social segment the Muslim Community as a whole that constituted the Congress (I)'s votebank. This indeed, remains a secure votebank for Mulayam Singh Yadav at this stage thanks to his having managed to work on a strategy given shape to by Madhu Limaye (in the context of the dual membership debate in the Janata Party). Mr. Yadav could achieve this thanks to his record in dealing with the VHP activists in Ayodha in 1990. But then, if only Mayawati can resist the temptation to strike a deal with the BJP in the months to come and remain steadfast to her agenda it is indeed possible for her together around her party a large section of the minority community in the state. In other words, Mayawati could enlist behind the BSP a combination of social groups the Dalits, the forward castes and the Muslims that enable the Congress (I) to emerge as the natural party of governance in Uttar Pradesh in the first couple of decades after Independence. This indeed is the critical performance in Uttar Pradesh this time such a development, however, will come with a crucial difference, while hi the case of the Congress (I) the prominent leader of the platform remained men from the forward castes—N.D. Tiwari, Kamlapati Tripathi, G.B. Pant, V.P. Singh etc., in the days ahead an assertive leader from the dalit community could finally take charge.[22]

But Mayavati's charisma as a new social engineer has shown result. She is heading the government of BSP in UP with her party's majority still now (2009).

REFERENCES

1. K.R. Bombwall, *National Power and State Autonomy,* p. 94.
2. K.S. Singh, *Indian Political System,* p. 248.
3. K.R. Bombwall, *op. cit.* p. 97.
4. Administrative, Reforms Commission, *Report on Centre-State Relationship* (New Delhi, 1969) p. 28.
5. *Ibid.,* p. 37.
6. *Ibid.,* p. 25.
7. *Ibid.*
8. *Ibid.,* p. 49.
9. K. Santhanant, *Union State Relations in India,* p. 7.

10. Dharam Vira, *Changed Role of Governor, The Mother land,* 22 December, 1972.
11. *Ibid.*
12. K.R. Bombwall, *op. cit.,* p. 94.
13. *Ibid.,* p. 95.
14. *Lok Sabha Debates, Fourth series,* Vol. XXXIX, No. 38,16 April, 1970. col. 147.
15. *Ibid.*
16. S.R. Maheshwori *President's Rule in India,* p. 119.
17. *The Times of India,* 21 March, 1970.
18. T.N. Chaturvedi, *Indian Journal of Public Administration* (Quaterly Journal of Indian Institute of Public Administration, Delhi), Vol. XXX, No.2, April-June 1984, p. 407.
19. K.R. Bombwall. *op. cit.*
20. *Report of the Centre-State Relations Inquiry Committee,* Tamil Nadu, Madras, 1971-72, p. 126.
21. *The Statesman,* 15 March, 2002.
22. *The Hindu,* 15 March, 2002.

4

Role of Central Government Under President's Rule in the State and Centre-State Relations

The Central Government plays the key role in the decision making process with regard to imposition, promulgation and extension of the president's rule in the state. With the taking over of the state Government following the imposition of President's rule, the President delegates the power of governance to the Governor of the concerned state. But this delegation is subject to the superintendence Direction and control of the president. The use of the word "President", however, is an euphemism, for the President is the constitutional head of state, and all powers really vest in the council of Ministers headed by the Prime Minister. What is therefore, said and done in the name of the President reflects really the thinking and action of the central Government. Since the central Government is a party Government many aspects of President's rule such as its proclamation and determination may not be understood isolation from the dynamics of politics, especially that of the ruling at the central level, Besides, consequent to the ringing out of the state Legislature the Parliament takes upon itself the functions of lawmaking and taxation for the state, and all this entails work and responsibilities for the central Government.

The Governor in his report to the president recommends the imposition of the President's rule in the state under Article 356 of the constitution stating the reasons thereof and justifying his action. This document is first received by the President's secretariat and seen by the President who forwards it to the Prime Minister for advice. In 1970, a departure from this procedure for transaction of business was made in one instance Uttar Pradesh Governor B. Gopala Reddy's report to President recommending President's rule was sent to the Prime Minister without being seen by the President V.V. Giri who at that moment of time was on a visit to the soviet union. This sparked off a political controversy in the country.[1]

According to the past practice, Prime Minister used to send the Governor's report to the Home Minister for examination and initiation of necessary action. The report comes up for discussion with a note by the Home Ministry. The Prime Minister decides whether the report should first be taken up in the Political Affairs committee of the cabinet or straightaway come before the parent body. But the recent practice is to place the Governor's Report in the Cabinet itself. The Prime Minister who presides over the meeting gives a summery of the political developments in the state including, of course, the Governor's recommendation and suggests also a course of action. Generally the meeting is brief and the Cabinet endorses the views of the Prime Minister. The Cabinet's decision is immediately conveyed to the President who then issues the Presidential proclamation clamping Article 356 on the State and simultaneously issues another order delegating his power to the Governor of the State, both the notification and the order being announced by the Ministry of Home Affairs. The whole exercise may ordinarily takes from over a week (for instance Punjab, 1 966) to a few hours depending upon the urgency which the Prime Minister may attach to this matter. Indeed, the quickness with which the entire cycles gets completed now is impressive. In the case of Gujarat (1976), the Babubhai Ministry fell on 12 March 1976. At 4.30 pm the Governor's report began tricking in Delhi through the telex and completed by 5.00 pm. The Cabinet meet at 6.00 pm to discuss the report. And at 7.30 pm the President signed the proclamation Bringing Gujarat under the operation of Article 356 of the constitution.[2]

In practice, it may not be more than a ritual, for the Governor keeps the centre informally apprised of the political developments in his state and the before sending his formal report recommending President's rule he assures himself about its acceptance by the central leadership. Similarly President's assent to the Cabinet decisions on the Governor's report is automatic but is an indispensable constitutional requirement, constitutionally speaking, it is only after the President has signed the proclamation that the President's rule becomes effective in the state. The President's action in clamping Article 356 on a state enjoys finality and cannot be judicially challenged. When, for instance, Rao Birender Singh took the matter to the High Court challenging the constitutionality of the President's proclamation by which in 1968 the President's rule was imposed in Haryana, the Punjab and Haryana High Court dismissed the writ petition observing that the President was not amenable to the jurisdiction of the judiciary and that the parliament which is invested with the power to approve or not to approve of the President's action lies outside the Court's jurisdiction.[3]

There are three patterns under which the President's rule may fall and the President's proclamation itself makes clear the pattern which has been opted for. The following patterns are followed:

(i) The President removes the Ministry but keeps the state Legislature under suspension, (ii) He removes the Ministry and abolishes the Legislature but the speaker of the Assembly continues in office, and (iii) He removes the Ministry, and the Assembly is merely suspended by the first proclamation but is later abolished. But while a suspended legislature may be abolished a reverse movement has never been attempted the Assembly abolished in the first proclamation but revised and kept under suspension by a subsequent one.

Once a state comes under President's rule it is required to be administered in accordance with the provisions of the constitution. Besides an administrative mechanism has to be devised and set in to motion to regulate the affairs incidental and consequential to these provisions. A study of the governmental mechanism at the central level to deal with the routines of administration pertaining to President's rule is the theme of the present chapter. The Governor has, as said earlier, been delegated the power to govern the President rule state. But his rule is subject to the superior authority of the President which means the council of Ministers. Besides, it is the Parliament which moves in to fill the gap created by the dissolution or even suspension of the state Assembly.[4]

Normally, the Governor administers all the 46 subjects figuring in the states list of the constitution. But important matters even in this sphere are referred to the functional Ministry at the central level for advice and even direction. The President ruled State's relationship with the centre is organised on a decentralised basis. The words superintendence, direction and control of the President are significant, meaning that under the President's rule the final voice in all matters rests with the centre. On the same token parliamentary questions on the state are replied by the functional Ministries soon on their receipt they are forwarded to the state for compelling the necessary information and draft replies. The state is under an obligation to send the relevant information to the functional Ministries on time. The replace are as a rule given by the functional Ministries. The Ministries with whom the state Government comes to have extensive relationship are, Home, Finance, Law and Planing Commission, and the ones dealing with developmental subjects.

But then, such a dispersed kind of relationship between the state and the functional Ministries point up to the problem of coordination at the central level. There is, thus the need for a nodal or focal at the level of the central Government, and the obvious choice for this role is of the Ministry of Home Affairs which it may be recalled, attends to matters relating to the emergency provisions of the constitution other than those relating of financial emergency under the Government of India Allocation of Business Rules 1961. Even otherwise, of all the central Ministries it is the Home Ministry with which the state have the most extensive and continuous relationship. Which the state under President's rule deals directly with the functional Ministries, copies of important correspondence are regularly dispatched to the Home Ministry.

On the same pattern the central Ministries deal directly with the state Government but make it a point to mark copies of all the correspondence to the Home Ministries. This arrangement is calculated to serve two purposes. First and foremost, the Home Ministry is kept informed on the whole range of administrative dealing with the various segments of the central Government, Besides it is also expected occasionally to get in touch with the functional ministries to expedite the proposals sent by the state and pending with them. This is the catalytic or trouble shooting role of the Home Ministry. All those and allied functions are in charge of a Division in the Ministry of Home Affairs, called the centre-state Relation Division known as the Political Division till 1972, the centre-state relation Division deals among others, with matters relating to President's rule. Though bearing the designation of centre state relation Division, it looks after certain other items of work as well and what is more, not all federal problems constitute its portfolio. This Division is headed by a joint secretary who is assisted by a complement of deputy secretaries including directors and under secretaries. The Joint Secretary reports directly to the secretary in the Ministry of Home Affairs.[5]

Does a functional Ministry enjoy sovereignty in its dealings with the state? This would be the questioned. This issue may be set in its proper perspective by posing another question. Does a Ministry enjoy complete freedom in the ordering of affairs put under its charge? While a Ministry is empowered to dispose of a large range of matters referred to it by the state the more important ones are as a rule, decided collectively i.e., by the Cabinet. Two such items transcending individual handling are legislation and budget. The procedure evolved for each of them is briefly as such.

As a rule, the state concerned prepared the draft legislation and forwards it to the functional Ministry with a copy to the Home Ministry. The functional Ministry begins considering it in consultation with all the concerned Ministries especially the Home, the Law and the Finance Ministries. As with any central Legislation, it finally comes before the Cabinet for its approval. It is only after the Cabinet has cleared it does the legislation gets placed before the consultative committee of M.Ps. In other words, the latter may suggest amendment to it or even disapprove it. No significant change are, however, expected at this stage.

Contrary to the parliamentary authority the committee has only a consultative role. From the committee the piece of legislation goes direct to the President for his assent. The committee being the surrogate of parliament the bill does not come before that body for its approval. On the contrary, the procedure for enactment of the budget is not short circulated. The budget proposals are as a rule prepared by the President-ruled state and sent to the Ministry of Finance. It is then discussed by a group of concerned ministries ^ which always includes the Finance, the Home and the Planing Ministers. It is significant to note that the budget proposals are never placed before the consultative committee of MPs for its comments. After it has been approved by the cabinet, the Finance Ministers presents it in the parliament and the procedure applicable to the central budget is observed in the case of the states budget but the time allotted is barely a few hours. After the passage of the budget in the two Houses it goes to President for his assent.

A word about the nature of the laws as well as of the budget enacted for the state under Article 356 may be relevant here in the context of the query whether the state Government under President's rule is a mere caretaker Government. A study of the laws and the budget passed for the states under Article 356 disclose that radical change in policy especially those having political implications and major taxation measures are generally not contemplated during the continuance of President's rule. It was while piloting the Punjab state legislature (Delegation of

Powers) Bill in the House of the people in 1951 the C. Rajagopalachari, the Home Minister, explained the scope of legislative work to be done by the centre when a state was placed under President's rule. It is not the intention of Government to take up all legislation simply because they have authority for a summery process and go on with every kind of thing simply for the sake of making laws. What they (centre) have to take is only that which is most urgent and most necessary either from the points of view of the present emergency or from the points of view of any emergency that may arise in the province. Their intention is only to take up absolutely essential legislation. But if they are controversial and are likely so to say to forestall the legitimate activities of a popular Ministry. I promise that such things will not be tackled and it is not a pleasure for Government to tackle such things. We shall only deal with necessary things."[6]

If, for instance, the popular Government had taken a policy decision to introduce prohibition in the state, it is extremely unlikely for this policy to be changed under President's rule. There have been two notable exceptions to this general convention. The communist Ministry in Kerala had completely dissociated itself from the scheme of common police reserved force implemented in the southern zone but Kerala joined this force when the state came under President's rule after the dismissal of the Namboodiripad Ministry in 1959. Similarly, on 2 April 1976, Nagaland under President's rule became a member of the North Eastern Council although the popular Government had solemnly decided to keep out of it. The ethics of these two instances are seriously questionable, President's rule ought not to be utilised for reversing the political decisions of major import made by the popular Ministry.

It sees that the laws enacted under the President's rule generally embody the provisions already included in the budget which has been passed by the parliament. A large number of laws passed for the state are in the nature of amendments to the existing ones certain taxation proposals passed by parliament demand corresponding revisions in appropriate existing acts.

Also revisions of acts become called for to take care of judicial decisions or to remove gaps and difficulties discovered in the course of their administration. Here most bills passed are really amendments to the existing acts. For example, during the period February 1974 to March 1975 when Gujarat remained under President's rule, the Parliament enacted the following laws for it: (i) the Bombay Inams (Kutch Area) Abolition (Gujarat second Amendment) Act, 1974. (ii) the Bombay Tenancy and Agriculture lands (Gujarat second Amendment) Act 1974. (iii) The Bombay Land Requisition (Gujarat Amendment) Act 1974, and (iv) The Gujarat Panchayat (Amendment) Act 1975.

It is thus apparent that the state under Article 356 remains in an extended relationship with and dependent upon, the central Government. While the Governor has been delegated powers of governance, at the same time, he has also been made dependent upon the central Ministries for major decisions and more particularly in the field of legislation and budget. The passing of the budget is a constitutional obligation and moreover, it makes but one demand on the centre in a year and so does not pose much of a problem to the state Government. The same however cannot be said about other matters while the state Government may give top priority to a matter the functional Ministry which has to approve of it may respond less enthusiastically, thus delaying action. The hurried Governor and other official of the state may visit Delhi and impress upon an early action but the Ministries may have other pressure and commitments and in this process even the Home Ministry's trouble shooting role, even when activated, may have limited effectiveness in the face of centre's own priorities.[7]

Extensive, thus becomes the Central Government's concern towards and participation in policy making in areas in the state list of subject of the constitution. The Central role under President's rule becomes vastly increased particularly in the case of the state which was ruled by an opposition party with varying degree of assertiveness, therefore, New Delhi emerges as the super-capital of the state and state Government officials are seen continually visiting Delhi to explain and pursue certain proposals. Similarly, but on a much reduced scale, the officials from central. Government Ministries also begin visiting the state to discuss matters and see things for themselves. Any way, one of the effects of such an administrative arrangement is delay in the processing of new policies and programs. To expedite decision making at the central level, a committee of secretaries was formed when Uttar Pradesh was placed under President's rule in 1973. But such contrivances while cutting short the delay in the disposal of issues, are hardly meant to promote original and vigorous thinking on matters of long term policies. The existing machinery of Government caters to matters of day to day administration but not suited for long term planning. Or, perhaps, the President's rule has never been meant for making policies on major issues.[8]

Parliament and President's Rule

As per established practice in consonance with the spirit of the constitution, Parliament decides on the promulgation and continuance (but not termination) of President's rule in the state unless of course, it is of more than two months duration. Since Article 356 strikes out the democratic processes and institutions in the state concerned, such an action must require the sanction of the people's representatives at the higher national level. The parliament also gets formally endowed with the functions of legislation and taxation which in normal lives are the responsibility of the state Legislative. Besides, the parliament must begin to act as a watch dog both on the central executive's activities in so far as they relate to the state under Article 356 and on the state Government's functioning. But this body is not associated even obliquely, with the termination of President's rule as no statement is made or placed in the two Houses when the President revokes it.

Approval of President's Rule: The Constitution obliges the President's rule to be formally endorsed by both Houses of Parliament within two months of its proclamation. While seeking this approval the Home Minister lays on the table of the House,

President's proclamation as well as the Governor's report, and initiates discussion with a-statement in which he explains the circumstances necessitating the imposition of President's rule in the state. This is followed by a debate in the House. This is the first and the most important opportunities for parliament to take stock of the situation calling for President's rule in the state. Its the imposition of Article 356 is the political move, the discussion in the House is understandable, charged with political overtones, being on party lives. The ruling party being safe behind its majority in the Houses, the debate which generally continue for a day or two ends with the expected endorsement of the governmental action the parliamentary approval remains valid for only six months and therefore, if the President's rule is continued for a longer period the central Government is obliged to come before it again to seek its consent, and a debate again follows.[9]

The second opportunity which parliament gets generally within a month or so of the imposition of President's rule is of a more substantive nature. One must recall that under President's rule the power of the state Legislature become exercisable by parliament or under its authority. The second occasion involves that august body in enacting a statute authorising delegation of legislative power of the state Assembly to the President. Originally, the state legislature Bill was passed like any other Bill with its usual three readings.

Now the parliament approves a resolution under which the Bill gets passed. This process takes much less time, but the parliament gets deprived of an opportunity of a detailed discussion of the affairs relating to the state under Article 356. There have been a few instances for example, Punjab in 1971, when the parliament was given a single opportunity to pass the statutory resolution as well as the bill delegating legislative power to the President coming back to this subject in consequence of this enactment the President, may from time to time. Whether Parliament is in session or not enact as a President's Act a bill containing such provisions as he considers necessary. The

President's Act when enacted is required to be laid before each House of Parliament and the latter passes a resolution within thirty days signifying its approval or making amendments. This statute also includes a provision for the constitution of committee consisting of members of Lok Sabha and of Rajya Sabha which the President shall whenever he considers it practicable to do so consult.[10]

However, it was not without serious misgiving that parliament agreed in 1951 to enact the Punjab state Legislature delegation of power bill. One member observed. I do not know of any kind of Government except a despotic government where the law making powers are given to one person. A standing committee of the House consisting of the elected members from Punjab in the House may be constituted and others will be associated with them. They may be given the power to prepare bills and it will be easy for parliament to pass them. Over the years the significance of this occasion the delegation of legislative power to the President has steadily declined and today it is comparatively a tame affairs. The debate takes place at a low key and the sailing of this piece of legislation is smooth. But the contents of the parliamentary statute are no less momentary. The act gives a blank cheque, as it were to the executive in the field of law making and the parliament's role becomes optional in the process getting restricted to mere passing. If it choose, of resolutions according approval of or modifications in the Act. The consultative committee of members of Parliament set up under this statute, remains seized with legislative matters of interest or concern to the state. This committee needs a somewhat detailed discussion.

Consultative Committees of MP's

A consultative Committee of Members of Parliament is set up generally to advise the Government on matters of legislation relating to the state under President's rule. Its function is to what the laws meant for the state before they are enforced. As a convention, however, it tends o functions like a mini parliament showing its concern towards all matters relating to the state. It is a committee nominated by the speaker of the Lok Shaba and

Chairman of the Raja Sabha but is not a Parliamentary committee. Its meetings are convened by the Ministry of Home Affairs. It meets two or three times in a year, some, sometimes in the state concerned itself. Since parliament has been constitutionally associated with the administration of President's rule in a state, it has to be consulted in matters relating to the latter. As it does not have the time to perform this role, its committees constituted for this purpose.

The Consultative Committee on State Legislation was not set up at the time of the first state namely Punjab, coming under President's rule in 1951. But a plea for some kinds of similar body was made in the Lok Sabha by Thakur Das Bhargava who said, I want to submit that this House may appoint a subcommittee comprising Sardar Mann, Bakshiji and four or five Members of Punjab, some Members from other states may also be included. That subcommittee should made laws for Punjab when two years later Pepsu was put under President's rule many Members of Parliament expressed their strong misgivings on the matter of delegating Parliament's legislative power to the President without having any consultation say in legislation making. In difference to their wishes K.N. Katju, the then Home Minister agreed to set up a consultative committee. As a result the PEPSU Legislature (Delegation of Power) Act 1953 delegated legislative power to the President provided that before enacting any such Act the President shall, except where it is not practicable so to do consult the committee constituted for the purpose consisting often Members of the House of the people nominated by the speaker and five Members of the council of state nominated by the chairman. The statute did not restrict the discretion of the speaker and the chairman to the MPs from the state concerned. But what we had in mind, K N. Katju said, was that Members who would be particularly acquainted with the local conditions, very likely their names would occur to the speaker and the chairman first so that they might be able to give their useful Advice.[11]

What was left to involve through a convention became a

statutory provision in the case of Kerala in 1956, when Parliament passed the Kerala State Legislature (Delegation of Power) Act According to this legislation, the President was to consult a committee constituted for the purpose consisting of all the Members of the House of the council of states who for the time being fill the seats allotted to the state of Kerala in the two Houses. Pandit Govind Ballabh Pant, the Home Minister, announced this change in December 1956 when moving the Kerala state legislature (Delegation of Power) Bill in the Lok Sabha. "Governor observed, as there is no local legislation, the Parliament has to devise some ready machinery for giving legislature sanction to necessary measures meant for the Kerala state. So it is proposed to give that power to the President. But before any such Bill can be accepted it will be placed before and considered by the committee consisting of all Members from Kerala. In fact, even before the formal acceptance of the proclamation. I have led the privilege of consultation with the Members from Kerala they have been good enough to give me very useful advice. Now, by virtue of this bill measures relation to Kerala will be placed before the committee, and than the President will give them the legal form and sanction."[12]

The composition of the consultative committee was to undergo further changes both in its pattern and in size in years to come, and a beginning in this direction was made with the passage of the Kerala State Legislature (Delegation of Power) Act 1959, which provided for a compromise between the two principles. Accordingly the consultative committee of MPs for Kerala consisted of thirty Members of the Lok Sabha nominated by the Speaker among whom were involved all members from Kerala and fifteen Members of the Upper, House nominated by the chairman among whom were included all the Members from that state. This marked a departure from the earlier practice of making this committee consist only of the Members of Parliament from the state under President's rule. Justifying the change B.N. Datar a Minister in the Ministry of Home Affairs said the Parliament also needed to be reflected in this committee, and the government's stand was accepted notwithstanding the opposition by members of parliament from Kerala. The compromise proved to be interim and by 1961 the composition of the consultative committee began to reflect the strength of various political parties in the parliament.

The Orissa state Legislature (Delegation of Power) Act 1961 was the first to lay down this direction and provided that before enacting any act the President shall whenever he considers it practicable to do so consult a committee constituted for the purpose, consisting of fourteen numbers of the House of the people nominated by the speaker and seven members of the council of states nominated by the chairman.[13]

Thus the provision for inclusion of all MP's from the state under Article 356 became conspicuous by its absence in the Orissa. Article 356 became conspicuous by its absence in the Orissa State Legislature (Delegation of Power) Act. At this time the MPs from Orissa numbered were thirty, twenty from the Lok Sabha and ten from the Rayja Sabha. This meant that some MPs from Orissa were to be kept out of the committee. Many MPs objected to this manner of constituting the committee. Even the speaker asked why all MPs from Orissa could not be put on it. Replying to him Lal Bahadur shastri, the Minister for Home Affairs said, The only point is the committee will become an unwieldy body. In there state's i.e., Kerala and Orissa it is a smaller number. But take, for instance, Uttar Pradesh, of course. 1 hope no President's rule would be introduced there. But suppose it happens like that, then we will have a very big body, a very big committee, if big committee, if all the Members from that state are to be included. So that it should not be the precedent.

In short, originally the consultative committee used to comprise all the members of parliament elected from the state concerned, regardless of their political affiliation. Such a composition could be viewed as a mechanism to introduce the popularly elected local element in the management of affairs of that state. This manner of constituting the committee did not pose any significant problem, far it tended to reflect, at the same time, the political complexion of parliament, When however, Kerala with its substantial communist following came under the President's rule in 1959, the constitution of the consultative committee along the about lines would have made it a communist dominated body, thereby completely upsetting the political balance between parliament and this committee this occasion was utilized by the ruling party to introduce a modification in the manner of constituting it and this process was completed in 1961. The consultative committee now reflects, in size and shape, the political complexion of the Parliament itself. Within the constraints of proportional representation of political parties in it the attempt is to put as many MPs from that state on it as possible.[14]

Whether the basis of membership should be nomination or election was also discussed. Direct election of the committee's members by the entire House was preferred by some on the ground that it was a more democratic process. Commanding this mode, a Member of Parliament said, I feel that power being given to the speaker or any body else to nominate members to the consultative committee is not in consonance with or in accordance with the spirit of the constitution. Once the President takes it the state Government up, it means that this parliament comes into the picture, and the President only acts through the advice of the party in power. So, far as the consultative committee is concerned it must completely reflected this House. It is the Parliament that rules Orissa now. It that is so, if the President is given the power, normally it means the power of the party which is in power. The whole responsibility is on parliament now. We are responsible for it, that is the party in power, If that is so the consultative committee also must completely reflect this Houses. So I submit that nomination would not be proper. It must be election. This suggestion was not accepted because it is only the mode of nomination which can ensure maximum representation to the national Legislature from the state under Article 356.

The meeting of the consultative committee is presided over

by the Minister for Home Affairs. The Governor accompanied by the Chief Secretary generally attends the meeting giving a resume of the work done in the state during the period President's rule, where there are advisers the latter attend on behalf of the Governor. Generally speaking, Members of Parliament belonging to the state under Article 356 are more vocal and take more interest in its activities than those who come from other states. Even the MPs of the first category show more concern for the problems effecting their constituency than in general matters of state-wide significance. Moreover, the legislators do not evince sustained interest in the work of this body.[15]

This committee must not be confused with the Informal consultative committee of MPs attached to each Ministry of the central Government, an arrangement devised in the year 1954. The latter committee is a standing one and discusses the problems and matters relating to the Ministry to which it is attached. As politically charged matters relating to President's rule fall within the jurisdiction of the Ministry of Home Affairs, the informal consultative committee attached to it begins showing interest in the state under Article 356. More questions on that state begins to be put in this committee, particularly by members who come from it. The informal consultative committees attached to other Ministries may discuss functional matters relating to the state. While members in both these bodies may seek information and give vent to their feelings they are unable to changes or even influence major policy decisions affecting the state.

The parliament has also the constitutional obligation of passing the budget of the state under President's rule. The budget is in fact prepared by the state Government itself but is presented by the Finance Minister. Formalities associated with the budget and the money bill are observed in the case of the pass of the state's budget. The MPs from that state are generally keener participants in the discussion, which, however, is not and cannot be even half as detailed as is usually the case when the central Government's budget is being passed. For instance, the Punjab budget for 1971-72 was passed by the Lok Sabha in 90 minutes.[16]

The Parliamentary committee have their jurisdiction extended to the state under President's rule. The Committee or Public undertakings for instance, examined the functioning of the public undertakings of Kerala when the state was under Article 356. The Public Accounts Committee also covered Kerala. In practices, however, the parliamentary committee have their hands already full, and extension of their concern to the state under President's rule is not a general event.

The foregoing is an analysis of the institutionalized opportunities available to parliament to discuss affairs of the state under Article 356. In addition, it can press into service all the other well known mechanisms of control such as adjournment motion, no confidence motion, half hour discussion parliamentary interpretations, etc. Not all these mechanism are Utilised in practice, and not by all or all the time. More active in invoking them are the Members of parliament coming from the state concerned , more particularly the opposition members. For instance, the number of Parliamentary interpellation focused on that state registers an appreciable increase under President's rule. An increase in the work load of individual MPs from the state is seen to occur consequent to the exit of state legislations. Their constituency linkage becomes more encompassing and they begin to spend more time in their state, visiting the state capital more often and meeting the officials, especially the Governor and the advisers. The MPs are never satisfied with seeing the Advisers only. They all come to see the Governor bringing all sorts of problem. But they are more individual case oriented and seldom do they come with general problems. It is to be noted that the solitary state level people's representative who ordinarily remains in offices even under President's rule is the speaker of the state Assembly, His principal functions remains took after the secretariat of the Assembly and has practically no role in influencing the ordering of affairs in the state.[17]

With these avenues open to parliament. Is this body able to ensure or enforce accountability of the state Government? The scheme of President's rule as designed in the constitution sought, while suspending the democratic process in the state, to make operative parliamentary control and surveillance over the state Government. The types as well as range of this control have already been discussed in the present chapter. But the mechanism is neither adequate nor effective to secure the equivalent of the vanished accountability of the state Government.

In the first place, parliamentary control, by the very nature, is remote-control, and is really no substitute for state level direction and monitoring of the state Government secondly, parliament does not have the necessary time and energy even to deal with if direct tasks, much less with this delegated responsibility. At any rate, all the problems of the state Government do not get highlighted in parliament.

Thirdly, it is too tall a demand on 500 and odd Members of parliament to direct their attention to the affairs of the state under President's rule. Jyotirmoy Basu expressed this dilemma this way. About the budget side, I would say that it is a great city because we know so little about Punjab's budget. We had no time to study it carefully. We do not know the facts that should be studied. Just we are doing something which should not be done.[18] At best, only the Members of Parliament belonging to that state show a measure of concern towards the administration of the state.

Fourthly, the parliamentary orientation is manifestly political and partisan and the Central Government does manage to remain completely sage behind it, majority in the parliament, thereby rendering the mechanism of parliamentary control of sporadic and occasional effectiveness, if not altogether devoid of impact. One therefore cannot help arguing that public accountability of the state inevitably becomes low, irregular, uneven, and shrewed when it comes under President's rule. Parliamentary control and surveillance become all the more restricted as a result of another practice which needs to be curbed and discouraged. There is a trend in the more recent past for the Executive to simultaneously seek parliamentary approval of the two resolutions on President's proclamation and on the state Legislation (Delegation of Power) Bill. On one occasion the parliament was called upon to take up for discussion, in addition to the two resolution, the budget for the state under Article 356. Paucity of parliamentary time is given as a reason behind this practice but any combining of these events inevitably curtails parliamentary scrutiny. Under President's rule the consultative committee of MPs becomes the bulwark of public accountability. But it does not seen to be effective in its functioning, and in this context. There is no evidence to suggest revision of the above assessment as Member of parliament said in 1971. During the six months of its consultative committee's (on West Bengal Legislation) existence only two sitting were held and that too for 6 or 7 hours. Important issue could not be discussed.

Some problems were placed before the consultative committee and they were got through in an hour. So, the definite demand is that the consultative committee should regularly meet and discuss the issue that are there and the important issue that come up daily. Similarly, more through should be given on the composition of this body. It may perhaps be so constituted that it reflects the strength of the political parties in the state Legislative concerned thereby making all spiritually closer to the state under Article 356. This does not necessarily mean gross irresponsibility on the part of the state public administration. President's rule provides for a new set of persons such as the Governor and his advisers to show continues regard for public interest and to exercise control state Government functionaries. As a result, the hierarchical accountability becomes more fully activated. As the governor emerges as the kingpin of state administration, he, more than any one else, may contributes most significantly towards making it efficient both in the technical and the social sense to ensure this he undertakes regular tours in the states and gingers up the public administration. He makes himself more accessible to more people and on occasions even gives summery decision in many matters. The advisers also tour the state and expedite decision making. Laudable as these efforts undoubtedly are, they are hardly a substitute for what has been constitutionally taken away from the people their popular Government. President's rule is at best a necessary evil the shorter its duration, the better it is.[19]

The supremacy of the Union Government over the state administration is a proven fact. However, states demand more autonomy on the rightful basis of federal provision within the framework of Indian constitution. The word federalism itself implies that, the share for state power should be conferred by the central government otherwise prolong controversy shall have to arise in between the centre and state struggling for power. Every centre-state relation studies starts from federal characters of constitution of India. Therefore, every scholars and writers have pointed their expression regarding the micro studies on federalism.

India is today a Union of 28 states 7 union territories. But the geography of the Indian federal system has been the product of a long period of development and even after it came in to existence, it has continuously changing, nor can one say with any degree of certainty that the boundaries have at least been drawn with finality. In historical perspective this was also true of the United States but contrast in the origins of the two systems in unmistakable.

In North America, the clones came together to establish a common Government for common purposes, reserving to themselves all those governmental functions not specifically allotted to the Federal Government and they held to themselves the residuary powers.

In contrast to this, the Indian federation has been the ultimate result of two separate forces at work for a century before the country became independent. One of these was the process of administrative decentralization and the gradual extension of the powers of the councils which gave shape to the provinces of British India. But this was only one part of the political geography of India, for at the time the country attained independence there was still in existence that colorful patchwork of princely India, large and small native states with different levels of administrative competence. The transfer of power from British to Indian hands left the native states in a precarious situation, willingly or under compulsion, they had to surrender their sovereignty.

The effect of these changes was to be seen in the constitution as it existed at the time of its inauguration on 26 January 1950. The constituent Assembly classified the states into definite categories, Part A States consisted of the autonomous provinces of British India with complete power over the items allotted to them under the division of powers. The native states of Hyderabad, Mysore and Jammu and Kashmir with five other Unions of princely states constituted Part B States with a position similar to those in the first category but the union Government had certain powers to regulate and direct their administrative and political institutions. There was another category of native states which were placed directly under the control of the union Government. A part from these categories, there were the union Territories directly administered by the central Government.

Since the enforcement of Indian constitution there has been several episodes and crisis in between centre and state, regarding the various issues and problems, which are remain unsolved till today. This is because of Indias doubtful characteristics of federalism nature towards the states. Central Government has never treated equally the states of India. As a result of which, constant problem for demanding the more autonomous, which is endowed by the federal principle. So centre state Relationship has been a burning topic and has been discussed and debated on various plate forms. The developments of widespread dissatisfaction with the existing state of centre-state relations. On the other hand, demand for autonomy at its core and criticism of centre's interference in the affairs of the states by some political and regional parties are the clear result of the profound indignation over the working of the constitutional provision in regard to centre state Relation.[20]

Though the problem of centre state Relation is not a new problem, the constitutional provisions in regard to centre state Relations worked comparatively smooth till 1967 due to the reason of same political party namely the Congress remaining in power both at the centre and the states which was an advantage to solve any differences among themselves at their party level. But in 1967, some of the state had either coalitions or non congress Governments in power and that has sparked off the differences between the centre and state. Though the constitutional provisions have not contributed so much to such disparity, the manner and method of working between the congress dominated centre and the non congress governments in some states is such that the relation began to deteriorate and as a result of such deterioration and in order to weed out the further dissatisfaction among the non-Congress(I) dominated states the Sarkaria Commission has been appointed by the central Government. But, as we all know, it will take a long time to have an exhaustive report of the Sarkaria Commission.

The main grievance against the centre's interference in the affairs of the states has been in regard to the office of Governor and his power. Instance of dismissal of Governor's by the centre has caused great dissatisfaction and apprehension among the states, having the non congress Government in power. Centre Government act as dictatorial behaviour in various ways, like in the recent trend is that 'the yes man' shall be appointed as Governor by the centre to act only as an agent ignoring the very principle that for a smooth working of federal structure it is necessary that the person to be appointed as the Governor should be such as to inspire confidence from both the centre and the state concerned and be independent of party affiliations. It is seen that in a situation where there arises a conflict between the Governor's role as the representative of the centre and that as the constitutional head in the state, then undoubtedly, the former obligation is taking president over the latter. The Governor is bound to submit to the dictates of centre and the same is highly objectionable, the practice being contrary to the philosophy of administrative autonomy to the states.[21]

Being a centre's representatives the Governor of a state in discharging his duties shall have to see as to whether the state is functioning according to the provisions of the constitution. If not, he shall inform such non-compliance to the centre and the President shall attract immediately Article 356 for its remedy. It needs no elaboration as to how many times President's rule has been imposed on this plea from the commencement of the constitution.

On the other hand, Article 356 is giving a clear way for imposition of President's rule in states for simple and tariffing reasons. Article 356 provide that where a state has failed to comply with or to give effect to any direction of the union under any of the provisions of the constitution, it shall be lawful for the President to hold that a situation has arisen in which the state Government could not be carried on. Such a finding on the part of the President could provide for a take over of administration of the state on any pretext which takes away the federal character of the constitution forcing it to work in a unitary system.

The present crisis of the centre-state relation has arisen mainly from failure of proper distribution of powers being the main characteristics of a federal polity. Subject from the state list, which is the domain of the state, have been transferred to the concurrent list delegating to centre more power depriving the state of their legitimate power. This centralization of power has put the states in confusion while exercising. Autonomy on administrative and political field. To deal with such problems Article 263 provides for establishment on an Inter State council, but for reasons best known to the centre, the same has not been honored. Perhaps centre may feel that such council would result in truncating the centres powers.

Undoubtedly to face emergency of any kind whether internal or external, or any eventuality, a strong centre is very much in need. But one cannot have a strong centre if it is a union of weak states. Autonomy in self government in the state might help to have a strong Government in the centre. The autonomy must operate at the grass-root level. A change in the system of administration is to be considered so that the people will really have a feeling of self-governance though the panchayati raj system was introduced to decentralise power, there was a feeling that decentralization was not effected in the right spirit and vigor.

Time has come to take a fresh look at the existing centre-state relations. The high handedness attitude of the centre might result in the growth of dangerous forces of regionalism threatening the national integrity and people's interest in general. It is submitted that the decentralization of power is essential to ensure harmonious functioning between the centre and state.

Most powers and responsibilities to the states would promote and strengthen the force of national integrity rather than encouraging divisive or centrifugal forces. It may be submitted that Governor's office whose integrity and independence in a federal set up are of vital importance, should be free from influence and dictation of the centre. His tenure shall be fixed and he shall hold the office without the pleasure of the President. Secondly, the invocation of Article 356 and 356 must be restricted and prevented and further governor's and president's powers to interfered in the administration of states under those Article ought to be taken away wherever necessary, amendment of the constitution is suggested. Thirdly, in the public interest the Inter state council should be established as provided by Article 263.

For promoting better cooperation and harmony among the states as well as centre, more administrative and political power to the states is suggested. Decentralization would only reduce tension and irritants that had surfaced in centre-state Relations as a result of arbitrary, discretionary and centralised control by the centre.[22]

India has many predominant unitary features such as common nationality, single judiciary with the supreme court as the highest constitutional as well as appellate court all India services etc, despite the federalism in characters in India.

The Centre-State Relations are, therefore, subject to inter-party conflicts. As a single party was in power at both the levels i.e. the centre and the states, for a long time since the coming in to force of the constitution, the centre state Relations were treated as an intra-party affairs. This prevented the growth of healthy conventions.

In the ruling Congress Party, the power has concentrated in the hands of the national leadership known as the High command. As a result of this, the state leadership has become more and more dependent upon the central leadership. The group rivalries and schisms for power in the states destablise the state Government, often we find a state leadership being protected or dismissed by the central leadership the infrastructure for federal government is therefore in crisis. A federal government is not necessarily a government in confrontational posture. But due to one party domination and the continued rule of such a party at the centre, the centre-state Relation are often projected in confrontational prospective. A federal or quasi-federal structure of Government means the distribution of powers between the national Government and the Government of the states which are supposed to be self-governing units.[23]

In India we have three lists of powers distributed between the centre and the constituent units of the federation. The central list contains ninety seven heads of subjects and the state list comprises of sixty six heads while in the concurrent list there are forty seven heads. Besides all unenumerated heads of powers come under the ambit of the National Government.

REFERENCES

1. A.C. Kapur, *Discretionary Powers of State Governors in India* (July-December 1973) 193-208, p. 169.
2. *President's Rule in the States and Union Territories,* Lok Sabha Secretariat New Delhi, 1989.
3. *Ibid.*
4. A.C., Kapur, *op,cit.* p. 220.
5. *Ibid.*, pp. 223-24.
6. *Parliamentary Debates, House of the People,* Part II, Vol. XIV, No. 10, 17 August, 1951, col. 783-84.

7. *Annual Report of the Ministry of Home Affairs for* 1968-69, p. 3.
8. *Ibid.*
9. *Parliamentary Debates, pt.* II, Vol. XIV, No 7. 13 August, 1951 col. 590.
10. *Lok Sabha Debates,* Pt. II, Vol. X, No 27,19 December, 1956, col. 3546.
11. *Lok Sabha Debates, Second Series,* Vol. LV, No 53, 25th April, 1961, col. 13613.
12. *Ibid.*
13. *Constituent Assembly debates,* Vol. IX, p. 177.
14. *Ibid.*, p. 178.
15. C.P. Bhambhri, *Political Parties and Centre-State Relations in India.* The Institution of constitutional and Parliamentary Studies, pp. 44-54.
16. *Ibid.*, p. 55.
17. *Ibid.*, p. 56.
18. *Lok Sabha Debates,* Fifth series, Vol. IV, No. 21, 21 June, 1971, col. 159.
19. S.R. Maheshwari, *President's Rule in India,* p. 151.
20. K. Santhanam, *Union-State Relations in India,* p. 7.
21. Sanajaoba Naorem, *Basic Issue on Centre-State Relations,* p. 112.
22. *Ibid.*, p. 113.
23. Durga Das Basu, *The Shorter Constitution of India,* Vol. I, p. 124.

5

President's Rule: Feedback and Reality

No one generally favours the idea of imposing the President's rule in the state as it affects the federal character of Indian constitution. It causes a stringed relationship between centre and state. Some times, the imposition of President's rule in the states curtails the fundamental rights of the citizens. And the Central Government exercises an extensive power over the state. However, there are certain advantages and disadvantages of the President's rule in the state. President's rule is invoked only when no political party is in a position to form the Government. Law and order is maintained firmly under President's rule. The functioning of the state, government becomes more efficient under President's rule than under popular rule. Political interference in the functioning of the administration is reduced under President's rule. Corruption in public administration disappears under President's rule. Developmental programs come to receive high priority under President's rule. The central Government's bounties to the state increase significantly under President's rule. Therefore, some times the people prefer President's rule to a popular regime.

Here we would like to analyse the situation which warrant the imposition of President's rule in the state. President's rule is invoked only when no political party is in a position to form the Government. Article 356 is invoked when the President is satisfied that a situation has arisen in which the Government of the state cannot be carried on in accordance with provisions of the Constitution. But a detailed analysis of the thirty-six occasions of President's rule in India focuses on the following situations leading to the suspension of popular rule in the states.

A Ministry was voted out of power, and no other party or coalition of parties was able or willing to form another Ministry consequent to the voting out of a Ministry the Governor recommended President's rule, altogether ignoring the plea of the second largest party in the Assembly for invitation to form an alternative Ministry. The Governor refused to call the largest alliance in the Assembly to form the Ministry. As this alliance alone was capably of forming the Government, the Governor recommended President's rule. The Ministry met with an adverse vote in the Assembly as a result of floor crossing by the legislators and tendered its resignation. The Governor regards the resultant situation as politically confusing and opts for President's rule through political parties make claims to form the Ministry. No single party won a majority in the legislature after election and the Governor straightway recommended President's rule without exploring the political processes to find out if a Ministry could be formed by a party processes to find out if a Ministry could be formed by a party with support from others or a coalition of parties. The state Assembly was not able to meet as a result of the speaker's action.

The most powerful and formidable party of the land, the congress, was smitten by internal factions and steeped out of office without any adverse vote in the legislature. On quite a few occasions President's rule was really not necessary in each such instance the ruling congress party, which alone was capable of forming the Ministry resigned, thereby forcing the Governor to claim Article 356 on the state. In such cases the Assembly was not generally dissolved. Punjab (1951) being an exception and the same party come forward to form the Government after a spell of President's rule. The Ministry was dismissed on the ground of mass upsurge against it in the state although it was enjoying majority in the Assembly. The ministry did not lose majority in the legislature but the Governor recommended dismissal on the ground that the ruling party was keeping itself in power by offering inducements to legislators to maintain its majority. The Ministry was discharged on charges of corruption though it commanded a majority in the legislature.[1]

Article 356 has thus subserved a wide variety of purposes. Some of these are not easily testable thus leaving an impression of being political in intent. At any rate, the uses to which it has been put and the frequency of its employment have virtually made the amplitude of this Article infinite, a situation never contemplated by the framers of the constitution on the contrary, the constituent Assembly had conjured up a state of rusty idleness for Article 356. Participating in the debate on this provision BR. Ambedkar chairman of the Drafting Committee, told that body. In regard to the general debate which has taken place in which it has been suggested that these articles are liable to be abused, I may say that I do not altogether deny that there is a possibility of these Article being abuse or employed for political purposes. But that objection applies to every part of the constitution which gives power to the centre to override the states and union territories.

That the application of Article 356 has not always conformed to the intentions of the framers of the constitutions is obvious. Even the acme of legal perfectionism, which a constitution is cannot escape being interpreted and operationalised in terms of the value from of its operators.

The two levels of Government, each separate and autonomous are apt to generate occasional functions in their mutual dealings, especially when different political parties are in powers at the two levels. In this contest, the very constitutional provision for the central take over of state administration deepens a propensity towards its use thereby weakening the latter position in the federal system.[2]

Law and order is maintained firmly under President's rule. Perhaps the greatest achievement of President's rule is discernible in the field of law and order shows an obvious improvement under President's rule for threat to peace like riots agitation anti social activities and the like get checked more successfully. This should not be surprising, for political leaders are in wilderness under President's rule and people with a grievance, genuine or fancied have no one to organise any agitation against the administration, President's rule is particularly welcome to the police which gets a freer hand in handling men and matters falling within its area.

As a result, it is not uncommon to come across instances of police zulum specially on the less organised less vocal section of the population. The over restive compasses remain quiet under the president's rule. Indeed, among those who have a sense of relief on the advent of Article 356 the harried Vice Chancellors of Universities figures very prominently. This happens not because the education budget get significantly stepped up, but those causing either directly or indirectly, discord and disturbance on the campuses find their teeth stripped, at any rate for the time being. The student leaders, who as a class are vocal, even aggressive during the popular regime sense the new environment and preferring low. In a sense, therefore, the President's rule may provide an ideal opportunity to the educational institutions to initiate important education reforms this however has not been the case.[3] In Manipur 10th President's rule in the state, the Governor Sri Ved Marwah and two other Advisor IAS retired K. Kipgen and IPS retired RE Rammohon and Chief Secretary Rakesh held many Governor's in-council and passed several pending resolution for state welfare. During the President's rule in Manipur two years long problems of Manipur public service commission Recommended Government college Lectures and Junior Medical officers have been solved and appointed. Surplus employees who are not regularised and appointed on contract basis, adhoc and several other master role work men were turn out in order to economic measure for the state. Unqualified part-time Lectures who were appointed in the different colleges in Manipur during the popular Ministry period have also been step down from the service. No appointment ban has been left during the President's rule in Manipur.[4]

All these, of course, does not imply that there is inevitably a deterioration of law and order under popular Government. Elected governments in the states are known to have maintained law and order reasonably well. It however, appears that law and order situation worsens considerably a leftist Government. This was the ease in Kerala (1959) and in West Bengal (1967-68) and (1969-70). The communist project their ideology on the functions and role of the police. The police under the communist Government is not expected to interfere in favour of the exploiting bourgeoisie classes in labour strikes agrarian disputes and other popular movements the communal philosophy on law and order was best expanded by S.A. Dange soon after the dismissal in 1959 of the Namboodripad Ministry in Kerala. He solemnly told the parliament. The sense of state power is the police. It enforce the class relation that exists. The laws are enacted they are outwardly impartial. But in effect they work against the worker peasant and middle class people and work in favour of the exploiting classes. In this the police is a vital element. The police is on in side of the rich, moneyed elements. Therefore, the first step taken by the Kerala Ministry was to make a police statement. We defend that statement and we shall make it again that the police shall not interfere in strikes in favour of the employers that the police shall not interfere in present disputes in favour of the landlords and the police shall observe the law in such a way that it is not a party against the worker and the toiling masses and in favour of the exploiting class.[5]

No wonder the President's rule in state after a communist Ministry accords top priority to law and order and scores a conspicuous success in maintaining it. The achievement is striking in the success in maintaining it. The achievement is striking in the back ground of inattention even though selective, to this as put under the earlier communist regime.

The functioning of the state Government becomes more efficient under President's rule than under popular rule.

That the President's rule has on occasions come in the wake of perceptible inefficiency in the public administration of the state and that it is characterised by a reduction in the levels of consultation and consideration may account for the prevalence of the above view. As one of the foremost declared objectives of President's rule is to ensure clean and efficient administration in the state, greatest attention is naturally given towards toning up of the machinery of the government at all levels. Indeed, within the first few hours of the introduction of President's rule, detailed instructions are normally sent to public servants all over the state asking them to discharge their duties in a fair and efficient way. Such a circular has always followed closely on the heels of every President's rule. When, for instance Article 356 was first introduced in the Punjab, the Governor issued a ten point letter of instructions to heads of department;, divisional commissioners, deputy commissioners, district and session Judges and other civil servants in the state. The civil servants were instructed not to accept recommendations, and not to tolerate communalism in any shape or form. The business of Government was to be conducted on the sole considerable of merit, Justice and fair play. The officers were told to speedily and effectively deal with corruption and arrange for summery punishment of corrupt officials.

The civil servants were further called upon to deal with all complaints promptly and to listen to all visitors and complaints with patience and courtesy. Stressing the need for economy, and avoidance of wasteful expenditure, the circular wanted the public personals to subordinate their convenience to the interests of the people and the state.

There is a measure of expenditure in decision making in the state administration but this is generally true in the case of implementation of policies and programs. In other words, the peace of execution of what had already been decided and initiated by the popular Government gets quickened under President's rule. But major level policy making gets generally postponed until the return of the popular Government. This comes about for two reasons. The Ministries of central Government which get directly involved in matters of major policy making do not have the time or interest or even knowledge of local problems to be able to initiate major moves in the field of state administration. More importantly there is a widely share view that the President's rule is more in the nature of a care taker Government and major policy decisions requiring political decisions or having political implications ought to be taken by the popular Government alone. For instance, the West Bengal Governor S.S. Dhavan, emphasised in his first radio broadcast after the imposition of President's rule in 1970 that he would regard himself as a caretaker. Similarly, the Chief Secretary of Uttar Pradesh, BB Lal, observed in 1968 that the state, under President's rule, would not adopt new policies but carry out the policies already laid down by the popular Government.[7]

In the 1994 President's rule in Manipur had done most valuable work for the state, like the destruction of encroacher of land and along the two sides of main road. It made cleared a new road from Keisampat Junction to Khoyathong main crossing, which has been occupied by intruders and encroachers. Several paca building has been cutoff by using heavy machine and excavator. This road has been planed for foot path in order to lessen the crowed in the city area. The road is constructed eastern bank of Nambul river it through fare the Kakhulong west, Usha Cinema hall west. Besides this various other and uncountable works has keen done sincerely. During these specific period, Imphal city beautification plan was established and had successfully completed. The than Governor. Retired, Army officer VK Nayar had planed the construction of paca wall both sides of Thanga pat, it is at the heart of city in front of the Raj Bhavan Imphal. No corruption was there in that stipulated period employees were in active and efficiency on them respective duties no question arises about financial crisis, over draft etc.

In the year 1992 The President's rule was imposed RK Ranbir was Chief Minister at that time and Chintamani Panigrahi was the Governor due to crossing in the floor R.K. Ranbir was minority in the confidence vote. Therefore, assembly as suspended on 7/192 and President's rule was imposed in the state. During the proclamation of President's rule in Manipur. Elected Legislative Members were very must repented with then misdeeds, and people were also remark to revenge to them in the next election, because, the elected members were so opportunist and highly corrupted, nepotism and favoritism. As a result of it, there were groupism and disunity among society in Manipur, Whereas, governor, Chentamani Panigrahi had constructed the Khwairamband Bazar (Nupi Keithel) up to standard level of foundation and good roofing, scientific method of electrification and certain other modification. The market has possess an year long crisis between (Pot Yonbi Ima) Trader women and popular government of Manipur regarding the storey building. The Women folk refused to construct the double storey building in place of old construction. The women traders were believed that the structure of this place should be preserved and should be protected as in the historical monument.

Because this place is the only market in the world. The Governor of Manipur could pleased the wishes and desire of women traders by constructing and preserving its former position. Thus President's rule in the state kept an apostle with year mark achievement in the state. On the other side, distribution of civil supply, such as rice, sugar, kerosine oil some other essential commodities were also regularised and cheeked.

Construction and repairing of roads were timely completed. The responsible officers of the Government were so effective and progress in the official work without delay. Drinking water, health and medicine, flood control and various other were maintain in well discipline during the President's rule. Where as -, the popular Minister have manipulated those all things. They never consider for whole out look of the state but only for his benefit of his/her constituency. They expend a lot of money and extravagant by to and for journey to his own affairs or purpose. Corruptions are rampant in the time of popular Ministers, all the secretaries in the office are waiting the such signal from the concerned Ministers. Therefore, no file is more smoothly.

Thousands of Government employees are escape from the duty and never attend the office in time during the popular Ministry period. Whereas, during the President's rule in the state, the employees are under the strict control and regular in their respective duties. Employees are afraid of President's rule period for suspension and other punishable. But which are not consider in the popular Ministry period. Short to say, in democratic country people who are not specially interested in politics have not faith and desire of popular Ministry in the state. Inspite of that President's rule is rather better for the future destiny of people in the state. Nor must one forget that the spurt in efficiency of state public administration does not remain perpetuated under President's rule for before long the state of affairs begins descending to the earlier, more familiar levels of operation. This aspects is discussed in detail under other subheads in this chapter.

Reduction of Political Interference in the Functioning of State Administration Under President's Rule

Political interference in public administration is a fact of life in the country. President's rule is characterised by a reduction in the number and intensity of political interference and also change in its style, especially in the beginning. This is particularly so when the legislature is dissolved, for the assertiveness of the politicians does not get completely extinguished in the case of the Legislatures kept under animated suspension, Also, there is a district sheft in the level from which interferences.

Begin to be faced by public administration. Under President's rule, The members of parliament assume state legislator's role too, and start meeting officials including the advisers as well as the governor more often generally to plead individual cases. The state level politicians, now in wilderness, exert pressures on the senior administrators through the central government leaders,

Even otherwise, the central ministers hailing from the state under Article 356 begin evincing active interest in the details of administration. Thus political interference appears to shift from the state capital to the centre.

But to say that political interferences come to a complete stop appears to be too idealistic a supposition in the single party dominance system of India. Knowing that the same political party and most probably the same persons would return to power once President's rule is lifted a number of civil servants do appear to be demonstrably receptive to the demands of the leaders of the ruling party. In this context one must point out that the personality of the Governor is the single most decisive factor determining whether public administration resist such advances made by politicians or succumbs to them. There have even been occasions when the President's rule attracted a measure of criticism on the score of being formally pro congress. Many of actions of the central Ministers for West Bengal Affairs (1971) were widely viewed as being political in design. Similar was the case of Uttar Pradesh in 1973. The out going Chief Minister, was permitted to continue as chairman and the former planing Minister in the out going ministry was appointed as adviser to the food department while the Minister for Hill Development Board. Besides certain action of the Governor, which were certainly avoidable were partisan look. In his presence a conference of officials held in Meerut in July 1973 was presided over by the President of the Uttar Pradesh Congress Committee. In another city, the Governor was present at a conference of congress city, the Governor was present at a conference of congress workers. It is but a truism that one should not only be fair but also appear to be so.[8]

Nor does President's rule seem to make any dent on the hidden like between the politician and the administrator. There are two long, too pervasive and much more local and the balance contrived between the politician and the administrator is too mutually beneficial to be disrupted by President's rule, clean and efficient administration under President's rule is not substantiable, at least in its entirely soon after the exist of his Ministry in Punjab (1951), Gopi Chand Bhargava reacted to the charge of corruption in public administration under popular regime by asserting. The general belief is that it will go on Ministry or no Ministry, its causes lying in the economic controls prescribed by the central Government. It can be safely observed that political corruption disappears, such of administrative corruption as is directly encouraged and patronised by the politicians abates substantially but individual corruption remain largely undiminished. A most distinguishing feature of President's rule is that public administration is in a firm position to cheek corruption and does in fact act swiftly and decisively against those with questionable integrity.

A fear of getting caught lurks in the minds of evil minded civil servants. Also, more civil servants get punished on charges of corruption under President's rule than under popular regime. What is more while there is a definite initial decline in corruption, it begins reemerging in its old vigour after a while. But the bulk of honest Government servants flourish under this regime. However, corruption is a much more inclusive phenomenon having sociological, economic and political ramifications and to regard President's rule as its cure is to exhibit, ignorance about its true native.[9]

Administrative Development Comes to Receive High Priority Under President's Rule

A verdict on the above question is not easy or unanimous. As the President's rule has been introduced in many cases on the break down of law and order in the state it has understandably remained preoccupied with the problems of general administration. Moreover, President's rule has unfailing seceded in maintaining peace and order,, and its achievement in the field of general administration has become so conspicuous that in popular minds it is indelibly associated with law and order administration. While the truth of this aspect cannot be denied the fact appears to be that President's rule acquires the colour chosen by New

Delhi its inputs are determined not locally but centrally. If, for instance, the President's rule has come after the ousting of an opposition party and is followed by a general election the central Government is seen to step up developmental activities, or at any rate concentrate on completing the socioeconomic programmes whose progress earlier was rather tardy. This is not unusually a politically calculated move of the ruling party at the centre to win the election. Again, if the application of Article 356 has followed widespread economic grievances on the part of the people in a state, development may come to receive a high priority. As the regional imbalance was the root of the popular agitation in Andhra Pradesh (1973) the President's rule was utilised by the centre to initiate and complete a large numbers of programmes of economic development. The central funds began flowing in massive doses.

Generally speaking, President's rule is characterised by a definite speeding up in the implementation of plans and programmes which had already been decided upon by the popular government, what remains held up on account of inter party disputes also gets resolved more easily. However, decisions on new major policies are normally allowed to wait until the return of the democratic Government in the state. Also, in certain states the in place of rural development became rather slow under President's rule and so was the case with the development of backward regions. This happens, for there is under President's rule an absence of watchful eyes to speak for them, take up their cause and insist upon implementation of suitable program. Generally speaking^ developmental administration does receive a set back under. This happens, for there is under President's rule an absence of watchful eyes to speak for them, take up their cause and insist upon implementation of suitable programmes, Generally speaking, developmental administration does receive a set back under President's rule more so when it is of a shorter spell.[10]

The Central Government's Bounties to the State Increase Significantly Under President's Rule

The central bounties do generally but not invariably increase under President's rule, there being apparently three principal reasons to account for this, under President's rule the centre comes in direct contact with the state concerned and in the process acquires a more intimate and detailed knowledge of the state's problems. The resultant awareness normally leads to action. Secondly, as grave deficiencies of the popular regime have generally led to its down fall and to the imposition of Article 356 the centre naturally anxious to make good at least the more glaring shortcomings of the previous regime. Thirdly, New Delhi is understandably more generous in allocation of grants to the state where the Chief Minister supplanted by President's rule was a persona nongrata with the central political leadership. In a calculated bid to brighten the image of President's rule New Delhi makes a conscious effort to give more funds to the state. Central funds flow more easily to a state which was ruled by an opposition party and where a general election is round the corner. Even when new grants are not made the legitimate schemes from the state which earlier could not be cleared by the centre for a variety of reasons get sanctioned quickly and also the funds already sanctioned but not hitherto released begin to flow easily. Of course, the exact magnetite of central grants depends upon the interest personality and assertiveness of the Governor and advisers and their equation with the central leaders.

Apart from this, there appears to be a better utilization of central funds or for that reason of the states own resources under President's rule than under popular regime. Two droughts of more or less equal gravity visited West Bengal recently, one when the state was President's rule under Dharam Vira and another when a popular Ministry was in office. The first one was managed with lesser resources.[11] This is a tricky question which can be answered only in the light of how much genuinely popular has been the preceding Ministry. Many a popular

Government remained engrossed in party wrangles, indulged in political horse trading, consciously encouraged political interferences in public administration, mismanaged the affairs of the state, and understandably, people at large breathed a sight of relief when the popular Ministry was jettisoned and President's rule was proclaimed. On the other hand, the President's rule was also viewed as a result of the political manoeuvreing on the part of the central government. The reaction to it has been one of resentment and anger, contributing even to a measure of alienation from the political system. Under the President's rule the state Government functionaries, especially the Governor and his advisers, undertakes extensive tours of the state and seek to meet people and redress their grievances. But the greatest weakness of this rule is the absence of an institutional avenue to assess popular will. Despite all its weakness, the constitutional machinery consisting of a popular Ministry and legislature is the single, most legitimate forum for articulation of people's problems and mobilizing popular opinion on them President's rule becomes for all practical purposes the rule of bureaucrats and with the best will in the world bureaucracy cannot but remain too tightly bound by rules and precedents to be able to see the human side of the problems under consideration. As a result, public administration becomes less open, less communicative and more secretive under President's rule. By and large the civil servants, especially those at middle and lower levels of administration, have no fear except the hierarchical one, and are seen by citizens to be rigid and even imperious in their demeanours. The bureau, even the noblest of it, is notoriously attuned to Justice than to mercy, and in this persecutive, the politician who has a human angle of viewing of affairs of the government has a complementary role to perform in the ordering of affairs of the Government. At any rate the novelty of President's rule is short lived and before long people do begin to years for the return of the popular regime.

That section of the society which has consistently remained for a variety of reasons, outside the active ambit of public administration all these long years and have neither dipped into the benefits made available by it under the various welfare programmes nor tasted its cussedness beyond a level to which they have by and large become accustomed, remain generally unconcerned about who rules them. But those who habitually come into contacts with administration directly rule. Though the restiveness is fairly widespread, it becomes manifest much earlier in urban areas. In this context, it is interesting to note that the State of Kerala which has listed President's rule much longer than any other state appears to have the political part of evolving the mechanism of coalition Government to ensure political stability in the state, the popular Ministry which came in to power since the election of 1971 is still continuing, valiantly avoiding the other alternative of succumbing to the President's rule.[12]

Even the elected representative have expressed the preference of President's rule in the state rather than the popular regime, to quoted his words from local daily news paper. The *Sangai Express* on 23-12-1999 Tuesday. That, Mr O. Joy the President of Manipur People's Party met the Governor and pressed to recommend for President's rule in Manipur because the present popular Ministry has unsatisfied and responsible for all aspects. The President have also expressed his views that, only the President's rule could magnified the state's affairs and could maintain the developmental plans for the state. Therefore article 356 is the opposite factors as in the federal characters in India even though, if the President's rule is more preferred to popular regime the people will surely devote for the imposition of Article 356 in very states of India.

Due to unlimited expenditure by the council of Ministers in the states the financial system has undoubtedly fallen down. Out of 60 MLAs some 34 or more MLAs are Ministers or equivalent rank of cabinet Ministers. This is because of fearing the brokening the Government so each and every ruling members are appointed any either cabinet or equivalent rank so all Ministers are expensed a lot of money by touring their respective constituencies and allotting security, equators, vehicles and daily expenditure. Moreover, ministers are trying fetch a lots of money by appointment whether it is legally or illegally. It is despite of union government instruction. Therefore the appointment band has been imposed in the state, however the state government of Manipur appointment many unqualified persons in different department. So due to wrong utilization of money central government has not further sanctioned the money even for the salary of March to May in 2000. It has been never happen in the history of politics in India.

In such situation has arisen the centre should be better to interfere of impose the financial emergency in Manipur. Each and every council of Ministers are highly corrupted and not for common welfare, but personal or individual happiness and nepotism for next election. All Ministers are holding the property for facing the next general election for win or success. Therefore in every section of people in Manipur have expressed the imposition of President's rule will be the only ways and means to settle and resolve the financial crisis and to prevent the corruption and cheek such malpractices in the state.[13]

Impartiality of President's Rule and One Party Dominance System

President's rule faces a dilemma not quite easy to resolve. This rule is expected to be completely impartial. In official circular and notifications issued on the introduction of President's rule the civil servants are specially asked to be absolutely objective in their dealings with members of the public as well as of the political parties. This, however, appears to be easier said than done. As the same political party, namely the congress, is most likely to return to office in the single party dominance system of the country and moreover, as virtually the same faces are likely to occupy ministerial positions many civil servants have learn to accommodate to varying degrees, the demands and encroachments of these erstwhile masters. Also the political colour of the center is of late increasingly projecting itself in its response to the state under article 356 and viewed in this context. President's rule runs the risk of opining up get another but most powerful channel for New Delhi's influence of course, the Governor may not as a buffer between the bureaucracy and these outside forces. Indeed, the stuff the Governor is made of is the most critical single factors determining the effectiveness and objectivity of President's rule. Whether persons having the necessary independence and personality would be preferred for the gubernatorial office, however, is a moot point while discussing this aspect one is irristably remained of a central innovation made in 1971 of appointing a ministers in-charge of the state under President's rule. This device is briefly discussed here.

Role of Central Minister in the State Under Article 356

Central Minister has however played dictatorial power with the imposition of President's rule in the state. It is on the contrary wishes of India constitution and violation of federal structure within itself. Here I would like to put an example of dictatorial behaviour of central Minister to interfere in the state during the imposition of President's rule. Simultaneously with the imposition of President's rule in the West Bengal on 29 June 1971. The central Government announced the appointment of Siddharth Shankar Ray, the Education Minister, as the Minister without portfolio in-charge of West Bengal Affairs. Announcing this appointment in the Lok Sabha, Prime Minister Indira Gandhi said, The central Government are anxious that all problems relating to West Bengal which are within their competence should be dealt with expeditiously very serious problems and an abnormal situation have been created in West Bengal and some other states by the massive influx of refugees in so short a period. These matters need to be given special attention and tackled urgently. It has therefore been decided to appoint a Minister of cabinet rank as minister without portfolio with immediate effect.[14]

The appointment of a central Minister to deal with the affairs of a state under Article 356 was first of its kind in the history of President's rule in India. The appointment of a Minister in-charge of West Bengal came in for sever criticism both in parliament and outside. This was viewed as undermining the status and standing of the governor as President's delegates under President's rule. Its constitutionality therefore, was subject to serious questioning. Nor was the soundness of this practice very apparent. By interposing functionary between the President and the governor it contained wether itself seeds of dyarchy and discord. What is more, President's rule should remain avoid of Political colours as far as possible, but the appointment of a Minister in-charge of West Bengal Affairs raised double over the political neutrality of such an administration. Hiren Mukherjee considered this appointment as constitutionally not above board. As West Bengal's super Chief Minister under President's rule, Mr Sidhartha Shanker Ray can scarcely add to the credibility of the President's non partisan role, what West Bengal needs and has indeed needed for a long time a new Governor and not a central Ministers to take over the governor's function.[15]

Although the Governor SS. Dhavan, was soon replaced by A.S. Dias who was a professional administrators himself, Sidhartha Sanker Ray continued as the Minister for West Bengal Affairs and even had an office in Calcutta to look after his work in the state. President's rule may not be a mere care taker Government but it is most certainly not on all fours with a popular Government. A popularly elected regime has to necessarily invoke the political and legislative processes while making policies and when assured of this support it is both politically and morally upright for it to decide on major policies and take up their execution.

No so anointed is the President's rule which is characterised, more than anything else, by a deliberate suspension of democratic processes in the state. This argument that parliament steps in the moment the legislature is snuffed out of existence is not convincing because the former is no substitute for the normal state level political institutions and processes. But at the same time, the other extreme of administrative immobilism and letting grass grow under the feet till the return of democracy is also to be avoided. The President's rule a balance between issue of long term nature and matters requiring short rang decisions and executive the latter. Equally pressing is the need for identification of problem entailing political implications and keeping away from them. By the same token, it kmust not ordinarily attempt to undo the policies and programmes set in motion by the previous popular Government President's rule must not be viewed as a corrective mechanism. Otherwise, democracy will have no inducement to evolue and apply self discipline.

Allied to the fore going discussion is a proclivity to enjoy President's rule to resume the ruling political party which was unable or unwilling to make embrassing choices. This case of Punjab under the Chief Minister ship of Ram Kishan in 1966 is an apt one. Before its bifurcation into the two states of Punjab and Haryana, Punjab and had the congress Ministry under the Chief Minister ship of Ram Kishan. The state Government had at this moment of time to take decisions on many tricky matters such as division of asst's and liabilities between the two embracing states which the popular Ministry was loath to do. It therefore, resigned forcing President's rule on the state should a popular Government shy away from tasks of governance even if there are difficult or embarrassing in the their nature. In all fairness, President's rule should not be invoked to accomplish the dirty work of administration. The aspect of accountability of state Government under President's rule has already been discussed in a separate importance in a democratic system. Under President's rule the accountability becomes remote, feeble, uneven and blurred. The duration of President's rule should therefore, be kept as short as possible. Additionally, the consultative committee of MPs which begins to function as a mini Parliament needs to be restructured to make it a more active body. Not only should it include all the Members of parliament representing the state under Article 356 but proceedings should also be published and reported in the press to educate the public opinion.

President's rule should shun another danger to which it has of late been exposed almost as a deliberate part of public relations. As obsession with the ruling elite to build up a bright image of President's rule and, by contrast, to score points over the presiding popular rule has occasionally led it to play political and administrative stunts such as large scale administrative transfers, out of proportion punishment to a few etc, the effects of which may prove to be gravely harmful in the long run. Indeed, such actions have become so common of late that many civil servant really do not known at the time when President's rule is announced whether they are on their head or their heels such as administrative surgery breeds a tendency towards window dressing which has an effects on diverting the civil servants from going to the roots of the problems. Nor should highly coloured success stories of President's rule be encouraged or connived at, for all this is bound to have an insavoury backlash. President's rule in a democracy is a necessary evil and must continue to be viewed as such. If a state government is fallible so is the centre. The central Government is equally subject to political pulls and pressures. After all, recruitment to the political cadres of the central and state Government takes place from the same source and it would be manifestly incorrect and unfair to ascribe political foibles to the state levels only. Except for weakening the stature of state Governments in the country's constitutional system, President's rule can hardly claim any long range effects. This of course, is subject to one correction which is discussed below.[16]

Regarding the political stability luring the President's rule, however distasteful it may sound, the very political use of Article 356 contributed towards a sort of stability in the state. Legislative floor crossing gets encouraged when a party other than the party in power enjoys a fair prospect of forming the Government. As demonstrated with telling effect by the Orissa episodes of 1973. This is firmly discouraged with President's rule especially floor crossing from amongst the ranks of the ruling party Normally, legislators defeats only when the alternative is a new Government, Not President's rule.[17]

Causes of President's Rule

President's rule has been imposed not only to cope with situations of political instability in the states but also to subserve other ends and that too on a liberal scale. The following table describes the immediate causes of President's rule in the states up to 1976 since the commencement of Indian constitution according to data available.

The causes of President's rule are given below state-wise and year-wise:

State	*Causes*
1. Punjab (1951)	Assembly was suspended. Internal disputes developed in the Congress Party and Dr. Gopi Chand submitted resignation of the Ministry on 16-6-51.
2. Pepsu (1953)	Assembly was dissolved simultaneously. There was shifting allegiance of members of the Legislature and Election Tribunals had decided petition against four Ministers of the council of Ministers including the chief Minister. The Chief Minister tendered the resignation of himself and his colleges to the RajPramukh. An numerous cases of defection. Ministry was not voted out. RajPramukh introduced President's rule.
3. Andhra (1954)	Assembly was dissolved simulteneously. Following the passing of a motion of no-confidence against it by the state Legislative Assembly. The Ministry headed by Shri T. Prakasam tendered its resignation, which was accepted w.e.f. 15-11-1954. The defeat for the government of the ruling coalition parties. Voting with the opposition on the no confidence motion. And further defections of the political party by the MLAs Governor did not invite the second largest party to form the Government and recommended President's rule in the state.
4. Travancore Cohin (1956)	Defection's. No party able to form Ministry. Raj Pramukh recommended President's rule in the state.
5. Kerala (1959)	Assembly was dissolved simultaneously. In his report to the President, the Governor had listed various acts of administration against the state government, such as (a) large scale release of prisoness and undesirable elements (b) new police policy depriving of protection to employers etc. (c) mass upsurge and public agitations indicating a definite shift in the mind of the people against Government.
6. Orissa (1977)	Assembly was suspended but subsequently dissolved

	on 23-1-1971. consequent upon the withdrawal of support by the Jana Congress in Orissa, the coalition Ministry headed by Sri RN Singh Deo lost its majority in the state. Assembly. The Chief Minister submitted his resignation. The proclamation issued on 11-1-71 was revoked and fresh proclamation was issued on 23-1-71 dissolving the Legislative Assembly of the state. The proclamation dated 23-1-71 ceased to operate on 22-3-71. As single party emerged with an absolute majority in the general election held in the state on 5th March 1971 as fresh proclamation introducing President's rule but keeping in the new Assembly under suspension 23-3-71.
7. Kerala (1956)	Assembly was dissolved simultaneously. The congress Ministry resigned on 11-3-1956 consequent on the resignation of six members from the congress party as a result of which the congress was not able to command a majority in the legislature. As the Raj Pramukh did not find any other party which loved form a stable Ministry, he recommended President's rule in the state.
8. Rajasthan (1967)	Assembly was suspended. After the General Election 1967 no party got an absolute majority. The leader of the largest single party Shri Mohanlal Sukadia of Congress was invited by the Governor to form the new Ministry but he declined although he claimed the support of the majority in the new Legislative Assembly. However Governor's refusal to call the largest alliance in the Assembly, the united front to form the Government, despite he recommended for President's rule.
9. Haryana (1967)	Assembly was dissolved simultaneously. In Haryana defections had become endemic. These had made mockery of the constitution and had brought democracy to ridicule. Though not valid out of office the Governor recommended dismissal on the Ground that the Ministry was maintaining itself in power by encouraging defections.
10. West Bengal (1968)	Assembly was dissolved simulteneously, position in regard to the relative strengths of various parties was fluid. There were double about the majority enjoyed by the Ministry of Dr. P.C. Ghose. The speaker's ruling made the functioning of the Assembly impossible. Thus Assembly was not able to meet. As a result of which Governor dismissed the Ajoy Mukherji Ministry on the

	ground that it did not convene the Assembly meeting to prove its majority.
11. Uttar Pradesh (1968)	Assembly was suspended an subsequently dissolved on 15-4-1968. Shri Charan Singh tendered his resignation from the office of Chief Minister. Neither the S.V.D. nor congress party was in a position to form a stable Ministry in the state. Therefore Governor of the state had recommended the President's rule in the state.
12. Bihar (1968)	Assembly was dissolved simulteneously. The Ministry headed by Shri Bhola Paswan Shastri resigned on 25-6-1968. Repeated defections by many Members of the Legislative Assembly made it clear that no stable Government was likely to emerge from out of the their membership of the Bihar Legislative Assembly.
13. Gujarat (1971)	Assembly was dissolved simulteneously. Indiscriminate defections and redefection by MLAs led to uncertainty about formation of stable Government. The council of Ministries held an emergency meeting on May 11. 1971 and passed a resolution advising the Governor to dissolve the Legislative Assembly, so governor recommended the President's rule in the State.
14. Karnataka (1971)	Assembly was suspended subsequently dissolved. On March 18. 1971, the Chief Minister Shri Veerendra Patil tendered has resignation from his office to the Governor stating: In the wake of unexpected and sudden changes, apparent floor crossings and defections from the Ruling party to other side and shifting of loyalties by some Members, which is highly distressing. I think it is not advisable on my part to continue as chief Ministers. The Governor accepted the resignation and after exploring possibilities of forming on alternative Ministry reported that is was not in the interest of the state to continue the present uncertain state of affairs.
15. Manipur (1972)	Third imposition of President's rule since after the declaration of fullfledged statehood, by virtue of the provisions of the North Eastern Areas (Reorganisation) Act 1971. Till the election were held to the Legislative Assembly of this state and a papular government came into office, it was not possible to carry on the administration of the state in accordance with the provisions of the constitution. President's rule was therefore, introduced in the state on the very day it came into existence.

16. Nagaland (1972)	Assembly was suspended and subsequently dissolved on 20-5-75. Unprincipled defections induced by lure of office, led to instability in the Ministry. In one year along eight members had defected once, another 8 had defected twice and had defected three times. As a matter of fact no majority party could not in a position to form the Government in the state. So Governor of the state recommended the President's rule in the state which was the only alternative resort to calm down the political deterioration in the state.
17. Tripura (1972)	By virtue of the provisions of the North Eastern Area (Reorganisation) Act 1971 the new state of Tripura was formed on 21-1-72. Till the election were held to the Legislative Assembly of this new state and a popular Government came in to office, it was not possible to carry on the administration of the state in accordance with *the provisions of the constitution. The* President's rule was therefore introduced in this state.[18]

REFERENCES

1. Durga Das Basu, *The Shorter Constitution of India,* Vol. 1, p. 224.
2. Druga Das Basu, *op. cit.,* p. 26.
3. KS Singh, *Indian Political System,* p. 126.
4. *Ibid.,* p. 127.
5. *Lok Sabha Debates,* Second Series Vol. XXXIII, No. 11, 17 August, 1959, col. 2867.
6. *The Statesman,* 27 June, 1976.
7. *The National Herald,* 29 February, 1968.
8. *The Times of India,* 16 November, 1976.
9. *The Statesman,* 27 June, 1951.
10. S.R. Maheshwari, *President's Rule in India,* p. 162.
11. *Ibid.,* p. 163.
12. S.R. Maheshwari, *op. cit.,* p. 94.
13. *Poknaphant Editorial,* Imphal, 4 May, 2000.
14. *Lok Sabha Debates, Fifth Series,* No 27, 29 June, 1971, col. 282.
15. *The Statesman,* 4 July, 1971.

16. S.R. Maheswari, *op. cit.*, p. 186.
17. *Ibid.*
18. *President's Rule in the State and Union Territories.* Lok Sabha Secretariat, New Delhi 1996.

6

Conclusions and Observations

After having thoroughly studied all the relevant aspects of the subjects we have drawn certain positive conclusions and made some observations.

The framers of our constitution anticipating that in the event of an extraordinary situation arising out of the failure on the part of a political party/political parties to form a government in the state or to maintain its stability or to run the state administration smoothly, the complete breakdown of constitutional machinery in the state, law and order problem in the state or so, the central government may be compelled to take over the state administration or to impose the President's rule in the concerned state, according to the provisions laid down in the constitution under Article 356 for setting the things right.

President's rule has been imposed in the states for various reasons which include the failure of a political party to form the government or a ministry after fresh election owing to lack of absolute majority or otherwise, breaking of ruling coalitions due to withdraw of support by alliance partners, passing of no-confidence motion against the council of Ministers and the fall of the government, complete breakdown of constitutional machinery, failure of the state governments to tackle law and order problem, public agitations in states leading to instability in the administration and absence of Legislatures in newly formed states. During the period 1951 -1976 several states came under President's rule on several grounds. Punjab was the first state to come under this rule which was imposed there on June 20,

1951. The other states include Bihar, Uttar Pradesh, Orissa, West Bengal, Rajasthan, Haryana, Gujarat, Andhra Pradesh, Tamil Nadu, Kerala, Mysore, Nagaland, Manipur and Tripura. Manipur alone came under this rule ten times, two times (first on 25-10-67 and then on 16-10-69) during the Territorial Assembly, and eight times since the attainment of full-fledged statehood in 1972. Since the coming into force of the constitution of India on Jan 26, 1950, President's rule has been promulgated seventy-five times up to 1989 in 23 states.

Since the coming into force of the Government of Union Territories Act 1963, President's rule have been promulgated ten times in four Union Territories. Pondicherry came under President.'s rule five times and former Union Territory of Mizoram and Goa two times each followed by Arunachal Pradesh (erstwhile NEFA) where it was proclaimed only once.

The Governor plays key role during the President's rule in the state. In accordance with the provisions of the constitution, after Article 356 is invoked he takes over the administration of the state.

All the powers of the state government are delegated to him by the President of India. It becomes his constitutional responsibility to manage the entire affairs of the state to the best of the satisfaction of the President and Union Government. He discharges his duties with the assistance of his advisers appointed by the central Government. The centre-state relations depend very much upon the functioning of the Governor during President's rule in the state. The role of central Government in President's rule in the state is of equal importance. The centre plays very important role in decision making process with regard to the promulgation, extension and revocation of the President's rule in the state.

Our disquisition into the subject leads us to conclude that there are both advantages and disadvantages of President's rule particularly when no political party is in a position to form the government. Law and order is maintained, political stability comes and development programmes receive high priority under President's rule in the state. But, on the other hand, the fundamental rights of the people are to a certain extent curtailed.

It may be observed here that sometimes when situation warrants the President's rule is not imposed in the state for various reasons and the very purpose for which provision has been made in the constitution for such rule is defeated. In the recent past, Bihar is a glaring example of it. After the last Assembly election in that state RJD (Rashtriya Janata Dal) formed the government with the active support of Congress (I). The latter not only extended the support to former but also joined the government. After law and order situation deteriorated there the then Governor S.S. Bhandari recommended the President's rule there which was approved by the Union cabinet and passed by Lok Sabha but unfortunately sabotaged by Congress (I) members, Left Front and other opposition parties in the Rajya Sabha for the reasons which are not far to discover. We may suggest here that in such a situation the President of India should go by the decision of a committee of constitutional experts and not by the decision of the members of the House concerned. But for that, constitutional amendments are necessary. In case of controversy in the Parliament over the recommendation of the Governor for the President's rule and its promulgation the opinion of constitutional experts should be the deciding factor. It is very unfortunate that only because sometimes it is not approved by one House or both the Houses of Parliament this rule warranted by the situation is not imposed in some states. Article 356 must be invoked for the purpose it has been laid down in the constitution otherwise the very basic spirit of the constitution will be lost and state concerned will immensely suffer. Constitutional provisions must be honored by the members of the parliament. The vested interest, partisan role and ideological commitments of the political parties, particularly those who actively support the ruling party/are alliance partners /are part of the coalition government in the concerned state, sometimes prove great hurdles in the way of promulgation of president's rule in the state. We, therefore feel that the constitutional amendment is the need of the hour to tide over the practical difficulties in making our constitution more functional., more operational and more effective.

In is a well-known fact that President's rule has been imposed in the states and Union Territories of India since the commencement of her constitution on 26th January 1950. By violating the federal structure in the constitution the central political leaders and its agent, i.e. the Governor sometimes misuse the article 356 and impose the President's rule in the states and union territories. After delving deep into the subject we find that no confidence motion against Chief Ministers., defection of MLA, and redefection, cross-voting are the major factors for the imposition of President's rule in the states. But it will be wrong to imagine that multiparty political system only is the factor responsible for changing of party and loyalty. The single majority party also finds it difficult to maintain the stable government in the state, for example the election to the Gujarat Assembly held in 1971 gave overwhelming majority to the congress with a strength of 137 members in a House of 167 and it assumed office under the Chief Ministership of Ghanashambhai Oza. Though victorious at the hustings, the party was not at peace with itself being riven with internal dissension in the middle of 1973. Due to internal party crisis the Chief Minister was changed and the political problem was brought in to a critical situation which paved the way for inviting the President's rule in Gujarat on 9 February, 1974.

Since first general election in this country most of the states could not have smooth sailing with a single majority. Therefore coalition form of government has been installed in some states. Divergent opinions and different ideologies causes a problem in the making of common minimum programme to run the government. Sometimes cabinet ministers choose the good portfolios in the ministry as a result of which the defection occur within the party. Every Chief Minister like to dissolve the assembly when he tenders his resignation to the Governor. Except for few states, the governors generally do not seek an alternative government. Opportunity is seldom given to the opposition party. In this matter, many writ petition has been filed even to the Supreme Court. The Governor played a vital role in shaping and sharing the formation of a new government in the state.

In a democratic form of Government, suspension of fundamental right is not only violation of democratic procedure but also that of federal behaviour. In reality the Governor is the agent of the centre. He does very little for the development of the state under the President's rule. He has dormant position in the popular ministry regime. He becomes active when the popular ministry is unstable or during the President's rule.

The Governor should not send his report immediately to the President recommending President's rule in the state, instead he should look for an alternative government. In order to subdue the political crisis, unstable ministry, changing of leadership, defection, redefection, crossvoting etc. The Assembly can be suspended for some time and meanwhile, the political solution could be found to the problem concerned. The dissolution of assembly and holding of fresh election do not always bring the political solution in the state. Article 356 of Indian Constitution should be invoked only when there is no option left. But the fundamental right of the people should be protected at all cost. Causes which have led to the imposition of President's rule in the states have been varied in nature, such as defections by members of Legislative, break up of coalition, passing of No Confidence motions against the council of Minister, resignation of Chief Minister for various reasons, absence of Legislatures in newly formed states, public agitations in states leading to instability in the administration etc. Though detections leading to imposition of President's rule became a matter of rather frequent occurrences only after the 1967 General Election, it was as early as November 1954 that the first instance of this nature occurred in Andhra Pradesh. Other states where similar situations have arisen over the years are Bihar, Gujarat, Haryana, Karnataka, Kerala, Manipur, Meghalaya, Mizoram, Nagaland, Orissa, Punjab, Sikkim and Tamil Nadu. Instance of President's rule being necessitated by break up of ruling coalitions are Kerala (1979, 1981 and 1982) Manipur (1992) Orissa (1961) and (1971) Punjab (1968) Tripura (1979) and Uttar Pradesh (1970). The passing of non confidence motions against the council of Ministers in the State legislatures of Andhra Pradesh and Kerala led to President's rule there in 1954 and 1964 respectively as no other party was then in a position to form a Ministry.

In Gujarat, President's rule was introduced in 1976 after Chief Minister resigned following and adverse vote in the state Assembly on a Demand for Grants. There have been other cases as in Kerala (1970 and 1979) Punjab (1951) Sikkim (1979) Uttar Pradesh (1968 and 1975) and West Bengal (1970) when the Chief Ministers resigned on their own due to various reasons which resulted in the Governor's recommendation for taking over the administration of there states by the President. Public agitations among other causes led to President's rule in Andhra Pradesh in 1973, in Assam in 1979, in Gujarat in 1974, in Kerala in 1959 and in Punjab in 1983 and 1987.

The formation of new states Kerala in 1956, Punjab in 1966, Manipur and Tripura in 1972 created situation in which the administration had to be taken over by the centre till the new Legislative Assembly could be duly elected and the popular Ministries ushered in.

It was in Kerala in 1965, in Orissa in 1971 and in Rajasthan in 1967 that in spite of the formation of new Legislative Assemblies after fresh elections no single party emerged with an absolute majority or was in a position to form a Ministry in collaboration with other parties. The solution recommended to meet such a situation was President's rule under Article 356.

Appendices

APPENDIX I

THE CHRONOLOGY OF PRESIDENT'S RULE IN MANIPUR WITH RELEVANT DETAILS

The President's Rule has been imposed so far ten times in Manipur, two times during the Territorial Assembly and eight times since the attainment of full fledged statehood. The following chart shows the proclamation of President's rule in the state indetail:

MANIPUR*

Sl.. No.	*Name of Lt. Governor*	*Name of Chief Minister and Party in power at the time of issue of Proclamation*	*Date of issue of Proclamation*	*Whether Assembly was dissolved or suspended*	*Circumstances leading of issue of Proclamation*	*Date of laying the Proclamation on the Table of*		*Date of Revocation of Proclamation*	*Ministry formed after the revocation of Proclamation*
						Lok Sabha	*Rajya Sabha*		
(1)	(2)	(3)	(4)	(5)	(6)	(7)	(8)	(9)	(10)
1.	Shri Baleshwar Prasad (1)	Shri Longiam Thambou Singh ((United Front)	25.10.67 (2)	Assembly was kept in Suspen-nded animation	The Assembly had 32 seats equally shared by congress and United Front. With the defection of a Member of United Front to the Congress Party and subsequent resignations of Speaker and Deputy speaker from their offices, both the groups refused to nominate a Candidate for Speakership as his election would automatically have given the otherside a majority, Presidents rule was necessitated. (2)	......	......	19-2-1968 (3)	The game of defections and counter defections brought the congress Party again in majority and Shri M. Koireng Singh assumed the office of Chief Minister on 19.2.1968. (3)

2.	Shri Baleshwar Prasad (4)	Shri M. Koireng Singh (Congress) (4)	16-10-69 (5)	Assembly was dissolved simultaneously (5)	A motion of nonconfidence was passed by the Assembly on 23-9-69 because of frequent changes in Party alignment by some Members Accordingly, the Chief Minister resigned and no Party was in a position to form stable Government.	......	......	(After the imposition of Presi dent's rule in 1969, Manipur was accorded a full-fledged statehood w.e.f. 21.1.72. Till the elections where held to the new Legislative Assembly and a popular govern-ment is formed, President issued a fresh proclamation on the was in a position to form same day under Article 356 of the Constitution) (6)	......

1ST MANIPUR LEGISLATIVE ASSEMBLY

Sl. No	*Name of Governor*	*Name of Minister Party in power at the time of issue of Proclamation*	*Date of issue of Proclamation*	*Whether Assembly was dissolved or suspended*	*Circumstances leading to issue of Proclamation*	*Date of laying the Proclamation of the Table of -*		*Date(s) of discussion approving the Proclamation in —*		*Date(s) of discussion further approving the continuance in force of the Proclamation in —*		*Date of revocation of Proclamation*	*Ministry formed after the revocation of Proclamation*
						Lok Sabha	*Rajya Sabha*	*Lok Sabha*	*Rajya Sabha*	*Lok Sabha*	*Rajya Sabha*		
(1)	(2)	(3)	(4)	(5)	(6)	(7)	(8)	(9)	(10)	(11)	(12)	(13)	(14)
3.	Shri B.K. Nehru (1)	—	21-1-72 (4)	—	By virtue of the provisions of the North Eastern Area (Reorganization) Act, 1971, the new state of Manipur was formed on 21-1-72. Till the elections were held to the Legislative Assembly of this new State and a popular government came into Office, it was not possible to carry on the administration of the State in accordance with the provisions of the Constitution. President's rule was, therefore, introduced in the State on the very day it came into existence. (3)	13-3-72 (4)	13-3-72 (5)	20-3-72 (6)	18-3-72 (7)	—	—	20-3-72 (8)	Elections to the Manipur Legislature Assembly were held in March, 1972 in which no Part)' emerged with a clear majority. However Shri Mohammed Alimuddin was elected leader of the United Legislature Party and he formed the Ministry on 20-3-72 (3)
4.	Shri B.K. Nehru (9)	Shri Mohamed Alimuddin (United Legislature Party) (9)	28-3-73 (10)	Assembly was dissolved	Various crossings of the floor and also formation of groups within the United Legislature Party led to an undesirable degree of instability in the Government. The Chief Minister, Shri Alimuddin submitted his resignation of 26-3-73.	28-3-73 (along with a copy of the Governor's Report to the President, dated 27-3-73 (11)	28-3-73 (along with a copy of the Governor's Report to the President, dated 27-3-73 (12)	15-5-73 and 14-5-73 (13)	31-3-73 (14)	31-3-73		4-3-74 (17)	After the elections held in the State in February 1974, Shri Mohammed Alimuddin formed the Ministry on 4-3-74 (18)

2ND MANIPUR LEGISLATIVE ASSEMBLY

Sl. No	Name of Governor	Name of Minister Party in power at the time of issue of Proclamation	Date of issue of Proclamation	Whether Assembly was dissolved or suspended	Circumstances leading to issue of Proclamation	Date of laying the Proclamation of the Table of -		Date(s) of discussion further approving the continuance in force of the Proclamation in —		Date(s) of discussion further approving the continuance in force of the Proclamation in —		Date of revocation of Proclamation	Ministry formed after the revocation of Proclamation
						Lok Sabha	Rajya Sabha	Lok Sabha	Rajya Sabha	Lok Sabha	Rajya Sabha		
(1)	(2)	(3)	(4)	(5)	(6)	(7)	(8)	(9)	(10)	(11)	(12)	(13)	(14)
5.	Shri L.P. Singh (19)	Shri R.K. Dorendra Singh (Congress) (19)	16-5-77 (20)	Assembly was suspended (20 and 21)	Due to defection, the Ministry lost the support of the majority of the Members of the State Legislative Assembly and accordingly, resigned. Subsequently, the Governor explored the possibility of forming another Ministry but did not succeed as the political situation in the State was very fluid and no party was in a position to form the Government	11-6-77 (along with a copy of the Governor's Report to the Vice President, acting as President, dated 15-5-77) (22)	11-6-77 (along with a copy of the Governor's Report to the Vice President, acting as President, dated 15-5-77) (23)	—	—	—	—	26-6-77	Shri Yangmasho Shaiza who was unanimously elected as leader of the Janata Party and had the support of the majority of the Members in the Assembly formed the Ministry on 29-6-77 (21)
6.	Shri L.P. Singh (24)	Shri Yang masho Shaiza (Janata Party)	14-11-79 (25)	Assembly was dissolved simultaneously (25)	The Governor had in his report, dt. 16-10-79 *interalia* stated "I have never known a Government which, according to my own best judgement has been so corrupt, devoid of integrity and unprincipled, and which is	23-1-80 (along with a copy of the report of the Governor to the President dated 27-10-79) (26)	23-1-80 (along with a copy of the report of the Governor to the President dated 16-10-79) (27)	—	—	—	—	13-1-80 (28)	Election to the state Assembly were held in January, 1980. A coalition Ministry headed by Shri R.K. Dorendra Singh assumed office on 14-1-80. (28)

(1)	(2)	(3)	(4)	(5)	(6)	(7)	(8)	(9)	(10)	(11)	(12)	(13)	(14)
					given functioning so continuously without any regard to the laws or considerations of justice and fair play". (24)								
3RD MANIPUR LEGISLATIVE ASSEMBLY													
7.	Shri L.P. Singh (29)	Shri Rishang Ksishing Congress-I (29)	28-2-81 (30)	Assembly was suspended animation (30)	Resignation of 10 Members from the Party reduced the ruling Congress-I party to minority. According to the Governor's assessment no party was in a position to form a stable Ministry.	2-3-81 (along with a copy of the report of the Governor to the President dated 27-2-81) (31)	2-3-81 (along with a copy of the report of the Governor to the President dated 27-10-79 (33)	19-3-81 (33)	26-3-81 (34)	—	—	19-6-80 (35)	A Congress (I) Government headed by Shri Rishang Keishing assumed office on 16-9-81. (35)

4TH MANIPUR LEGISLATIVE ASSEMBLY. NO PRESIDENT'S RULE.

Sl. No	Name of Governor	Name of Minister Party in power at the time of issue of Proclamation	Date of issue of Proclamation	Whether Assembly was dissolved or suspended	Circumstances leading to issue of Proclamation	Date of laying the Proclamation of the Table of -		Date(s) of discussion approving the Proclamation in —		Date(s) of discussion further approving the continuance in force of the Proclamation in —		Date of revocation of Proclamation	Ministry formed after the revocation of Proclamation
						Lok Sabha	Rajya Sabha	Lok Sabha	Rajya Sabha	Lok Sabha	Rajya Sabha		
(1)	(2)	(3)	(4)	(5)	(6)	(7)	(8)	(9)	(10)	(11)	(12)	(13)	(14)
5TH MANIPUR LEGISLAI'IVE ASSEMBLY													
8.	Shri Chintamani Panigrahi (36)	Sh. R.K. Ranbir Singh (United Legislature Front) (36)	7-1-92 (37)	Assembly was suspended (38)	The ULF Ministry lost it majority with the resig nation of Janata Dal Legislators from the party. (38)	24-2-92 (along with a copy of the report of the Governor to the President dated 25.1.92) (39)	24-2-92 (along with a copy of the report of the Governor to the President 25-1-92) (40)	28-2-92 3-3-92 (41)	25-2-92 (42)	—	—	8-4-92 (43)	A Cong. (I) Coalition Ministry headed by Shri RK. Dorendra Singh was sworn in (44)
9.	Shri V.K. Nayar (45)	Sh. R.K. Dorendra Singh [Indian National Congress (I) headed the Coalition Govt. (45)	31.12.93	Assembly was suspended (47)	In the wake of continued Naga-Kuki clashes, resulting in about 1000 deaths, the President rule was imposed in the State. (47)	21-2-94 (48)	21-2-94 (49)	11-5-94 (50)	10-5-94 (51)	—	—	13-12-94 (52)	Sh. Rishang Keishing (Congress Party) was sworn in on 13-12-94 ending 346 day's old President's Rule in the state. (53)

(1)	(2)	(3)	(4)	(5)	(6)	(7)	(8)	(9)	(10)	(11)	(12)	(13)	(14)
6TH MANIPUR LEGISLATIVE ASSEMBLY NO PRESIDENT'S RULE.													
10.	Shri O.N. Srivastava	Congress (I) Ministry form 25-02-95 1.15 pm and led by Rishang Keishing Resigned on 15-12-97 after losing the motion for confidence. Then United Front Government was form the Ministry on 16-12-97 (11.30 am) led by W. Nipamacha Singh. (Manipur Sate Congress Party)	......	......	......	......	......	......	......	......	......	......	......

(1)	(2)	(3)	(4)	(5)	(6)	(7)	(8)	(9)	(10)	(11)	(12)	(13)	(14)
7TH MANIPUR LEGISLATIVE ASSEMBLY													
11.	Shri Ved Marwah	People Front Government led by Samata Party headed by Radha binod Koijam 3 months old Ministry	2-06-01	Assembly was dissolved simultenously	Unprecedented events was took place that out of 60 members legislative Assembly in Manipur, 58 58 MLAs had been supported to his ministry, but within a short period of three months the government was crack between the partner of BJP Ministers and defeated in the vote of confidence.	......	......	......	......	......	......	......	When after the revcation of proclamation the mid term election was held on 14-2-2002 for seeking people mended fresh election. After the election Congress Party got larger members and Shri Congress party formed the coalition government in the state.

APPENDIX II

President's Rule in States and Union Territories

1. STATES

ANDHRA PRADESH

Sl. No.	Name of Governor	Name of Chief Minister and Party in power at the time of issue of Proclamation	Date of issue of Proclamation	Whether Assembly was dissolved or suspended	Circumstances leading to issue of Proclamation
(1)	(2)	(3)	(4)	(5)	(6)
1.	Shri C.M. Trivedi (1)	Shri T. Prakasam (Coalition Ministry of Congress and Andhra Praja Party) (1)	15-11-54 (2)	Assembly was dissolved simultaneously (2)	Following the passing of a motion of no confidence against it by the State Legislative Assembly, the Ministry headed by shri T. Prakasan tendered its resignation, which was accepted w.e.f. 15-11-54. The defeat of the Govt. was caused by some members of the ruling coalition parties voting with the opposition on the no-confidence motion. (3)
2.	Shri Khandubhai K. Desai (9)	Shri P.V.Narasimha Rao (Congress) (9)	18-1-73 (10)	Assembly was suspended (11)	On 17-1-73 the Chief Minister tendered the resignation of his Cabinet in the wake of Mulki Rutes agitation in the State, though the Congress Legislature Party enjoyed an absolute majority (271) in a House of 288. (12)

ASSAM

Sl. No.	Name of Governor	Name of Chief Minister and Party in power at the time of issue of Proclamation	Date of issue of Proclamation	Whether Assembly was dissolved or suspended	Circumstances leading to issue of Proclamation
1.	Shri L.P. Singh (1)	Shri J.N. Hazarika (asom Janata Dal Suported by the congress (U) congress (I) and C.P. I. (1)	12-1279 (2)	Assembly was suspended. (1+2)	In his report, dt 11-12-79 to the President, the Governor had stated that Shri Hazarika had the support of only 8 persons and was no longer even the leader of the Asom Janata Vikhayani Dal and that the leaders of all the political parties he was

					able to consult were of the view (hat the State should be placed under President's Rule for a brief period so that they may consult one another and come with a proposal to form a viable Ministry. While recommending issue of Proclamation under Article 356 he however, added that the Legislative Assembly may be kept in suspended animation. (1)
2.	Shri L.P Singh (11)	Smt. Anwara Taimur (Congress-I) (11)	30-6-81 (12)	Assembly was suspended (11+12)	In his report dt. 29-6-81 to the President the Governor had stated that Smt. Anwara taimur had tendered resignation on 28-6-81 and that no other party was in position to form a stable Ministry.
3.	Shri Prakash Mehrotra (20)	Shri Keshab Chandra Gogoi (20)	19-3-82	Assembly was dissol-ved simultaneously (21)	The Ministry headed by Shri Gogoi resigned on 18-3-82 before facing the no-confidence motion in the Assembly. (20)
4.	Shri D.D. Thakur (29)	Shri Prafulla Kumar Mohanta (AGP) (29)	27-11-90 (30)	Assembly was kept in suspended animation (30)	Due to deteriorating law and order situation the President felt that the Government of the State cannot be carried on in accordance with the provisions of the Constitution. (29)
BIHAR					
1.	Shri Nityananda Kanungo (1)	Shri Bhola Paswan Shastri (Samyukta Vikhayak Dal)	29-6-68 (3)	Assembly was dissol-ved simultaneously (3)	The Ministry headed by Shri Bhola Paswan Shastri resigned on 25-6-68. Repeated defections by many Members of the Legislative Assembly made it clear that no stable Government was likely to emerge from out of the then membership of the Bihar Legislative Assembly. (I) and (2)

contd...

Sl. No.	*Name of Governor*	*Name of Chief Minister and Party in power at the time of issue of Proclamation*	*Date of issue of Proclamation*	*Whether Assembly was dissolved or suspended*	*Circumstances leading to issue of Proclamation*
(1)	(2)	(3)	(4)	(5)	(6)
2.	Shri Nityanand Kanungo (12)	Shri Bhola Paswan Shastri (Lok Tantrik (14) Dal), who had formed a coalition Ministry with the support of other parties, submitted his resignation on 1-7-69 after being in office for 9 days only (13)	4-7-69 (14)	Assembly was suspended (13 and (15)	Continuous defections by the Members of the Legislative Assembly led to uncertainty about stable Government. (15)
3.	Shri D.K barooah (22)	Shri Bhola Paswan Shastri (Coalition Ministry) resigned on 27-12-71 (22)	9-1-72 {Proclamation dated 9-1-72 remained in force for 2 months after which it ceased to operate. A fresh Proclamation was issued on (9-3-72)} (23)	Assembly was dissolved on 20-12-71 (24)	The Chief Minister tendered the resignation of his Council of a more stable Government in the State. (22)
4.	Shri Jagannath Kaushal (28)	Dr. Jagannath Mishra (Congress) (28)	30- 4-77 (29)	Assembly was dissolved simultaneously (29)	In the March 1977 Lok Sabha elections, the Congress the ruling party in the State-could not win any seat from Bihar. The Union Government took the view that this implied a complete lack of confidence on the part of the electorate in the Government of that State. (30)

No.	Governor	Chief Minister	Date	Assembly	Reason
5.	Shri A.R. Kidwai (35)	Shri Ram Sunder Das (Janata) (35)	17-2-80 (36)	Assembly was dissolved simultaneously (36)	The Union Government felt that having suffered an overwhelming defeat in the Lok Sabha Elections held in January, 1980 the ruling party in the State no longer represented the people. (37)
6.	Shri A.R. Kidwai (44)	Shri Laloo Prassad Yadav (44)	28-3-1995 (44)	The term of State Assembly expired on 15-3-95 (44)	Due to non-completion of Election to State Assembly before 31-3-95 the Governor recommended imposition of President's Rule to enable Parliament to pass the Vote on Account. (44)
GOA					
1.	Shri Khursheed Alam Khan (1)	Dr. Luis Proto Barbosa (P.D.F.) (1)	14-12-90 (2)	Assembly was kept in suspended animation (2)	The MGP withdrew its support to the ruling P.D.F led by Dr. Barbosa whose disqualification Orders also upheld by the High Court and no other party was in a position to form the stable Government. (1)
GUJARAT					
1.	Shri Shriman Narayan (1)	Shri Hitendra [Congress (O)] (1)	13-5-71 (2)	Assembly was dissolved simultaneously (2)	Indiscriminate defections and redefection by MLAs led to uncertainty about formation of stable Government. The Council Ministers held an emergency meeting on May 11-1971 and passed a resolution advising the Governor to dissolve the Legislative Assembly. (1)
2.	Shri K.K. Viswanathan (11)	Shri Chimanbhai J. Patel (Congress) (11)	9-2-74 (12)	Assembly was suspended but subsequently dissolved on i 5-3-74	Due to persisting agitation in the State the Chief Minister submitted his resignation on 9-2-74 though the Congress Party enjoyed an absolute majority of

contd...

Sl. No.	*Name of Governor*	*Name of Chief Minister and Party in power at the time of issue of Proclamation*	*Date of issue of Proclamation*	*Whether Assembly was dissolved or suspended*	*Circumstances leading to issue of Proclamation*
(1)	(2)	(3)	(4)	(5)	(6)
				(13)	140 Members in a House of 168. (11) and (13)
3.	Shri K.K. Viswanathan (22)	Shri Babubhai Jashbhai Patel (Janata Front), following the midterm elections held in the State in June 1975, five parties, *viz*, Congress (O). Bhartiya Jana Sangh, Bhrtiya Lok Dal. Socialist Party and Rashtriya Mazdoor Paksh and 77 independents had formed the Janata Front Legislature Party with a strength of 86 in the 181 member State Assembly. The Front has also secured the support of 5 independents and 12 members of the Kisan Mazdoor Lok Paksh. (22)	12-3-76 (23)	Assembly was suspended (22) and (23)	The Kisan Mazdoor Lok Paksh, which had been supporting the Janata Front Government was dissolved on 11-2-76, when the demands for grants of food and Civil Supplies Department came to be voted in the Assembly, the Ministry suffered a defeat and the Chief Minister tendered his resignation. As no party or combination of parties was in a position to form a stable Government, the Governor recommended imposition of President Rule. (22)
4.	Smt. Sharda Mukherjee (31)	Shri Babubhai Patel (Janata) (32)	17-2-80 (33)	Assembly was dissolved simultenously 33)	The Union Government felt that having suffered an overwhelming defeat in the Lok Sabha elections held in January, 1980 the ruling party in the State no-longer represented the people. (34)

HARYANA					
1.	Shri B.N. Chakra-varty (1)	Shri Birendra Singh (Samyukta Dal)	21-11-67 (2)	Assembly was dissol-ved simulteneously (2)	In Haryana defections had become endemic. These had made mockery of the Constitution and had brought democracy to ridicule. (1)
2.	Shri Jaisukh Lal Hathi (9)	Shri Banarsi Das Gupta (Congress) (10)	30-4-77 (11)	Assembly was dissol-ved simultaneously (11)	In the March 1997 Lok Sabha elections, the Congress, the ruling party in the State-could not win any seat from Haryana. The Union Government took the view that this implied a complete lack of confidence on the party of the electorate in the Government of that State. (12)
3.	Shri Dhanik Lal Mandal (17)	Shri Om Prakash Chautala (JD-S) (17)	6-4-91 (18)	Assembly was dissol-ved simultaneously (18)	After the disqualification of three MLAs by the Speaker of the Assembly, the government led by shri Chautala reduced to a minority. The Governor, therefore, asked the Chief Minister to prove his majority on the floor of the House before April 3,1991. The Chief Minister had turned down the Governor's directives as he had already recommended the dissolution of the Assembly. After the deadline, the Governor recommended the imposition of President's Rule. (17)
HIMACHAL PRADESH					
1.	Shri Amin-un-Din Ahmed Khan (1)	Shri Ram Lal (Congress) (2)	30-4-77 (3)	Assembly was dissol-ved simultenaously (3)	In the March, 1977 Lok Sabha elections, the Congress the ruling party in the State-could not win any seat from Himachal Pradesh. The Union Governmenttook the view mat this implied a complete lack of confidence on the part of the electorate in the Government of that State. (4)

contd...

Sl. No.	Name of Governor	Name of Chief Minister and Party in power at the time of issue of Proclamation	Date of issue of Proclamation	Whether Assembly was dissolved or suspended	Circumstances leading to issue of Proclamation
(1)	(2)	(3)	(4)	(5)	(6)
2.	Shri Virender Verma (9)	Shri Shanta Kumar (BJP) (10)	15-12-92 (11)	Assembly was dissolved simultenaously (12)	On Dec. 6, 1992 the disputed structure at Ayodhya was demolished by Kar Sevaks. The Union Government felt that a Government headed by members of banned organizations could not be allowed to continue. President dismissed the Government and State was brought under President's Rule under Article 356. (13)
JAMMU AND KASHMIR					
1.	Shri Jagmohan (1)	Governor's rule followed by President's rule (1)	7-9-86 (2)	Assembly was kept in suspended animation (3)	Considering the report of the Governor and other information received by him, the President was satisfied that situation had arisen in which the Government of the State could not be carried on in accordance with the provisions of the Constitution of India as applicable to that State and of the provision of the Constitution of J&K. (3)
2.	Shri Girish Saxena (7)	Governor's rule followed by President's rule	18-7-90 (8)	Assembly was dissolved on 19-2-90 during Governor's Rate (7)	The President was satisfied that the Government of the State could not be carried on in accordance with the provisions of the Constitution of India as applicable to that State and of the Constitution of Jammu & Kashmir on account of widespread terrorists activities which deteriorated security and political situation in the State. (7)
KARNATAKA					
1.	Shri Dharama Vira (1)	Shri Veerendra Patil (Congress-O)	27-3-71 (2)	Assembly was suspended but sub-	On March 18,1971, that chief Minister (Shri Veerendra Patil) tendered his resignation from his Office to the

		(1)		sequently dissolved on 14-4-71 (3)	Governor stating: "In the wake of unexpected and sudden changes, apparent floor crossings and defections from the Ruling Party to the other side and shifting of loyalties by some Members. Which is highly distressing. I think it is not advisable on my part to continue as Chief Minister/" The Governor accepted the resignation and after exploring possibilities of forming an alternative Ministry reported that it was not in the interest of the state to continue the present uncertain state of affairs. (1)
2.	Shri Govind Narain (12)	Shri D. Devraj Urs (Congress) (12)	31-12-77 (13)	Assembly was dissolved simultaneously. (13)	Due to internal dissensions, large number of Members of the Congress Legislature Party Publicly announced in December, 1977 their decision to withdraw their support to the Chief Minister. After reviewing the development, the Government decided to leave the question whether or not tire Ministry enjoyed Majority support to be decided only in the Assembly. Latter the Governor reported that there were grave apprehensions whether the proceedings in the Assembly which was to meet on 3-1-78 should be free and orderly. He also expressed serious misgivings questioning the *propriety* of reading an address prepared for him by a Ministry which had forfeited the confidence of the majority in the Assembly. He therefore, recommended to the President to issue a proclamation under article 356 of the Constitution. (14)
3.	Shri P. Venkata-subbiah (17)	Shri S.R. Bommai (Janata Dal) (17)	21-4-89 (18)	Assembly was dissolved simultaneously (18)	Dissension was surfacing in the Ruling Janata Party in the State which became evident when out of its 139 Members, only 27 remained in the Janata Party

contd...

Sl. No.	*Name of Governor*	*Name of Chief Minister and Party in power at the time of issue of Proclamation*	*Date of issue of Proclamation*	*Whether Assembly was dissolved or suspended*	*Circumstances leading to issue of Proclamation*
(1)	(2)	(3)	(4)	(5)	(6)
					in the wake of formation of Janata Dal. Newly formed Janata Dal with the support of 7 Independents became ruling parry. Soon after the expansion of the Ministry, 18 Members withdrew their support and brought the government in minority. The Members were lured to join Janata Dal by adopting-some unethical method. This led to imposition of President Rule. (17)
4.	Shri Bhanu Pratap Singh (26)	Shri Veerendra Patil (Cong-I) (26)	10-10-90 (27)	Assembly was kept in suspended animation (27)	Due to sudden outbreak of communal violence, the ruling Congress-I Legislature Party formed dissident group and demanded change in leadership. Some of the Ministers attended meetings of both the groups. Thus head counting and horse-trading resulted in utter confusion in the administration arid the spirit of joint responsibility of the Cabinet totally shattered which led to imposition of President's Rule. (26)
KERALA					
1.	Shri Rama Verma (Rajpramukh) (1)	Shri Panampilli Govinda Menon, Chief Minister in Travancore-Cochin State (Congress)	23-3-56 (3)	Assembly was dissolved simultaneously (3)	The Congress Ministry resigned on 11-3-56 consequent on the resignation of the members from the Congress Party as a result of which the Congress was not able to command a majority in the Legislature. As the Rajpramukh did not find any other Party which could form a stable Ministry, he recommended President's Rule (l) and (6)

2.	Shri P.S. Rau (Acting Governor from 1-11-56 and Dr. B. Ramakrishna Rao w.e.f 22-11-56)	—	1-11-56 (11)	—	The States were reorganized on 1 -11 -56 when the new State "Kerala" came into being. President's Rule in Travancore-Cochin was formally revoked on 1-11-56 accordingly and reimposed on the same day in the newly formed Kerala State as there was no legislature for the new State. (12)
3.	Shri B. Ramakrishna Rao (18)	Shri E.M.S. Namboodriapd (Communist) (18)	31-7-59 (19)	Assembly was dissolved simultaneously (19)	In his report to the President, the Governor had listed various acts omission and commission against the State govt. such as, {a) large scale release of prisoners and undesirable elements; (b) new police policy depriving of protection to employers etc.;(c) "mass upsurge" and public agitations indicating definite shift in the mind of the people against government. (18)
4.	Shri V.V. Giri (26)	Shri R. Shankar (Congress) (26)	10-9-64 and 12-1-65 (27)	Assembly was dissolved simultaneously (27)	The Ministry tendered its resignation to the Governor on 10-9-64, the motion expressing want of Confidence to the Council of Ministers having been passed by the Assembly on 8-9-64 (28)
5.	Shri V.V. Giri Shri A.P. Jain (from 2-4-64 to 6-2-66) Shri Bhagwan Sahay (w.e.f. 6-2-66) (34)	—	24-3-65 (35)	Assembly was dissolved simultaneously (35)	In the general elections to the Kerala Legislative Assembly held on 4th March, 1965, no single party had secured an absolute majority and therefore no party by itself was in a position to form a Government. Even combination of parties were not able to form a Ministry. (36)
6.	Shri V. Viswa nathan (45)	Shri G. Achutha Menon (C.P.I.) (45)	4-8-70 (46)	Assembly was dissolved on 26-6-70 (46)	On the advice of the Chief Minister, the Governor dissolved the Assembly on 26-6-70. While arrangements to hold fresh elections were in progress, the Chief Minister tendered his resignation on 1-8-70, whereupon the Governor recommended President's Rule.

contd...

Sl. No.	Name of Governor	Name of Chief Minister and Party in power at the time of issue of Proclamation	Date of issue of Proclamation	Whether Assembly was dissolved or suspended	Circumstances leading to issue of Proclamation
(1)	(2)	(3)	(4)	(5)	(6)
					(45)
7.	Shri Jothi Venka-tachellum (50)	Shri C.M. Mohammed Koya (Coalition Government)	5-12-79 (51)	Assembly was dissol ved on 30 -11 -79 (51)	The Muslim League and other groups had formed a coalition Ministry led by Shri Mohammed Koya but Shri Koya resigned on 1-12-79 when he found he was in a minority. He recommended to the Governor to dissolve the Assembly. (50-51)
8.	Smt. Jothi Venka-tachellum	Shri. E.K. Nayanar (Coalition Government) (56)	21-10-81 (57)	Assembly was suspen-ded animation (56) & (57)	The ruling left formed coalition lost majority conse-quent on the withdrawal of support by Congress (S) Legislature Party and thereafter by Kerala Congress (Mani Group). (56)
9.	Smt. Jothi Venka-tachellum (64)	Shri K. Karunakaran (UDF) (64)	17-3-82 (65)	Assembly was dissol-ved simultaneously	The ruling UDF Party reduced to 69 in the 140 member Assembly and the possibility of stable alternative Ministry in the State was remote after resignation of chief Minister.
MADHYA PRADESH					
1.	Shri S.N. Sinha	Shri S.C. Shukla (Congress)	30-4-77	Assembly was dissol ved simultaneously	In the March 1977 Lok Sabha Elections, the Congress-the ruling party in the State-could win only 1 seat from Madhya Pradesh. The Union Government took the view that this implied a lack of confidence on the part of the electorate in the Government of the State.
2.	Shri C.M. Poonacha	Shri Sunder Lal Patwa (Janata)	12-2-80	Assembly was dissol-ved simultaneously	The Union Government felt that having suffered an overwhelming defeat in the Lok Sabha elections

					held in January 1980, the ruling party in the State no longer represented the people.
3.	Shri V.B.L Mathur	Shri Sunder Lal Patwa (BJP)	15-12-92	Assembly was dissolved simultaneously	On Dec. 6. 1992 the disputed structure was demolished by Karsevaks. The Union government felt that a government headed by members of banned organisations could not be allowed to continue. President dismissed the Government and the State was brought under President's Rule under Article 356.
MAHARASHTRA					
1.	Shri Sadiq Ali	Shri Sharad Pawar (Peoples Democratic Front)	17-2-80	Assembly was dissolved simultaneously	The Union Government felt that having suffered an overwhelming defeat in the Lok sabha elections held in January, 1980 the ruling Party in the State no longer represented the people.
MANIPUR					
1.	Shri B.K. Nehru	—	21-1-72	—	By virtue of the provisions of the North Eastern Areas (reorganization) Act, 1971, the new State of Manipur was formed on 21-1-72. Till the elections were held to the Legislative Assembly of this new State and a popular Government came into Office, it was not possible to carry on the administration of the State in accordance with the provisions of the Constitution. President's rule was, therefore, introduced in the State on the very day it came into existence.
2.	Shri B.K. Nehru	Shri Mohammed Alimuddin (United Legislature Party)	28-3-73	Assembly was dissolved simultaneously	Various crossings of the floor and also formation of groups within the groups within the United Legislature Party led to an undesirable degree of instability in the Government. The Chief Minister, Shri Alimuddin submitted his resignation on 26-3-73.

contd...

Sl. No.	Name of Governor	Name of Chief Minister and Party in power at the time of issue of Proclamation	Date of issue of Proclamation	Whether Assembly was dissolved or suspended	Circumstances leading to issue of Proclamation
(1)	(2)	(3)	(4)	(5)	(6)
3.	Shri L.P. Singh	Shri R.K. Dorendra Singh (Congress)	16-5-77	Assembly was suspended	Due to defections, the Ministry lost the support of the majority of the Members of the State Legislative Assembly and accordingly, resigned. Subsequently, the governor explored the possibility of forming another Ministry but did not succeed as the political situation in the State was very fluid and no party was in a position to form the Government.
4.	Shri L.P. Singh	Shri Yangmasha Shaiza (Janata Party)	14-11-79	Assembly was dissolved simultaneously	The Governor had in his report, dt. 16-10-79 *interalia stated* "I have never known a Government which, according to my own best judgement has been so corrupt, devoted of integrity and unprincipled, and which is given functioning so continuously without any regard to the laws or considerations of justice and fair play"
5.	Shri L.P. Singh	Shri Rishang Keishing (Congress-I)	28-2-81	Assembly was suspended animation	Resignation of 10 Members from the Party reduced the ruling Congress (I) party to a minority. According to the Governor's assessment no party was in a position to form a stable Ministry.
6.	Shri Chintamani Panigrahi	Sh. R. K. Ranbir Singh (United Legislature Front)	7-1-92	Assembly was suspended	The ULF Ministry lost its majority with the resignation of Janata Dal Legislators from the party.
7.	Shri V.K Nayar	Sh. R.K. Dorendra Singh [Indian National Congress (I)] headed the Coalition Govt.	31-12-93	Assembly was suspended	In the wake of continued Naga-Kuki clashes, resulting in about 1000 deaths, the President rule was imposed in the State.

MEGHALAYA					
1.	Shri Hiteswar Saikia	Shri Laldenga (MNF)	7-9-88	Assembly was dissolved simultaneously	The break-away group of nine Legislators of the ruling MNF formed a new MNF (D) party reducing the strength of ruling party to 16 in the 40 member House. Moreover, Speaker created a constitutional crisis by suspending eight of these members during the pendency of proceedings for their disqualification. These developments, paved the way for President's rule in me State.
NAGALAND					
1.	Shri L.P. Singh	Shri J.B Jesookie (Nagaland Nationalist Organisation)	22-3-75	Assembly was suspended but subsequently dissolved on 20-5-75.	Unprincipled defections induced by lure of Office, led to instability in the Ministry. In one year along eight members had defected once, another 8 had defected twice and two had defected three times.
2.	Gen. K.V. Krishna Rao	Shri Hokishe Sema (Congress-I)	7-8-88	Assembly was dissolved simultaneously	Defection of 13 ML As from the ruling Cong-I party brought the Government in minority in the 60 member house. The manner in which the dissident group formed a new party overnight and its merger with the other opposition parties without any ideology or objective of service to the people paved they way for President's rule in the State.
3.	Shri. M.M. Thomas	Shri Vamuzo (National People's Council)	2-4-92	Assembly already dissolved by the Governor on 27-3-1992	President's Rule was imposed in the wake of the fluid party position in the State and deterioration of law and order situation in the State.
ORISSA					
1.	Shri Y.N Sukhthankar	Dr. Harekrushna Mahtab (Congress and Ganatantra: Parishad Coalition Ministry)	25-2-61	Assembly was dissolved simultaneously	The coalition between the Congress Party and the Ganatantra Parishad which together had formed the Ministry came to an end and the Chief Minister, Dr. Mahtab, tendered his resignation on 21-2-61.
2.	Dr. S.S. Ansari	Shri R.N. Singh Deo,	11-1-71	Assembly was suspen-	Consequent upon the with drawl of support by the

contd...

Sl. No.	Name of Governor	Name of Chief Minister and Party in power at the time of issue of Proclamation	Date of issue of Proclamation	Whether Assembly was dissolved or suspended	Circumstances leading to issue of Proclamation
(1)	(2)	(3)	(4)	(5)	(6)
		(Swatantra-Jana gress Coalition Ministry).	23-1-71 23-3-71	ded but subsequently dissolved on 23-1-71.	Jana Congress in Orissa, the coalition Ministry headed by Shri R.N. Singh Deo lost its majority in the State Assembly. The Chief Minister submitted his resignation. The Proclamation issued on 11-1-71 was revoked and a fresh Proclamation was issued on 23-1-71 ceased to operate on 22-3-71. As no single party emerged with an absolute majority in the general elections held in the State on 5th March, 1971 a fresh Proclamation introducing President's Rule but keeping in the new Assembly under suspension, was 3-3-71.
3.	Shri B.D. Jatti	Shrimati Nandini Satpathy (Congress)	3.3.73	Assembly was dissolved simultaneously.	Taking into account the frequent political defections by M.L.A.'s and finding no party which could form a stable government after the submission of resignation by the Chief Minister on 1-3-1973, the Governor recommended President's Rule.
4.	Shri S.N. Shankar	Smt. Nandini Satpathy (Congress)	16-12-76	Assembly was suspended (29 and 30)	Defections in the ruling Congress Party and sharp divisions in the Cabinet had created political uncertainty in the State which had its repercussions on the administration and the law and order situation. The Governor in his report to the President recommended imposition of President's rule to meet the "extraordinary situation."
5.	Shri Harcharan Singh Brar	Shri Binayak Achary (Congress)	—	Assembly was dissolved simultaneously	In March, 1977 Lok Sabha election, the Congress S-the ruling party in the State-could win only 4 seats from Orissa. The Union Government took the view

					that this implied a lack of confidence on the party of electorate in the Government of the State.
6.	Shri B.D. Sharma	Shri Nilamoni Routary (Lok Dal)	17-2-80	Assembly was dissolved simultaneously.	The Union Government felt that having suffered overwhelming defeat in the Lok Sabha elections in January, 1980, the ruling party in the State no longer represented the people.
PUNJAB					
1.	Shri C.M Trivedi	Dr. Gopichand Bhargava (Congress)	20-6-51	Assembly was suspended	Internal disputes developed in the Congress Party and Dr. Gopichand submitted resignation of his Ministry on 16-6-51.
2.	Shri Yadavindra Singh, Rajpramukh of PEPSU	Shri Gyan Singh Rarewala (United Party)	4-3-53	Assembly was dissolved simultaneously	There was shifting allegiance of members of the Legislature and the Election Tribunals had decided petition against four Ministers of the Council of Minister including the Chief Minister. The Chief Minister tendered the resignation of himself and his colleagues to the Rajpramukh.
3.	Shri Dharam Vira	Shri Rama Kishan (Congress)	5-1-66	Assembly was suspended	On the decision to reorganize the State, the Ministry resigned on 22-6-66.
4.	Dr. D.C. Pavate	Shri Lachhman Gill Singh (Punjab Janata Party)	23-8-68	Assembly was dissolved simultaneously	Shri Lachhman Singh Gill resigned on 21-8-68 due to the withdrawal of support by the State Congress Legislature Party. No other Parry was able to form the Ministry.
5.	Dr. D.C. Pavate	Shri Parkash Singh. Badal (Akali Dal)	15-6-71	Assembly was dissolved on 13-6-71	Defections from the ruling party *i.e. Akali* Dal made the Chief Minister Shri Parkash Singh Badal to tender the resignation of his Council of Ministers on 13-6-71.
6.	Shri M.M. Choudhary	Giani Zail Singh (Congress)	30-4-77	Assembly was dissolved simultaneously	In Man, 1977, Lok Sabha elections the Congress the ruling party in the State could not win any seat from Punjab. The Union Govt. took the view that this implied a complete lack of confidence on the

contd...

Sl. No.	Name of Governor	Name of Chief Minister and Party in power at the time of issue of Proclamation	Date of issue of Proclamation	Whether Assembly was dissolved or suspended	Circumstances leading to issue of Proclamation
(1)	(2)	(3)	(4)	(5)	(6)
					party of the electorate in the government of the State.
7.	Shri Jaisukh Lal Hathi	Shri Parkash Singh Badal on (Akali Dal)	17-2-80	Assembly was dissolved simultaneously	The Union Government felt that having suffered an overwhelming defeat in the Lok Sabha election held in January, 1980 the ruling party in the State no longer represented the people.
8.	Shri A.P. Sharma	Shri Darbara Singh	6-10-83	Assembly was suspended animation and dissolved on 26-6-85	Situation arising out of the agitation of the shiromani Akali Dal and the activities of extremist elements in the State.
9.	Shri S.S. Ray	Shri Surjeet Singh Barnala (Akali Dal)	11.5.87	Assembly was suspended and later on dissolved on 6-3-88	
RAJASTHAN					
1.	Dr. Sampumanand	Caretaker Government under Shri Mohanlal Sukhadia (Congress) as general elections were held in 1967.	13-3-67	Assembly was suspended	After the general Elections in 1962 no party got an absolute majority. The leader of the largest single party Shri Mohanlal sukhdia (Congress) was invited by the Governor to form the new Ministry but he declined although he Maimed the support of the majority in the new Legislative Assembly.
2.	Shri Ved Pal Tyagi (Acting Governor)	Shri Harideo Joshi (Congress)	30-4-77	Assembly was dissolved simultaneously	In the March, 1977 Lok Sabha Election the Congress the ruling Party hi the State-could win only one seat from Rajasthan. The Union government took the view that this implied lack of confidence on the part of the electorate in the government of the State.

3.	Shri Raghukul Tilak	Sh. Bhairon Singh Shekhawat (Janta)	17-2-80	Assembly was dissolved simultaneously	The Union Government felt that having suffered an overwhelming defeat in the Lok sabha election in May, 1980 the ruling party in the State no longer represented the people.
4.	Shri Bali Ram Bhagat	Sh. Bhairon Singh Shekhawat (BJP)	15-12-92	Assembly was dissolved simultaneously	On December 6,1992 the disputed structure at Ayodhya was demolished by Karsevaks. President on the recommendation of Union Government, which felt that a Govt. headed by Members of banned organisations could not be allowed to continue, dismissed the Govt. and State was brought under President's Rule under Article 356.
SIKKIM					
1.	Shri B.B Lal	Shri Kazi Lhendup Dorzi (Janata Party)	18-8-79	Assembly was dissolved on 13-8-79	On the advice of the Chief Minister, the Governor dissolved the Assembly on 13-8-79. Thereafter, the Chief Minister tendered his resignation which was accepted on 17-8-1979. On 18-8-79 the State was placed under President's Rule.
2.	Shri H.J.H Telyar Khan	Shri Bhim Bahadur Gurung (Congress)	25-5-84	Assembly was dissolved simultaneously	Defection of 17 ML As from the ruling Congress Party made a situation *in* which the Govt. of the State cannot be carried on in accordance with provisions of the Constitution.
TAMIL NADU					
1.	Shri K.K. Shah	Shri M. (Dravida Kazhagam)	31-1-76	Assembly was dissolved simultaneously	In the report, the Governor had stated that the DMK Ministry had by a series of acts of maladministration, corruption and misuse of power for achieving partisan ends, had set at naught all canons of justice and equity. The Maladministration under DMK Ministry was broadly categorized (a) Administrative and financial improprieties committed by the Government; (b) Flagrant misuse of authority and high handedness

contd...

Sl. No.	Name of Governor	Name of Chief Minister and Party in power at the time of issue of Proclamation	Date of issue of Proclamation	Whether Assembly was dissolved or suspended	Circumstances leading to issue of Proclamation
(1)	(2)	(3)	(4)	(5)	(6)
					to further parry interests; and (c) Deliberate attempts to thwart the basic objectives of a national policy, disregard of the instructions o the Central Government in relation to emergency and misuse of emergency powers.
2.	Shri Prabhudas Patwari	Shri M.G. Ramachandran (AIAKMK)	17-2-80	Assembly was dissol ved simultaneously	The Union Government felt that having suffered on overwhelming defeat in the Lok Sabha Elections held in January, 1980 the Ruling Party in the State no longer represented the people.
3.	Shri S.L. Khurana	Smt. Janaki Ramachandran (AIAKMK)	30-1-88	Assembly was dissol-ved simultaneously	The State faced a political deadlock after the death of the then chief Minister, Shri M.G. Ramachandran and unwarranted happenings in the Assembly broke down the constitutional machinery to run the State Government.
4.	Shri S.S. Barnala	Shri M. Karunanidhi (DMK)	30-1-91	Assembly was dissol-ved simultaneously	Growing LITE activities in the State resulting in deterioration law and order situation and State government's ineffectiveness in containing these activities.
TRIPURA					
1.	Shri B.K. Nehru	—	21-1-72	—	By virtue of the provisions of the North Eastern Areas (Reorganization) Act, 1971, the new State of Tripura was formed on 21-1-72. Till the elections were held to the Legislative Assembly of this new State and a popular Government came into Office, it was not possible to carry on the administration of

					the State in accordance with the Provisions of the Constitution. The President's rule was therefore introduced in this State on 21-1-72.
2.	Shri L.P. Singh	Shri Radhika Ranjan Gupta [Coalition Ministry of Janata Party and CPI (M)]	5-11-77	Assembly was dissolved simultaneously	On 28-10-77, the CPI (M) announces its decision to withdraw support from the Coalition Ministry. On 3 11-77, the Chief Minister tendered his resignation along with other members of the Council of Minister. Since no party was in position to form the Ministry, the governor recommended to the President for the issue of Proclamation under article 356 of the Constitution.
3.	Shri Raghu Nath Reddy	Shri Samir Ranjan Barman	11-3-93	Assembly was dissolved simultaneously	The caretaker Congress TUJS Ministry resigned in the wake of Political Uncertainty' in the State. President rule was imposed on the recommendations of the Governor.
UTTAR PRADESH					
1.	Dr. B. Gopala Reddi	Shri Charan Singh (Samyukta Vidhyak Dal)	25-2-68 (subsequently varied on 15-4-68).	Assembly was suspended and subsequently dissolved on 15-4-68	Shri Charm Singh tendered his resignation from the Office of Chief Minister on 17-2-68. Neither the S.V.D. nor the Congress Party was in a position to form a stable Ministry in the State.
2.	Dr. B. Gopala Reddi	Shri Charan Singh B.K.D.-Congress coalition.	1-10-70	Assembly was suspended	Differences arose between B.K..D. and Congress. On the Chief Minister requesting the Governor to remove 13 Congress Ministers from the coalition Ministry, the Congress, the major partner in the coalition, withdrew support from the coalition Ministry.
3.	Shri Akbar Ali Khan	Sh. Kamlapati Tripathi (Congress)	13-6-73	Assembly was suspended	As a result of serious situation that arose out of the incidents of grave indiscipline in some companies of the P. A.C. the Chief Minister felt that the direct involvement of the Central Government was necessary. Consequently, the Chief Minister whose Party enjoyed

contd...

Sl. No.	*Name of Governor*	*Name of Chief Minister and Party in power at the time of issue of Proclamation*	*Date of issue of Proclamation*	*Whether Assembly was dissolved or suspended*	*Circumstances leading to issue of Proclamation*
(1)	(2)	(3)	(4)	(5)	(6)
					an absolute majority in the Assembly, resigned.
4.	Dr. M. Chenna Reddy	Shri H.N. Bahuguna (Congress)	30-11-75	Assembly was suspended	Shri H.N. Bahuguna, Chief Minister of the Congress Party which was enjoying absolute majority in the State Assembly had tendered the resignation of his Ministry on 29-11-75. No other party was in a position to provide stable Ministry.
5.	Dr. M. Chenna Reddy	Shri Narain Dutt Tewari (Congress)	30-4-77	Assembly was dissolved simultaneously	In the March, 1977 Lok Sabha elections, the Congress- The ruling party in the State, could not win any seat from Uttar Pradesh. The Union Government took the view that this implied a complete lack of confidence on the part of the electorate.
6.	Shri. G.D. Tapase	Shri Banarsi Das (Lok Dal)	17-2-80	Assembly was dissolved simultaneously	The Union Government felt that having suffered an overwhelming defeat in the Lok Sabha elections held in January, 1980 , the ruling Party in the State no longer represented the people.
7.	Shri Satya Narayan Reddy	Shri Kalyan Singh (BJP)	6-12-92	Assembly was dissolved simultaneously	Following the situation arise after the demolition of disputed structure at Ayodha on 6-12-1992 and the resignation of Sh. Kalyan Singh owning moral responsibility for the damages caused to the deposed shrine, President on the recommendation of Union Cabinet invoked article 356 of the Constitution and dissolved the State Assembly.
8.	Shri Motilal Vora	Ms. Mayawati (Bahujan Samaj Party)	18-10-95	Assembly was kept in suspended animation and later on dissolved on 27-10-95	On withdrawal of support by the Bhartiya Janata Party no parry-was in a position to form the Government.

WEST BENGAL

1.	Shri Dharma Vira	Dr. P.C. Ghosh (Progressive Democratic Front)	20-2-68	Assembly was dissolved simultaneously	Position in regard to the relative strengths of various parties was fluid. There were doubts about the majority enjoyed by the Ministry of Dr. P.C. Ghosh. The Speaker's ruling made the functioning of the Assembly impossible.
2.	Shri S.S. Dhawan	Shri Ajoy Kumar Mukherjee (United Front)	19.3.70	Assembly was suspended and subsequently dissoved on 30-7-70	Following die (1) resignation of Shri Ajoy Kumar Mukherjee, Chief Minister on 16-3-70 the Governor explored the possibility of formation of an alternative Ministry in the State. He came to the conclusion that there was no prospect of such an alternative Ministry and recommended President's rule in the State.
3.	Shri S.S. Dhwan	Shri Ajoy Kumar Mukherjee (Democratic Front)	29-6-71	Assembly was dissolved on 25-6-71	On 25-6-71 the Chief Minister who enjoyed a thin majority in the Legislative Assembly advised the Governor to dissolve the Legislative Assembly and subsequently on 28-6-71 tendered the resignation of his Council of Ministers.
4.	Shri Anthony Lancelot Dias	Shri S.S. Ray (Congress)	30-4-77	Assembly was dissolved simultaneously	In the March, 1977 Lok Sabha elections, the Congress ruling party in the State could win 3 seats from West Bengal. The Union Government took the view that this implied a lack of confidence on the part of the electorate in the Government of that State.

2. UNION TERRITORIES

[Including Erstwhile Union Territories Which have Since Become States]

Sl. No.	Name of Lt. Governor	Name of Chief Minister and Party in power at the time of issue of Proclamation	Date of issue of Proclamation	Whether Assembly was dissolved or suspended	Circumstances leading of issue of Proclamation	Date of laying the Proclamation on the Table of		Date of Revocation of Proclamation	Ministry formed after the revocation of Proclamation
						Lok Sabha	Rajya Sabha		
(1)	(2)	(3)	(4)	(5)	(6)	(7)	(8)	(9)	(10)
ARUNACHAL PRADESH									
1.	Shri R.N Haldipur	Shri Tomo Riba (United People Party)	3-11-79	Assembly was dissolved simultaneously	Consequent upon the defections from the ruling party, the strength of UPP reduced to 15 in the 33 member House. On the resignation of the Chief Minister, President's Rule was imposed.	24-1-80	24-1-80	24-1-80	After the election to the Assembly Congress-I Government headed by Shri Gangon Apang assumed the office on 18-1-80. 18-1-80
GOA, DAMAN & DIU									
1.	Shri K.R Damle	Shri Dayanand Bangodkar (MGP)	3-12-66	Assembly was dissolved simultaneously	To ensure free and fair conduct of opinion poll in Goa to merge with Maharashtra and Daman & Diu with Gujarat. The territories had also the options to continue as Union Territory.	3-12-66	3-12-66	5-4-67	After the elections to the Assembly held in February, 1967, the Maharashtrawadi Gomantak Party headed by Shri Dayanand B. Bandodkar formed the Government on 5-4-67.
2.	Shri P.S. Gill	Mrs. Shashikala G. Kakodkar (MGP)	27-4-79	Assembly was dissolved simultaneously	Following the defeat of the Government on 23-4-79 in the Assembly due to defections from the ruling party on trial of strength, the Chief Minister resigned and no other party was in a position to form the stable Government.	30-4-79	30-4-79	16-1-80 (The proclamation ceased to operate on 16-1-80 and no order rescinding the order of 27-4-79 was issued)	After the elections to the Assembly Congress-I party headed by Shri Pratap Singh Raoji Rane assumed the office of Chief Minister on 16-1-80.

MANIPUR									
1.	Shri Baleshwar Prasad	Shri Longiam Thambou Singh (United Front)	25-10-67	Assembly was kept in Suspended animation	The Assembly had 32 seats equally shared by Congress and United Front. With the defection of a Member of United front to the congress Party and subsequent resignations of Speaker and their offices, both the groups refused to nominate a Candidate for Speakership as his election would automatically have given the otherside a majority, President's rule was necessitated.	—	—	19-2-68	The game of defections and counter defections brought the Congress Parry again in majority and Shri M. Koireng Singh assumed the office of Chief Minister on 19-2-1968.
MANIPUR									
2.	Shri Baleshwar Prasad	Shri M Koireng Singh (Congress)	16-10-69	Assembly was dissolved simultaneously	A motion of nonconfidence was passed by the Assembly on 23-9-69 because of frequent changes in Party alignment by some Members. Accordingly, the Chief Minister resigned and no Party was in a position to form a stable Government.	—	—	21-1-72	(After the imposition of President's rule in 1969, Manipur was accorded a full-fledged statehood w.e.f 21-1-72. Till the elections were held to the new Legislative Agsembly and a popular government is formed, President issued a fresh proclamation on the same day under Article 3 56 of the Constitution).
MIZORAM									
1.	Shri S.K. Chhibber	Shri C.H. Chhunga (Congress)	1 1-5-77	The Assembly ceased to exist after expiry of its normal tenure on 11-5-77	Consequent upon the expiry of the term of Legislative Assembly, the Chief Minister along with the Council of Ministers resigned and demanded fresh elections.	—	—	2-7-78	After the elections to the Assembly the MFC Party headed by Brig. T. Sailo formed the Government on 2-6-78.
2.	Shri RP Mathur	Shri T. Sailo (Mizo Peoples	11-11-78	Assembly was dissolved simul-	Due to the split in the ruling party, the chief Minister recom-	20-1-78	20-1178	8-5-79	After the elections to the assembly the Mizo Peoples

contd...

Sl.. No.	Name of Lt. Governor	Name of Chief Minister and Party in power at the time of issue of Proclamation	Date of issue of Proclamation	Whether Assembly was dissolved or suspended	Circumstances leading of issue of Proclamation	Date of laying the Proclamation on the Table of		Date of Revocation of Proclamation	Ministry formed after the revocation of Proclamation
						Lok Sabha	Rajya Sabha		
(1)	(2)	(3)	(4)	(5)	(6)	(7)	(8)	(9)	(10)
		Conference)		taneously	mended for dissolution of the Assembly and holding of fresh elections.				Conference Party headed by Brig. T. Silo assumed the office of Chief Minister on 8-5-79.
PONDICHERRY									
1.	Shri S.L. Silam	Shri V. Venkatabsubha Reddiar (Congress)	18-9-68	Assembly was dissolved simultaneously.	After having lost the majority in the Asssembly due to defections, the Chief Minister resigned on 11-9-68 and no other party was in a position to form the stable Government.	—	—	17-3-69	After the midterm Poll to the Assembly DMK-CPI Coalition Government headed by Shri Farook formed the Government on 7-3-69.
2.	Shri Chhedi Lal	Shri M.O.H Farrok (DMK)	3-1-74	Assembly was dissolved simultaneously.	On withdrawal of support and resignation from the Ministry by the CPI, the Chief Minister resigned on 30-12-73 and no other party was in a position to form the Government.	—	—	6-3-74	Elections to the Assembly were held in February, 1974 in which ADMK-CPI alliance emerged as a Largest group having no absolute majority. ADMK Party headed by Shri S. Ramaswamy formed the Government on 6-3-74.
3.	Shri Chhedi Lal	Shri S. Ramaswamy (ADMK)	28-3-74	Assembly was dissolved simultaneously.	In a trial of strength, the Government was 28-3-74 defeated on the floor of the Assembly by 14 votes to 15 and consequently the chief Minister resigned.	28-3-74	22-4-74	2-7-77	After the elections to the Assembly, a Minority Government beaded by Shri S. Ramaswamy of 2-7-77.

4.	Shri B.T. Kulkarni	Shri S. Rama-swamy (AIADMK)	12-11-78	Assembly was dissolved simul-taneously	The AIADMK Government was formed 20-11-78 with the supp-ort of alone CPM member, following the defections of 4 members from the ruling party, the Government was defeated in a trial of strength. As no other party was in a position to form the government President's rule was imposed.	20-11-78	25-7-83	16-3-85	After the elections to the Assembly DMK Congress coalition Government he-aded by Shri D. Rama-chandran formed the Government on 16-1-80.
5.	Shri K.M. Chandey	Shri D. Rama-chandra (DMK)	24-6-83	Assembly was dissolved simul-taneously	President's rule was necessitated when congress-I party withdrew support to the DMK led coal-ition government.	26-7-83	25-7-83	16-3-85	The elections to the Asse-mbly held on March, 1985 in which Congress Party won 15 seats, the largest group in a 30 members house. Congress gover-nment haded by Shri M.O.H Farook formed the Government on 16-3-85.
6.	Shri Har Swamp Singh	Shri D. Rama-chandran	12-1-91	Assembly was suspended but sub-sequently dissolved on 4.3.91	The DMK-led coalition Govern-ment had been reduced to minority following the withdra-wal of support to it by three Janata Dal Legislators. Consequ-ently, the Chief Minister had sub-mitted the resignation of his Council of Ministers on 27-12-90, the date line fixed by that Lt. Gov-ernor to prove his majority on the floor of the Assembly. As no party was in a position to form the stable Government. President's rule was imposed.	4-7-91	—	4-7-91	After the elections to the Legislative Assembly, held in June 199 1, the Cong-ress-I party formed the Ministry under the Chief Ministership of Shri V. Vaithilingum on 4-7-91.[1]

1. *President's Rule in the States and Union territories,* Lok Sabha Secretariat (New Delhi, 1996), pp.78-89; S.R. Maheshewari, President's *Rule in India,* pp. 33 ff.

Bibliography

PRIMARY SOURCES

Administrative Reforms Commission, *Report on Centre-State Relationship,* New Delhi, 1969,1977.

Annual Report of the Ministry of Home Affairs, Govt. of India, Delhi, 1968-1978.

Constituent Assembly Debates, Vol. DC. *Governor's Reports to the President,* 1951-2001.

Lok Sabha Debates, 2nd series, Vol. LV, No. 53, April 25, 1951.

————Pt. II, Vol. VIII, No. 5, Nov. 19, 1954.

————Pt. II, Vol. Ill, No. 31, March 29, 1956.

————Pt. II, Vol. X, No. 27, Dec. 19, 1956.

————2nd series, Vol. II, No. 19, March 8,1961.

————2nd series, Vol. LV, No. 53, April 25,1961.

————3rd series, Vol. XXXIV, No. 12, Sept. 23,1964.

————4th series, Vol. XX, No. 25, August 1968.

————4th series, Vol. XXXIX, No. 38, April 16,1970; 4th series, Vol. XVI, No.45.

————5th series Vol. II. No.l, May 24, 1971.

————5th series, Vol. IV, No. 21, June 21, 1971.

————5th series, No. 27, June 29, 1971.

————5th series, Vol VII, No.55, Aug.5, 1971; 5th series, Vol. XXIII, No.8.

————5th series, Vol. XX, No. 13, Aug. 8, 1973.

————5th series, Vol. XLIV, No. 37, Sept. 7, 1974-1978.

Parliamentary Debates, Pt. II, Vol. XIV, No. 4, Aug. 9, 1951; Pt. II, Vol. XIV, No. 7, Aug. 13,

House of the People, 1951; Pt. II, Vol. XIV, No. 10, Aug. 17, 1951.

————Vol. II, No. 4, March 12,1953

President's Rule in the State and Union Territories, Lok Sabha Secretariat, New Delhi, 1989,1996.

Rajya Sabha Debates, 1957-1958.

Report of the Centre-State Relations Inquiry Committee, Madras, 1977.

Report of Parliamentary Committee on the Demand for Punjabi Suba, Lok Sabha Secretariat, New Delhi, 1966.

SECONDARY SOURCES

Avasthi, A and Ranga Rao S.P., *Crisis Administration in India,* Delhi, 1983.

Basu, D.D., *The Shorter Constitution of India,* Vol. 1, 7th edn, Delhi 1976.

Bhatt R.K.K., *Political and Constitutional Development of Jammu and Kashmir State,* Delhi, 1984.

Bhambhri, C.P., *Political Parties and Centre-State Relations in India,* The Institution of Constitutional and Parliamentary Studies, Delhi, 1969.

Bombwall, K.R., *National Power and State Autonomy,* Delhi, 1969, reptd 1977.

Crohin, T.E., *The State of Presidency,* Delhi, 1980.

Dharam Vira, "Changed Role of Governor," *The Motherland,* Dec. 22,1972.

Edwards III George C., *Presidencial Influence in Congress,* San Francisco, 1980.

Franda, M., *Small is Politics,* Delhi, 1979.

Fraser, A., *Government and Politics in Bengal,* Delhi, 1979.

Frye, A., *A Responsible Congress, The Politics of National Security,* New York, 1975.

Gani, H.A. *Centre-State Relation and Sarkaria Commission,* New Delhi, 1990.

Hanumantha Rao, G.V., *Party Politics in Andhra Pradesh,* Hyderabad, 1983.

Kashyap, Subhash C., *History of Parliament of India,* Vol. I, Delhi 1994.

History of Parliament of India, Vol. II, Delhi, 1995.

Kumar, A.P., Murly, V.L and Ravi, K., *Government and Politics in Andhra Pradhes,* Delhi, 1982.

Maheshwari, S.R., *President's Rule in India,* Delhi, 1977.

Markandan, K.C., *The Preamble,* Delhi, 1984.

Mishra, K.P., *Janata's Foreign Policy,* 1979.

Mishra, M.S., *Politics of Regionalism in India (with special reference to Punjab),* Delhi, 1988.

Maisel, L and Sacks Paul, M., *The Future of Political Parties,* London, 1975.

Pal, Chandra, *Centre State Relation and Co-operative Federation,* Delhi, 1983.

Phukon, G., *Politics of Regionalism in North East India,* Guwahati, 1996.

Prasad, A.B.B., *Political Organization of Northern India* (AD 950-1194), Patna,1979.

Prasad, A., *Central-State Power under Indian Federation,* Delhi, 1981.

Ray, A Maj. Gen., *Kashmir Diary,* Delhi, 1997.

Rao, R.V.R. Chandra Sekhara and Prasad V.S., *Indian Constitution and Polity,* Delhi, 1991.

Sahni, S., *Centre State Relation,* Delhi, 1984.

Saini, M.K., *Politics of Multinationals,* Delhi, 1981.

Scott, R., *The Politics of New States,* London, 1970.

Sanajaoba, N., *Basic Issues On Centre-State Relations,* Delhi, 1985.

Santhanam, K., *Union-State Relation in India,* Bombay, 1960.

Singh, K.S., *Indian Political System,* Delhi, 1985.

Sogani, M., *Chief Secretary in India,* Delhi, 1984.

Singh, T. *The Soviet Federal States: Theory, Formation and Development,* Delhi, 1982.

Teng, MK Bhatt, RKK and Kaul, S., *Kashmir Constitutional History and Document,* Delhi, 1977.

Journal

Indian Journal of Public Administration (Quarterly Journal of Indian Institute of Public Administration, *Delhi),* Vol. XIX, No. 4, Oct-Dec 1973; VoL XXX, No. 2, April-June, 1984,

Newspapers and Periodicals

The Hindu

The Hindustan Standard

The Hindustan Times

The Motherland

The National Herald

The Statesman

The Times of India

The Tribune.

Local Dailies

Poknapham

Sangai Express.

Index

A

Administrative Reforms Commission (1966-70), 108

Ambedkar, BR, 16

Andhra Pradesh, 28-30, 79

Article 154, 99

Article 188, 10, 11

Article 200, 3, 123

Article 201, 3, 123

Article 249, 2

Article 256, 2

Article 257, 2, 123

Article 312, 2

Article 356 (of Indian Constitution), 1, 2, 4, 5, 16, 17, 109, 122, 123, 165, 166, 200
- Governor's interpretation of, 106-
- scope of, 114, 151, 163, 165

Assam, 122

Assembly dissolution,
- pattern of, 14

B

Bengal, 9

Bihar, 57-59, 77-79, 102
- Governor's report to the President, 124-125

British Raj, 9

C

Central minister, 179

Centre-State relations, 101, 137-162

Chief Minister, 14, 50, 105, 108

Commission of Inquiry Act, 1952, 93

Constituent Assembly, 10, 11, 13, 16, 157-

Constitution, 2, 3, 4, 6, 14, 99, 105, 100, 109, 111
- Order 1954, 7

Consultative Committees, 147

Council of States, 15

D

Datar, BN, 149

Dharam Vira, 105, 111, 112

E

Enquiry Commission, 123

G

Gandhi, Indira, 22, 111, 179

Government of India Act (1935), 8, 9, 99
Governor, 13, 100, 105, 109, 115, 129, 140
    and advisors, 118
Governor's Advisors,
    appointment of, 116-118
    qualities of, 119
    relations of with state Govt. personnel, 120
Govt of Union Territories Act (1963), 189
Great Britain, 115
Gujarat, 71-72, 88-91, 94-95

H

Haryana, 44-48, 107
High Courts, 10, 12

J

Jammu and Kashmir, 7, 13

K

Katju, KN, 148
Kerala, 30-34, 36-38, 64-65, 107

L

Lal, BB, 169
Law and order, 165, 189
Legislature,
    right to summon, 105
Lok Sabha, 5, 7, 13

M

Madhya Pradesh, 103
Manipur, 1, 79, 83-84
Ministry of Home Affairs, 141
Mysore, 69-71

N

Nagaland, 91-92
NER, 122
New Delhi, 111, 144, 175, 179
North America, 156
North Eastern Council, 143

O

Orissa, 34-, 53, 68-69, 81-83

P

Parliament, 102
    and President's rule, 145
PEPSU, 26-27
President's rule, 1
    a glimpses at history of, 20
    approval of, 145
    attitude of central govt., 14
    causes of, 182-183
    early history, 8-
    feedback and reality, 163-187
    in states/UTs, 44-98
    modality of, 16
    nature of functioning of Governor during, 112-
    position & role of Governor during, 99-136
    high priority to administrative development during, 172
    reduction of political interference during, 171
    role of central govt. under, 137
Public Accounts Committee, 153
Punjab, 24-26, 39-41, 59-61, 72-74, 102

R

Rajagopalachari, C. 143
Rajasthan, 41-44, 103
Raj Bhavans, 115
Rajya Sabha, 13
Rao, PS, 28

S

Samyukta Vidhayak Dal, 21, 53, 54, 55, 57
Sarkaria, RS, 93
State Legislation (Delegation of Power) Bill, 155
Supreme Court, 6, 50, 93, 103

T

Tamil Nadu, 92-94, 107, 108
Tripura, 79

U

Union Government, 156
Uttar Pradesh, 53-56, 65-68, 85-88, 92, 130
    Governor's report to the President, 126-128
    State Legislature Act, 56

W

West Bengal, 48-53, 61-63, 74-77, 102

■■■